THE
COMPLETE
BOOK OF
GOLF

THE
COMPLETE
BOOK OF
GOLF

A

GUIDE TO EQUIPMENT
TECHNIQUES
AND COURSES

JOHN ALLAN MAY

GALLERY BOOKS
An Imprint of W. H. Smith Publishers Inc.
112 Madison Avenue
New York City 10016

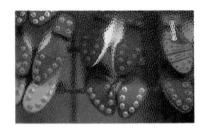

First published in the UK in 1991 by
The Hamlyn Publishing Group Limited.
a division of Reed International Books
Michelin House, 81 Fulham Road, London SW3 6RB.

This edition published in 1991 by Gallery Books
An imprint of W.H. Smith Publishers Inc
112 Madison Avenue
New York
New York 10016

ISBN 0-8317-1536-7

Produced by Mandarin Offset
Printed in Hong Kong

CONTENTS

INTRODUCTION

St Andrews, the home of golf, and the Headquarters of the Royal Ancient, whose clubhouse (on the left) nestles behind the 18th green.

*G*olf, the game for all ages, is truly a mystery which *Webster's* English dictionary defines as "something that cannot be explained" ... "A profound secret" ... "Rites and practices revealed only to initiates, having an inexplicable quality and character."

Its origins are just as mysterious. It seems clearly to have evolved from club-and-ball games played in very distant times, such as *paganica* in the Roman Empire, from which developed *chole* and *kolven* in what became Belgium and Holland and *palle-maille* in France, Italy and England, (The last, an indoor game, even gave its name to a London street, Pall Mall, where a large purpose-built palle-maille court was built in the 17th century.) But just *when* people began playing golf, the game with a hole in it, is undiscoverable. The impenetrable mists of centuries obscure its origin.

It seems certain, however, that the sport on which modern golf is based began in Scotland and was a game of the people. By the middle of the 15th century so many Scots were playing it during the long northern summer twilight on the rabbit-cropped common-land links between the seas and the towns that King James II of Scotland decreed that "it be utterly cryit dune and not be used." Like football, another popular sport banned at the same time, golf was seriously interfering with archery practice, the first duty then of all loyal Scotsmen.

But the game had already developed an almost fatal fascination. People started playing it again. Nearly 30 years later another royal ban was imposed. Before long that too was being ignored. And by the middle of the 16th century Scottish nobility and royalty had also become the great game's captives.

Queen Mary of Scotland was cinsured for playing on the links a day or so after the murder of her husband. Records show that King James VI of Scotland played matches for what was then big money. In 1602, he lost two golden pounds, then a substantial amount, to the Earl of Bothwell. Customs dockets of the time reveal that Scotland was importing at least some golf balls from Holland. So now that kings and courtiers also played the game, the people's pastime entered "history"; that is, became the subject of records, literature and art. From that time on we know most of the story.

James VI, on becoming James I of England, brought the game south with him. He played at Blackheath near his palace at Greenwich. A regular group of "goffers" was formed there in 1608, although the official Blackheath Club was not formed until a century and a half later. In England the game was largely the preserve of the gentry for a very long time. It was played mostly on heathland, heather and pine country unsuitable for agriculture. Linksland is rare in England and the first true English links – at Westward Ho! in Devon and Sandwich in Kent – were not much used for golf until the 19th century. Adjoining Royal St George's at Sandwich is the Prince's course; the two names neatly characterise the early history of golf in England.

Meanwhile the building of the British Empire took the game around the world. It has been played in India, for example, for 200 years. There are faint echoes of golf talk in Virginia in the 17th century when that American state was a colony. And a newspaper advertisement of the time suggests that some golf was played regularly in New York in the 1770s, as it was further north in Canada.

In Europe, the Duke of Wellington's officers played golf in their spare time during the Napoleonic wars, notably at Pau in the south of France, where the first European club was formed in 1856.

Then quite suddenly, as railways and steamships made communications very much faster and easier, the golf game spread like wildfire. Before the end of the 19th century England had almost as many golf courses as Scotland. In the United States the first acknowledged golf club was founded at Yonkers, New York (the St Andrews Club) in 1888; Shinnecock Hills on Long Island was opened in 1891. The first U.S. Open championship was held at Newport, Rhode Island in 1895. Only another six years passed before the first course was opened in Japan.

In the earliest times golf had been played only on courses designed by nature. There had not even been any specially prepared putting surfaces. The very first Rules of Golf (1745) told players to tee up within a club's length of the previous hole. The entire course within the confines of the rough was termed "the green," an expression which has lasted through to modern times in the term "through the green." But so rapid was the expansion of the game by 1900 that special courses had to be designed and built wherever there was suitable land available.

And today golf has become quite insatiable. In France for instance some 300 new courses have been opened or started since 1985. In Britain the Royal and Ancient Gold Club of St Andrews, the country's supreme authority, has calculated that nearly 700 new courses will be needed in England and Wales by the year 2000 if the demand for golf is to be satisfied. There are now green oases of golf in the deserts of Arabia. And there is a Golf Academy in Moscow.

So golf now is a game on which the sun never sets. It is played in the still-spartan conditions of the original links; in pine and heather country; in glorious parklands; over redesigned farmland and reconstituted desert; among the lakes and mountains. It is the whole world's game.

Yet golf faces perhaps its biggest challenge – to return the game to the people. Club membership is becoming so expensive in many areas that only the rich can afford to play there. The world needs thousands more public and municipal courses, where green fees are modest. It is after all a game for Everyman, Everywoman and Everykid – literally a game for all ages. Challenging. Rewarding. Frustrating. Addictive. Beautiful. Golf is still as mysterious as it ever was.

THE AIM OF THE GAME

The aim of the game is to strike a ball into a number of distant holes in the ground — usually 18 — in the fewest number of strokes. The ball is 1.68 inches (42.67 mm) in diameter; each hole is 4¼ inches (108 mm) in diameter and 4 inches (100 mm) deep.

Various sand and water hazards may lie in the way between each "teeing ground" and the hole, along with trees, bushes and rough grass. At matchplay the number of strokes taken by players on each hole determines the winner or winners of that hole and the number of holes won the winner or winners of the round: At strokeplay — also called medal play — the total number of strokes taken for the round determines the winner. Most professional tournaments extend over 72 holes or four rounds.

THE CONCEPT OF PAR

Par is a notional standard representing the number of strokes a good player should take on each hole and for each round of 18 holes, allowing two putts per green. Originally the term was "bogey," which has come to mean one over par.

For men par is rated purely on distance. Up to 250 yards (228 m) the par is 3; up to 475 yards (434 m) it is 4; beyond that it is 5. (one or two extremely long holes may be rated par 6).

Distances for women golfers are shorter but Ladies Committees are allowed some latitude in fixing pars for their courses.

A Standard Scratch Score (SSS), however, is now used for handicapping purposes by both men and women, and this adjusts par on the basis of difficulty.

EQUIPMENT INTRODUCTION

A selection of old equipment kept in the Royal and Ancient's golf museum at St Andrews.

"The game consists of putting little balls into little holes with instruments very ill-adapted for the purpose." The disillusioned quote has been attributed to many famous men, including Winston Churchill. In fact, it was the judgment of a Professor of Logic at Oxford University, probably in about 1870. He happened to be tutor to the eminent golfer and writer Horace G. Hutchinson.

The joke is, of course, that the professor was quite wrong. Golf equipment is superbly well-adapted for its purpose. It's just that some golfers are not well-adapted to use them. Probably the very earliest discovery, which applies to all club-and-ball games where the ball is stationary until hit, was that the striking surface had to be offset from the shaft. Otherwise, the shaft being slender, no player could get the ball off the ground except by accident. Nor indeed could he or she connect with the ball regularly. The basic shape therefore had to be much as it is today.

Early golfers could and did exchange clubs and balls with players of *kolven*, a Dutch game which in many ways was similar to golf but not played to holes in the ground. But if the offset nature of the clubface is what makes the game possible, it is also one of the things that can make it difficult.

A further discovery was that the clubface should be tilted backwards at an angle and that this tilt, called "loft," could differ from club to club, producing a variety of shots. This, again, increased the possibilities for the player and at the same time the difficulties. Finally it was found that the shaft needed to be rather whippy if the ball was to be hit any distance – and that the amount of flex to produce optimum results varied from player to player.

The first shafts were made from a variety of woods – ash, hazel or even malacca cane – until hickory became the norm. You had to select the correct clubs for your personal swing by feel alone – by "the music," as "Old Tom" Morris put it. The very first clubs were made by bowmakers – another

good reason for the Scottish kings trying to outlaw the game in times of conflict with the English. Not until the onset of the industrial revolution did iron-headed clubs arrive in any great numbers.

On the old links they literally "played the ball as it lay" and soon needed special clubs for the awkward occasions. So they had "rutting irons" and "track irons" for use where carts had left their marks on the links commonland, also "blasters" and "spade mashies." Some clubs had concave faces and were known as "spoons." Indeed it was not until the mid-19th century that a Mr Henry Lamb invented the convex or rounded clubface on his woods, which were called "bulgers" and were the ancestors of most modern woods. (They provided a gear effect and were more forgiving with slightly off-center shots).

The "cleek" was a driving iron with little loft; and because of the rough nature of the early greens many players had a "putting cleek," a slightly lofted putter, in their bags. With "mashies" and "niblicks" and "mashie-niblicks" it was not uncommon in the late 19th century for a player to have as many as 20 clubs in his bag.

Happily by that time caddies had arrived in force. The term "caddie" is universally believed to have derived from the French word *cadet*, meaning a younger son, and to have resulted golfwise from the fact that Mary Queen of Scots was an avid golfer. She returned to Scotland from France with a large retinue of courtiers and most no doubt had a "cadet" to do the carrying for them on the links. But there is also evidence that in Scotland about that time porters and carriers in general were known as "cawdies," so there is some room for doubt as to the true origins of the word.

It is possible that the golf balls the ordinary folk used in the game's early stages were wooden, but "featheries" soon became the order of the day. These were balls with leather casings stuffed with feathers, an idea said to date back to Roman times and possibly to the game of *paganica* (about

which we know nothing else). The stitching on the leather covers helped to keep the balls in the air and possibly to provide some element of side-spin when needed, although nobody appreciated that at first.

The earliest gutta-percha balls when they arrived in the 1840s had smooth surfaces, gutta-percha being a substance resembling rubber. Players soon discovered however that they played better when the "gutties" had been hacked around a bit. So before long ball-makers deliberately hammered and nicked their products before finally painting the outsides.

Then came the Haskell ball, named after its American inventor. This was the first truly modern ball. It had a small inner core of gutta-percha around which was wound a great length of elastic rubber. The outer covers were variously marked with pimples rather than dimples and sometimes a latticework of etched lines. The ancestor of today's golf balls had been born. It took some time, however, before Haskells were thoroughly accepted in Britain. As Horace Hutchinson remarked in 1890, "we move less rapidly than America."

That Horace Hutchinson was only too right was proven later when in the 1920s the steel shaft arrived and then in the 1930s the standardised larger ball (1.68 in). It took about 10 years for steel shafts to come into regular use in

Britain and 40 years to standardise the American ball.

So the search has continued year after year through the centuries for ways of making this enchanting but often frustrating game less difficult for the average player.

New clubs, new shafts, new clubheads; new balls that fly farther and better; special gloves, special clothes, special spiked shoes; pull-trolleys, golf carts . . . the golfer is spoilt for choice. Yet the game remains even for the greatest players as much of a challenge as ever. It is indeed a mystery and, thank goodness, nobody has solved it yet.

Hickory-shafted putters and irons. These are examples of the type of clubs prevalent in the late 19th and early 20th century.

CLUBS

The difficulty of golf is this: one has to strike and to control a very small ball, not two inches in diameter, with the even smaller "sweet-spot" of a flexing and twisting club which is between three and four feet long. The wonder of golf is that one can often actually do this – provided one swings well *and has clubs exactly suited to that swing.*

Some 120 years ago "Young Tom" Morris, in winning his third Open championship, holed the 578-yard opening hole at Prestwick, Scotland, in only three shots. More than 50 years ago Gene Sarazen, on the way to winning the second-ever Masters tournament at Augusta National, Georgia, holed-out with his second shot on the 505-yard 15th hole. At 50 years of age Jack Nicklaus gained an astonishing 40 extra yards off the tee by using a high-technology Japanese graphite-shafted driver.

Clubs in general are categorised as woods, irons and putters. The maximum number any player may take round in his or her bag is 14, but they may be mixed in any fashion desired. The orthodox mix for the average club player is three woods, 10 irons including both a wedge and a sand-iron and a putter. But some players leave out one of the woods and take an extra wedge or sand-iron, while others take four or five woods and leave out a couple of irons. Many older players and beginners carry a "short" set of only five clubs and a putter. It is a matter of individual choice.

The 1-iron is the equivalent of the old driving iron and is often used by professionals when the drive off the tee requires good distance but absolute control.

The shaft is much shorter than that of the 1-wood (usually 39 inches); the loft is a little greater and the clubface is more heavily grooved, so that the 1-iron is felt to grip the ball more solidly than the driver, thus allowing greater ball control.

The shafts of the 2-, 3- and 4-irons are progressively a little shorter still, and each clubhead is slightly more lofted; the usual loft for a 4-iron is 26 or 27 degrees.

Right: A range of irons from a 3-iron on the left to sand-wedge on the right. This shows the varying degrees of loft on a standard set of irons. "Loft" is necessary because the more the loft the more the underspin put on the ball. And the more underspin the higher the ball will fly.

But these are all known as "long irons" and are used when good distance is required along with a higher flight. As the iron numbers get higher, a consistent player will hit the ball about 10 yards shorter with each club.

The 5, 6 and 7 are "medium irons" and these are used for middle-distance shots. At close range – from about 130 yards in to the green – the "short irons" are

used, the 8- and 9-irons, the wedge and the sand-iron.

A wide variety of wedges is now available. These are used for special shots around the greens. The pitching wedge will usually have a loft of 50 degrees, but alternative wedges are available with lofts of up to 62 degrees. Sand-irons, for use mainly in bunkers, vary in loft from 53 to 60 degrees; each has a rounded flange behind

the leading edge in order to insure that the clubface slides under the ball and does not stick in the sand.

All these clubs are heavily grooved so that, properly used, they will apply considerable back-spin to the ball, making it easier to control the exact distance it will travel when it lands on the green, making it stop dead or bounce backwards whichever is required.

Above: A standard range of iron clubs showing both the backs and the faces. A regular set of irons will comprise nine clubs: the 3 to 9-irons, pitching wedge and sand-iron. There are a number 1- and 2-irons but they are more difficult to use. The faces are grooved so that the club grips the ball providing the right amount of spin and control.

WOODS

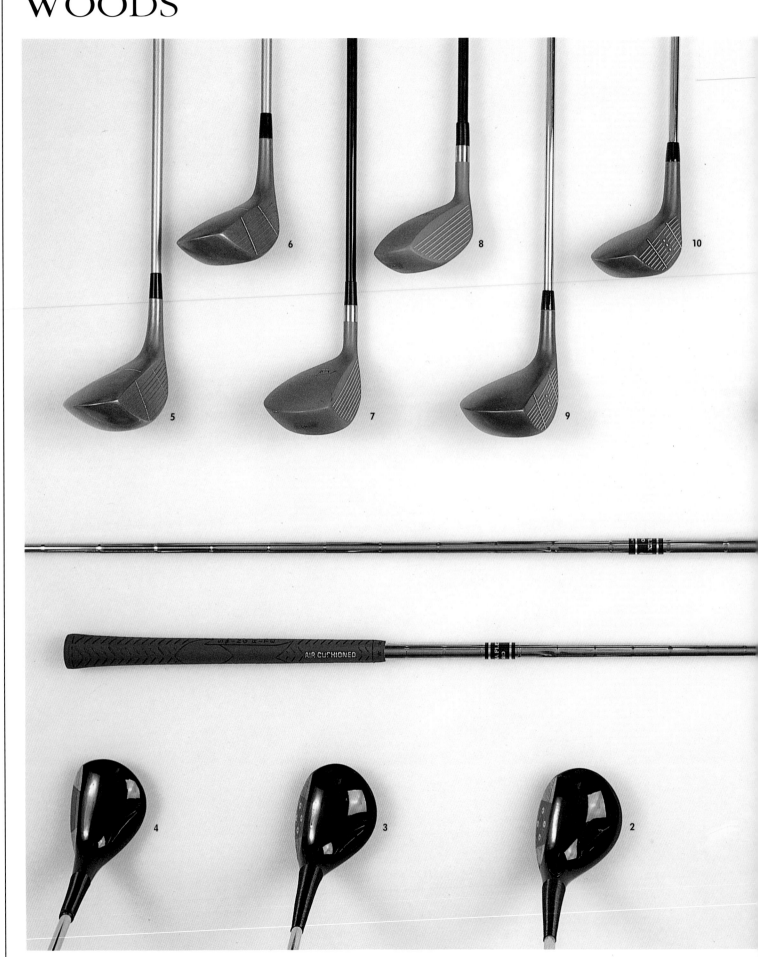

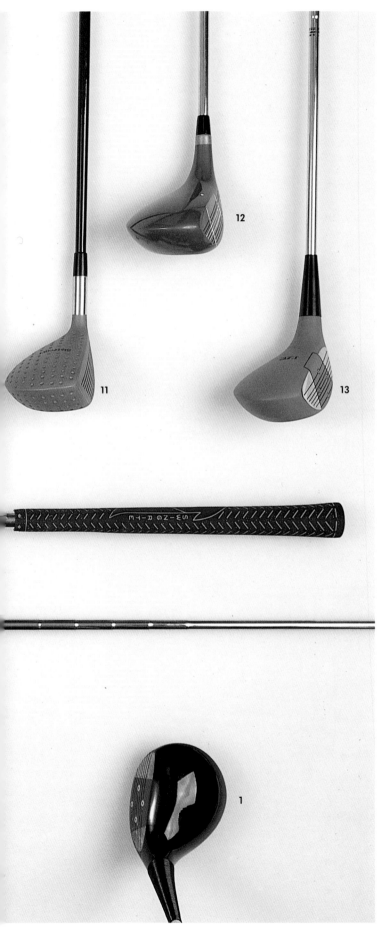

Woods, which these days are often made of metal, hark back to the earliest days of golf. The clubheads are larger and the clubfaces usually deeper than the blades of irons, but, interestingly, they weigh less than irons. They are used mainly off the teeing grounds and the fairways for long-range shots, although special woods that can be used effectively from long grass have recently become very popular.

The driver, or 1-wood, is the longest club. It usually has a deep face and the least "loft" (the angle at which the face slopes backward, measuring from bottom to top). For drivers, 10 degrees of loft is customary, although many professionals use drivers with only 8 degrees of loft, while some with up to 12 degrees are used by amateurs. Much depends on whether the player's personal action means he tends to hit the ball high or low.

Theoretically the driver should hit the ball farther than any other club in the bag. The usual length of shaft is 43 inches (109cm) and the usual weight about 13¼ ounces (376g); but lighter modern shafts allow greater weight to be put in the clubhead without altering the total weight of the club.

The driver is used mainly from the tee, its lack of loft and general design making it difficult to use off the fairway. But if gripped well down the shaft the driver is also useful if a player has to hit under the low branches of trees but needs to hit the ball a reasonable distance.

The 2-wood is little used by tournament professionals today. It has a shallower face and slightly more loft than the driver, and the shaft is a little shorter. But since many drivers are now made with a 2-wood's loft, the latter club seems to most people to be unnecessary. It's interesting to note, though, that the old-time hero Harry Vardon used driving clubs that were lighter and shorter than those of his contemporaries. (The term "2-wood" was not then in common use).

The 3-wood is the most popular of its genre. It usually has a 42-inch shaft, 16 degrees of loft and a 13- to 14-ounce clubhead. It has become the basic fairway-wood. Many amateurs find it easier to use off the tee, where many professionals also use it when they require greater accuracy than they can be certain of when using a driver.

The 4-wood is another club that has gone out of fashion. Most professionals prefer an iron club with which they can hit the ball a similar distance but with greater control. The 4-wood's loft is usually 20 degrees.

More popular now is the 5-wood with a 22-25 degree loft and a slightly smaller head. It is particularly useful for shots out of poor lies on the fairway, when it seems difficult with other clubs to get under the ball.

Among amateurs 7-woods and even 9-woods are increasingly used, possibly because the shorter shafts and larger heads make medium range shots from the fairways look easier and there is no need to hit down on the ball, as there is with an iron club. These clubs can also be used from poor lies in the rough. Nowadays, Lee Trevino uses a 7-wood as a general-purpose club.

Woods come in a wide range of materials. Many are no longer really woods at all but metals. On the bottom row are real woods with persimmon heads, much loved by traditionalists: driver (**1**), 3-wood (**2**), 5-wood (**3**) and 7-wood (**4**).

On the top row is a selection of metal-headed woods: boron-shafted driver and 3-wood (**5** and **6**); metal-shafted drivers and 3-woods (**9**, **10**, **11** and **13**); graphite-shafted ladies driver and 3-wood (**7** and **8**); and a metal-shafted 1½-wood (**12**). With the different materials each club has a different feel to it, so that the wise golfer tests every club before buying.

PUTTERS

The final club in the bag – and some would say the most important – is the putter. This is used, of course, for the final act of putting the ball into the hole. There are so many different designs that it is impossible to enumerate them all – one manufacturer alone offers what is basically the same design in 48 different guises.

There are four main categories. Blade putters are of traditional design, like unlofted irons. Center-shafted putters, as the name implies, have the shafts fixed to the middle of the blades. Mallet putters are designed rather like miniature drivers. And heel-and-toe-weighted putters have a wide striking surface with a larger "sweet spot" (the tiny area that give the truest strike).

There are no rules governing the length of the shaft for a putter and many modern players have adopted the "broom-handle" type, which can be used as a pendulum, with the fulcrum either under the player's chin or at the sternum in the chest. In years gone by one Joshua D. Crane used a putter with a shaft only a foot long and putted with it one-handed, resting his other hand on his knee. But the Crane putter is rarely used these days.

The croquet-mallet putter has been ruled illegal, and the shafts of any and all putters must diverge at least 10 degrees from the vertical when the sole of the clubhead is flat on the ground.

Most putters have a slight loft, usually about 3 degrees; but there are putters with reverse loft, which is intended to insure the ball is hit slightly above center and thus is caused to roll more

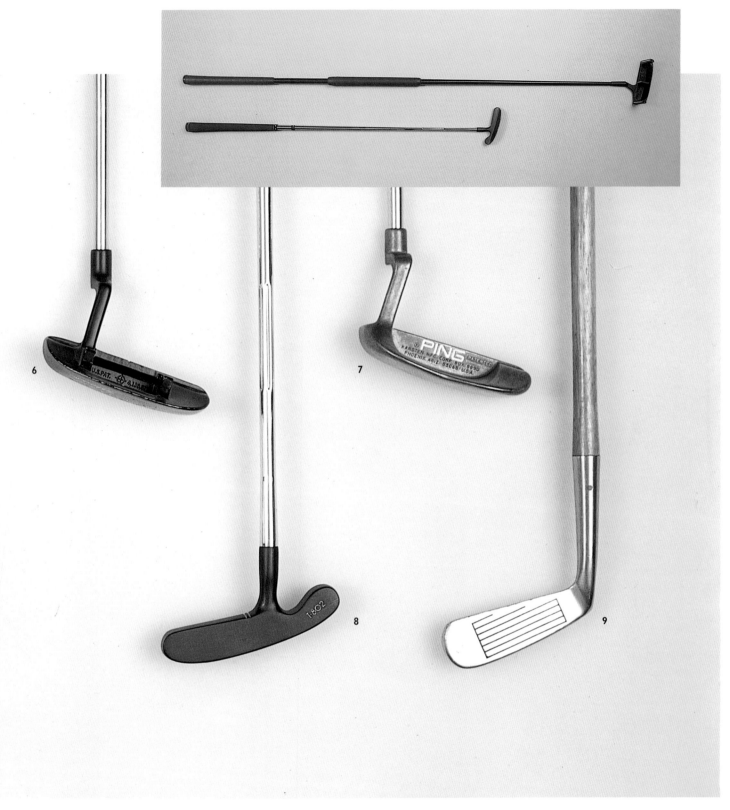

truly. (The center of gyration of a circular object is five-sevenths of the diameter up from the ground). The danger with this type of putter is of hitting down on the ball and causing it to bounce.

The man reckoned to be the greatest tournament putter of all time, the South African Bobby Locke, believed he put "true top-spin" on each putt. But American amateur champion at the turn of the century Walter J. Travis, who was possibly Locke's peer, used a lofted putter so that he put a touch of underspin on his putts. In this way, he insisted he could always make a firmer stroke.

As the old saying has it, "You pays your money and you takes your choice." In the last analysis it is not the club that makes the putt, but the player.

Seen here there are a variety of putters: the old fashioned hickory-stemmed blade putter (**9**); the center-shafted putter (**8**); variations of the goose-necked putter (**1**, **4**, **6** and **7**); and variations of the heel and toe weighted putter (**2**, **3** and **5**).

Inset: The "broom handle" putter which can be held under the chin or at the sternum between the ribs and used like a pendulum, compared to a standard putter.

SHAFTS

Every clubshaft flexes and twists to some extent during the course of a full swing. Clubmakers through the centuries have done their level best to control these movements in order to achieve the right results on contact. In modern times, as science and technology have become more understanding and more sophisticated, the possibilities of control have greatly improved and it sometimes seems that the greatest difficulty manufacturers have is in exercising control within the parameters of custom, tradition and the Rules of Golf. Probably if each individual did not swing differently to some degree this seeming difficulty would be a real one.

The facts are, however, that each swing is different to some degree, each shaft material is different, each shot is different and temperament varies as often and as much as temperature. It is just not possible to make the game easy for every player all of the time. Hence the wide disparity of clubshafts now on offer.

After shafts made of hickory, steel took over. Aluminum also had its day. Both of these metals are still used today, but the accent has now been placed on graphite, plastic and various mixes and alloys. The new materials allow lighter shafts. That means that clubheads can have more weight without increasing the total weight or the "swingweight" of the club.

The length of a shaft is also a factor. A longer shaft should permit a wider swing which in theory should increase the speed of the clubhead. But it may alter the flex and torque factors of the shaft in such a way as to affect the swing. So there are some makers who offer, and some players who in fact prefer, shorter shafts than the standard. The first of the great modern players, Harry Vardon, used clubs which were both shorter and lighter than those used by his contemporaries.

With a high-speed swing it has been shown that there is a tendency for the shaft to bend forward and to "close" (turn inward toward the player) slightly. This

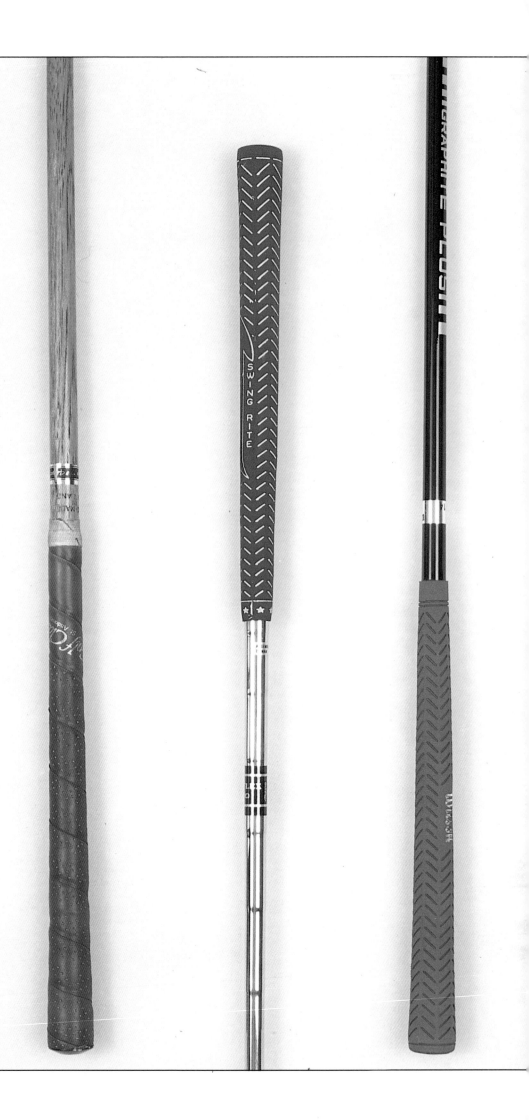

may account for the fact that all good natural golfers hook the ball (that is, cause the ball, if they are right-handers, to move right-to-left in the air). This makes it all the more puzzling why virtually 90 per cent of all golfers slice, causing the ball to curve away from them in the air. To answer the puzzle some clubmakers provide a bent hosel so that the clubhead arrives at the ball a little behind the shaft. Others hook-face their woods, turning the clubface inwards to compensate for the slicing tendency.

So where and how the shaft flexes is vitally important. With graphite and composite shafts, layer after layer of fibres are woven and wrapped together to make a tapered "stick." Very great care is then needed to insure that the flex-point does not vary from shaft to shaft and club to club within a set. Any variation will not only alter the "feel" of a club but also the results of a strike. As a consequence, some of the most expensive clubs use boron, graphite and other composite materials for their shafts. But the very high cost of these materials means that most popular club models are still made of steel.

Shafts Of Light
Pictured here are a variety of club shafts: from the old-fashioned hickory on the left, through steel and three types of graphite to boron on the right. Most shafts, however, are still made from steel. Different flexes suit different swings but the chief advantage of the lightweight graphite and composition shafts is that they allow a heavier club head without increasing the total weight of the club. This theoretically increases the value of the kinetic energy applied to the ball.

If theory is applied correctly in practice a lightweight shaft will indeed add to the distance the ball can be hit, as Jack Nicklaus discovered after he had passed 50. But not all actions apply theory correctly. Buy what suits your action.

CLUBHEADS

Clubheads also are made from a variety of materials. For traditional woods – the wooden ones – persimmon, maple and laminates are generally used. The heads of metal woods however may be of steel, alloys, graphite, ceramics, plastics, cobalt, beryllium, byzanium, Kevlar (a poly-plastic), magnesium, carbon fibre or a combination of such materials.

Wooden woods usually have an inset in the impact zone, sometimes of plastic, often of persimmon; but metal woods must be plain. No material which could act as a spring is allowed.

Many modern woods have a "bore-through" hosel instead of a shank and socket. In these the shaft penetrates right through the head and is fixed underneath, in the intention of making the clubs more stable and more consistent in the way they flex. Others have oversize clubheads. Some use a double bulge, being slightly rounded both vertically and horizontally. Such modern "bulgers" should in theory be more forgiving to off-center strikes.

The heads of most makes of irons are cast, but some of the better models are forged in the traditional manner. Most now are hollow-backed and either perimeter-weighted or heel-and-toe weighted. The aim of perimeter weighting is to spread the "sweet spot," the truest striking area, and to allow more actual weight in the sole of the club, which should enable one to hit the ball higher.

Many soles are now rounded, making the exact lie of the clubhead when soled on the ground by different individuals less important. But traditional irons with flat soles and plenty of weight in the back are still available and are preferred by many better players. The thought is that these designs put more weight directly behind the sweet spot.

An Important Fact
The faces of all iron clubs are grooved so that the club head grips the ball. The backs of some are perimeter-weighted to reduce off-center hits, the backs of others flat with the main weight behind the sweet-spot. This adds power.

With a flat sole the lie of the club becomes very important. If when the club is soled the toe is up in the air, so to speak, the player will tend automatically to stand too upright or to push his or her hands forward, making a consistent strike unlikely. With too flat a lie on the other hand the stance may not be upright enough. With these it is therefore vital to choose clubs with lies suitable to the individual, or to have them custom-made.

Most iron clubheads these days are of steel; but various alloys such as beryllium-copper and cobalt-copper are becoming popular, as is titanium. All are more expensive than steel.

The faces of all clubs are grooved, the better to grip the ball and to produce the required spin. The shape of these grooves and the distance between their edges have for many years been regulated by the Royal and Ancient Golf Club of St Andrews and the United States Golf Association. In the 1980s the American manufac-

turer Karten Solheim, one of the most innovative of club manufacturers, introduced "U-grooves" or "square grooves" on his Ping Eye 2 clubs, and these appeared not to conform precisely to official specifications. When they were declared illegal, law suits resulted. A settlement was reached which allows clubs with these grooves to be used by amateurs in the United States for as long as they like, and by amateurs in Britain (and all other countries accepting the R & A's authority) until 1996. Professionals may no longer use them. And the Karsten Manufacturing Corporation has agreed to return to conforming grooves in the future.

WOMEN'S CLUBS

Clubs specially designed for women players are now much in vogue. Many have color-coordinated shafts and clubheads. But it is not just the look of the clubs that matters. They are specially weighted so that it should be easier for women to hit the ball into the air, specially angled to make slicing less likely, and specially shafted so that they are lighter to use without sacrificing clubhead weight.

BALLS

An unending search goes on for ways to improve the performance, the "playability," of golf clubs within the parameters set by the world golf authorities.

Every ball has to be a certain size, weight and shape. And in terms of the distance it can be struck it must not exceed the tolerances set by a particular mechanical driving machine ("Iron Byron" of the True Temper Company). But the construction, design and aerodynamics of different balls can, within these limits, give different results.

On a full-blooded drive the clubhead may be traveling at 150 feet per second (around 100 mph). The ball is compressed, flattened against the clubface. As it recovers its shape it leaps off the clubhead, adding this compression-bonus to the clubhead's speed. The compression of the ball is thus one factor in distance. But so are the ball's particular design characteristics in flight. If it has a low spin-rate it will tend to fly lower than one with a higher rate, it will tend to roll farther on landing, and it will not slice or hook quite so readily. A ball with a high spin-rate will fly higher, land more softly, roll less far and bite better on the greens. However, it will tend to slice and hook more readily unless it is hit with absolute precision.

Golf balls these days are three-piece, two-piece or (as at most driving ranges) one-piece. The three-piece ball has an inner core, either liquid or solid, around which is wound elastic thread. The cover is usually balata, natural or synthetic, although some three-piece balls are covered with the harder Surlyn (a patented thermoplastic material).

The two-piece ball is of moulded solid rubber, usually with a Surlyn cover. It is virtually cut-proof, spins slightly less than the three-piece ball and runs farther.

Until now the balata-covered three-piece ball has been preferred by most professionals and low-handicap amateurs because it has a softer "feel" and guarantees more control at short range. But research suggests that these

Left and below: The three-piece ball remains the favorite for perhaps most professionals. It has the best "feel" to it and, it is said, is easiest to control. But it is very expensive to produce. It has a small core or center, which may be liquid-filled or of solid rubber, and then a tight winding of high-velocity rubber thread. A cover of balata or surlyn is then applied.

Bottom: The modern two-piece ball lasts longer, spins more slowly and runs further. It is the favorite of most handicap golfers and those who wish to maximize the distance they hit the ball. With these balls the number and design of the dimples becomes quite critical and hooks and slices can be reduced.

BALL SPECS

The ball must be at least 1.68 inches in diameter.
It's weight must not be more than 1.62 ounces.
It's initial velocity when used on the "Iron Byron" ball-hitting machine must not exceed 250 feet per second.

Dr.ives by the machine must not exceed 280 yards carry-plus-roll.
The ball must be symmetrical and behave consistently in flight, regardless of its orientation on the tee.

NOTE "Iron Byron" is set to swing at a clubhead speed of 160 ft/sec.
Players achieving greater speeds will hit the ball further.

The Feathery ball dates back to about the year 1400 and lasted as the stock golf ball until the middle of the 19th century. The leather cover was stuffed with wet goose feathers and then soaked. As it dried it hardened into a good golf ball.

Around 1860 the first "Gutty" came into use. This was made from gutta percha, a rubbery substance, which was heated and moulded by hand into a solid one-piece ball. Players found to their delight that the more they cut these balls the better they behaved.

advantages may be shared in time by the harder two-piece balls.

Dimple patterns also affect the performance of the balls. Originally all dimples were imprinted on the ball in a regular straight-line pattern. But now sophisticated designs are available which give the balls slightly different but highly significant flight characteristics.

The compression factor also differs between various types of ball. The factor is rated at 100-compression, 90-compression and 80-compression and measures the ball's resistance to the forces generated at impact. The differences are manifested mainly in the "feel" at impact: the lower the compression factor the softer the "feel." There is little difference in the distance the various balls will fly if each is hit at the same clubhead speed. (The importance of "feel" to golfers proves that the game is played mainly in the mind. For by the time the player feels the moment of impact the ball has gone a yard or two on its way already: there is nothing he or she can do about it.)

Temperature also affects a golf ball. But it is the temperature of the ball that matters, not that of the air around it. Much depends on the temperature at which the ball has been stored over the last 12 hours or so. The optimum temperature appears to be 75 degrees. But it is no good a player just putting a ball in his trouser pocket at the clubhouse and thinking it will have warmed up successfully by the time he gets to the first tee.

Extreme cold affects balls – particularly three-piece ones – far more than extreme heat. It may take nearly 50 yards off a medium-handicap golfer's tee shots. But who keeps their golf balls in the fridge? Left in a cold car for long periods, however, they may become too cold for their owner's good. And again, no hand warmer is going to warm them up in time when the player arrives at the course.

The moral seems to be to find some way of keeping golf balls warm all the time. Keep half a dozen on the central heating boiler perhaps or keep all of them in the airing cupboard all the time. When traveling keep them warm in the car.

Wind effects the flight of the ball, particularly the more sensitive balls with a high spin rate. Those who are really serious about the game will therefore play the type of ball that suits their game, and the weather conditions, best. Most handicap golfers need more distance and more roll most of the time. They also need protection from their mishits. So on average they would probably do best to use two-piece balls with a low spin rate. Golfers for whom control is more important than distance will usually opt for the three-piece ball unless conditions demand more run on the ball after landing.

The wise golfer tries out several different types of ball for himself or herself. On the other hand, your average Sunday golfer is inclined to replenish his stock from the cut-price "found-ball" rack at his pro shop – and what *he* is looking for is something that is reasonably shiny, not too scuffed and bears a familiar brand name.

By about 1880 the ballmakers cottoned on and hammered their gutties with ready-made nicks and cuts. The stock golf ball now flew about 50 per cent further than it used to.

The "Bramble" ball then appeared. This was moulded rather than hammered and had pimples rather than dimples. This was the first manufactured ball in the modern sense of the word.

These developments led to the Haskell ball and the modern wound rubber ball. The earliest ones had a solid rubber core around which great lengths of rubber thread were wound. But in the first years of the 20th century there was no uniformity either in size or weight. There is today.

BAGS

The golf bag did not make its appearance on the course until toward the end of the 19th century. Until that time golfers or their caddies carried a few clubs in the crook of their arms. A photograph of a famous fourball taken around 1880 – Jamie Anderson, Allan Robertson, "Old Tom" Morris and Major Boothby at the Swilcan Bridge at St Andrews – includes two caddies carrying some seven clubs apiece. Another of club players on Wimbledon Common, London in 1900 shows each caddy with a bag. And it was the sudden spread of the game after a national railway network had been established that made carry-bags essential.

Legend has it that the first canvas bag was produced by a sail-maker of Appledore, North Devon. (Appledore is close at hand to Westward Ho!, the first English links course where a club was set up in 1864). These canvas bags were soon provided with cane stiffeners, iron frames and one pocket at least for balls and a towel.

In spite of the fickle British climate raingear did not appear until the 1920s. Immediately, larger bags became necessary – and some were very large indeed. One or two players had their caddies carry as many as 25 clubs. These enormous bags were often made of leather and the total weight of them was literally staggering. Happily for caddies the Royal & Ancient and the USGA agreed in 1930 to make 14 clubs the maximum that could be used at any one time.

These days there are three main types of golf bag – the tournament bag, the trolley bag and the carry bag. And the serious traveling golfer will also own a bag cover, a holdall, a shoe bag and a practice-ball bag.

A tournament bag will have a 9-inch rim and at least a six-way divider at the rim to separate the clubs (some bags, however, boast a channel for each club). It will have a carrying strap which can be detached when a golf car is used. The inside will be lined to protect the clubs. There will be a large pocket for weather-proof clothing and smaller pockets for accessories, balls, cards, pitchmark menders, tee pegs, gloves and possibly refreshments. Two rings at the side will secure an umbrella. There will also be a rain hood available.

Trolley bags are similar in design to tournament bags but rather smaller, with rims of 8 or 8½ inches in diameter. Six-way dividers are common. The bags are usually made of lightweight PVC or polyurethane. There are the usual pockets for clothing and equipment.

Carry bags are narrower and lighter. Some are collapsible but with an optional stay to keep them rigid on the course. Most these days are made from nylon or a similar lightweight material.

Very light carry bags are still made which are smaller and lighter still and are called "Sunday bags" or "drainpipes." They are useful if a player is taking out only seven or eight clubs.

Some of these carry bags will be supplied with folding aluminum bagstands already attached; otherwise stands can be purchased separately.

Bags are best carried so that the weight is evenly divided across the small of the back. It may also be helpful to one's golf to carry the golf bag with the strap over the leading shoulder (the left shoulder for right-handers and the right shoulder for left-handers). The reasoning is that at the address position the leading shoulder should be slightly higher than the other and carrying the bag from that shoulder encourages this correct posture and makes it habitual.

Keep your bag or bags in good condition and never leave wet clothing or damp clubs in the bags. A good golf bag should last a golfing lifetime.

A selection of golf bags. On the top row are a variety of tournament and standard trolley bags, from the expensive on the left to the relatively cheap on the right. On the bottom row are a lightweight "carry" bag on a metal stand and two holdalls. The holdalls are useful for carrying shoes, practice balls and other accessories.

SHOES

Special shoes for golf did not come into fashion until about 70 years ago. Before that golfers wore their ordinary shoes or boots. Many gentlemen golfers wore spats or leggings over their calves and ankles and most ladies wore high-buttoned boots. The lower orders wore working or gardening boots.

By the 1930s special rubber-soled shoes came on the market along with the first spiked shoes. Originally the spikes were short and fixed into the soles, but soon the value of replaceable spikes became apparent as some spikes wore down much more quickly than others. Later rubber studded shoes similar to those worn on board ship by sailing buffs were introduced and have become very popular on courses where the ground is hard.

Which type of shoe is best depends not only on the state of the turf and the usual weather conditions but also on a player's swing. The soil needs to be gripped firmly and good balance must be maintained, particularly when the swing is extremely powerful, but at the same time there must be fluidity in the swing from the feet up.

In olden days players turned legs, hips and shoulders fully on the backswing almost as if they were going to walk away; then on swinging through turned everything equally fully, as though they were going to walk forward after the ball. These days while the hips turn on the backswing there is a feeling of resistance in the right leg and indeed in the right instep. Then on the downswing the right leg pushes the hips to the left, in-

itiating a powerful release of the club into and "through" the ball.

This action has to be taken into account when choosing shoes. But shoes that are specially built-up on one side to promote it have been ruled illegal.

The traditional golf shoe is what used to be called a "brogue," with an extra tongue or "kiltie" over the laces; but shoes resembling the popular "trainers" are taking over in some countries. Rubber or plastic waterproof shoes are the cheapest but have the disadvantage tht they do not "breathe." With active footwork they are also likely to split before the spikes need replacing.

Most shoes nowadays have weather-proofed leather uppers and composition soles. Some have insulation against the cold. Many have special lightweight

spikes. The latest lightweight shoes have synthetic uppers and dual-density soles.

The most important attributes of golf shoes are that they should be flexible, comfortable, and weatherproof and should provide the individual golfer with a suitable grip of the turf. Unless one is using a powered golf cart, shoes have to be comfortable for walks of four, five, six or even seven miles.

Golf shoes are usually of the "brogue" design, with a flap over the laces, and metal studs to help maintain balance. Recent developments have led to the the dimpled sole, which does the same as a metal-studded sole but needs no maintenance (replacing studs etc).

GLOVES

The left-hand golf glove has become a seemingly essential part of the right-handed golfer's uniform. It first came into use in the United States in the late 1920s and was popularised in Britain by Henry Cotton. He had made his first visit to the United States in 1928. Prompted by Tommy Armor, he made some crucial changes in his swing but retained his own personal two-knuckle left-hand grip and his firm belief in the absolutely crucial role of the left hand in a right-hander's swing.

Cotton taught that "tackiness" of the palms can affect the degree of touch and control available to a golfer on any particular day. Therefore, he said, everyone should wear a thin-skinned glove to provide the same grip whatever the conditions. A glove, he said, also saves a good deal of wear-and-tear for the hand, although in his own case he noted that his hands were free from callouses because he never allowed the club to move in his hand.

Henry Cotton, of course, was the supreme "hands player," whereas most modern golfers use the hands in reflex, subconsciously. This itself may account for the almost universal use of the glove today. For it is perhaps easier when wearing a skin-tight glove to forget the left hand altogether. However the ball is hit, the hand will not shift on the club.

Gloves are now available in a

Gloves look smart and colorful but have a purpose — to help the player keep a secure grip on the club in all conditions. They are only worn on the left-hand if you are right-handed and vice versa.

wide variety. The soft leather glove probably gives the best feel, but all-weather gloves in other materials are popular. Some players now wear gloves on both hands, at least in cold, wet and windy conditions.

Almost all players take the glove or gloves off when putting. The feel in the fingers is then considered crucial and there is obviously no chance of the club slipping in the hands when the ball is struck.

One or two "heretics" claim that the feel in the fingers is so important anyway that gloves should be discarded altogether and that most people would be able to play better without them. But the general conviction is that wearing a glove on the leading hand keeps that hand's vital role continuously in mind. The left wrist must be firm at impact when the ball is struck and always so related to the clubface that the face is precisely square (or open or closed) if that is what is needed for the shot in hand.

Henry Cotton would have added this: the left hand must *resist* the hit with the right — and a good glove is invaluable, helping it to do just that.

RAIN GEAR

Golf is one of the few games which does not stop for rain. Only if the course is flooded and play impossible, or if there is danger from lightning, is play suspended. Therefore the wise always come prepared.

A golf umbrella is useful (unless very high winds accompany the rain). But a good rain suit is mandatory. The best will not only keep the rain out but will "breathe," so that in humid weather condensation does not make the player wet within even though dry without.

The suit must be light in weight. It must be foldable without losing its shape or keeping the resultant creases. And the trousers must be sufficiently wide that they can be put on or taken off with ease over spiked golf shoes.

The best suits don't rustle, either. P.G. Wodehouse wrote of the golfer disturbed by the noise of the butterflies in the adjoining field. Rain trousers that cheep like a cricket can be even more disturbing.

In these days of casual wear a clean, well-styled jacket may be acceptable in the clubhouse, too, although it is advisable to make sure of this before entering. It will certainly be acceptable for general wear outside.

A good rain suit will boast pockets not only for one's hands but also for a scorecard, golf balls, tee pegs and so on. Space for a soft towel will also be valuable.

In cold climates some players prefer an oiled sweater to a rain jacket, but in any climate where rain is possible trousers are a must.

A rain hat is useful too. It should be waterproof and foldable and should have a sufficiently wide brim to stop water running down one's neck and, if possible, keep rain away from spectacles.

When playing in the rain it is important to keep the grips of one's clubs dry, and to dry them thoroughly if they get wet. One's golf bag should have a rain-hood; but even so water often penetrates the bag in some mysterious fashion and as the grips are at the bottom of the bag they often get surprisingly damp. If a bag is not supplied with a rain-hood it is advisable to buy one with an elasticated girth that will fit any size of bag. In wet weather one also needs a small brush or other device to keep shoe-spikes clear of mud and cut grass.

If the weather is cold as well as wet take a hand-warmer with you. Most of these now run on small fuel rods of slow-burning material. You just light them up, close the lid and put them in a pocket. They stay warm for several hours. Some players use them to keep their golf balls warm, reckoning that a warm ball will fly farther than a cold one. And so it will – but only if it has been warmed for at least 12 hours beforehand. A hand-warmer will however help keep a golf ball dry. That's almost as important. It may pay to have one or two extra pairs of gloves with you too.

Golf umbrellas are rather cumbersome things and if you do not have the benefit of a caddy it might be wise to buy an attachment which will fit the umbrella on to the handle of your golf trolley. Unless there is a wind blowing it should keep everything dry, including yourself, and leave at least one hand free.

Golfers who wear spectacles MUST invest in a form of rain visor either for the spectacles themselves or one that fits under the brim or visor of a golf cap.

When playing in the rain adjust your considerations of distance to suit. Not only will the turf be wet but the rain itself will take a few yards off every shot.

It should go without saying, but after playing in the rain every sensible golfer dries all his or her gear. Do not put the clubs anywhere near direct heat. Let them air-dry in a warm dry place. But dry the bag. Dry the umbrella. Take the rain gear out of the bag and dry that.

Dry any damp golf balls too. And, if you can, keep them warm. Warm golf balls play better than cold ones, but it is all-time warmth they need, not just a quick dry-off on radiator.

Right: A wide range of rain suits is now available. Some are simple and economical, others well-styled and fairly expensive. Those at the top of the range will keep you dry inside and out, while the most economical will probably produce a little condensation in warm weather. The man is wearing a Gore-Tex suit that "breathes," the lady a smart but more economical one.

Rain hats that you can fold up and carry in your bag are useful.

Umbrellas these days are as colorful as they are necessary.

TROLLEYS

After the Second World War the number of golfers increased dramatically, but in most countries the number of caddies diminished; the golf trolley or pull-cart arrived on the scene. The first trolleys had narrow pram wheels and were not very popular with head greenkeepers and course superintendents because they marked the fairways in wet weather. But soon the wide-wheeled trolley was introduced which, in spreading the weight, made the wheel tracks less obvious.

Lightweight metals have improved both the look and the performance of modern trolleys, most of which fold easily and can be packed in the boot of a car in seconds. Some have foldaway seats attached so that players can rest easy during those increasingly frequent hold-ups while they wait for the fairway or the green ahead to clear.

The first electrified trolleys appeared around 1970. They have become increasingly popular and, with the improvement of the dry battery, increasingly useful. Most will now do 36 holes without recharging, even on a hilly course. These trolleys, too, take apart and can be packed easily into the car boot. An electric trolley with a step so that the player can ride up the steepest hills is now also available.

The inevitable development of this trend has been the motorised golf-cart, which will carry two players and their clubs in ease and

style around the course. The only walking the players have to do is from the cart to their golf balls; on most courses special cart-paths are necessary so that fairways and even rough are not damaged.

In the United States the use of carts is compulsory on many courses. On some courses, admittedly, they are a boon, especially where distances between greens and tees are too great for comfort. But this has led to a reaction in other places, and on some courses the caddie is making a comeback; Pebble Beach in California is one of these. Other clubs like Pinehurst allow members to carry their own bags if they tee off at special times in the afternoons.

In Britain and Ireland motor-ised golf carts are mainly limited to the elderly and disabled, although they are becoming increasingly available for general use, especially at clubs owned by Japanese business interests. But the general opinion in Great Britain is that the game was made for walking and buying or renting an electric pull-trolley is as far as most Britons are prepared to go.

For the walking golfer the trolley or pull-cart is one of the great inventions of the age, particularly now that many have been electrified like the one in the center here. But the other two are at least light and easy to pull even on quite hilly courses. They also fold when you"ve finished and want to put them in the car.

OTHER ACCESSORIES

Once upon a time there was on open box on every tee filled every day with wet sand by the green-keeping staff. Alas, no more. These days everybody uses tee pegs and needs to have a reasonable number with them every time they step on to the first tee.

Most tee pegs are plastic, which is probably a sign of Hutbers Law in operation: Improvement means Deterioration. Plastic pegs can damage persimmon woods; if left on the ground can harm the blades of mowers; and on hard

ground will bend rather than penetrate the surface. Wooden tee pegs are relatively less harmless, but they do tend to break rather easily.

Tee pegs come in a variety of sizes, long ones for drivers, short ones for irons. But it is also possible to buy "castle tees" which hold the ball up on tripod legs or are made of rubber and can be used again and again. Some, known as Scotsman's tee pegs, have a tassel so that they can be readily recovered every time. If

using the last, remember that it is illegal to arrange the tassel at exact right angles to your line-of-aim when driving off.

You should also carry several ball markers for use when lifting a ball on the green; they have a habit of vanishing. A pitchfork for mending ballmarks on the greens is another vital accessory. A special small brush for keeping clubfaces clean is useful. A towel for drying the ball, and perhap's one's hands as well, is a necessity. A sponge ball-cleaner attached to

the bag can be helpful as well.

While many players carry the scorecard and a pencil in their pockets it is even better to tie a scorecard-holder to one's bag or trolley. At many clubs one can buy a distance chart as well to keep alongside the card. This will give exact distances from various landmarks fringing each fairway to the center of each green.

If the course being played is usually crowded a seat-stick will come in handy. And if there is fierce rough – gorse, thorn

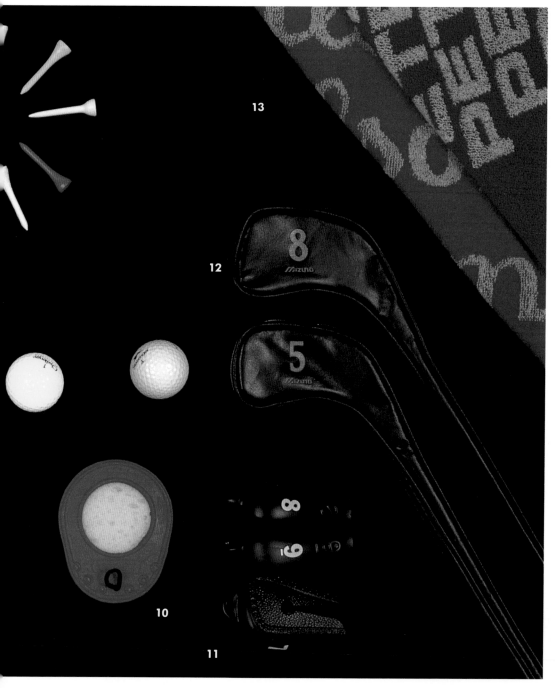

When the ball lands on the green it will usually make a pitchmark.

Lift the dented turf around the edges with your pitchmark mender. Then tap the area flat.

When you lift your ball on the green place a ball-marker *behind* it on the line of the putt.

bushes, and so on – so will a small box of sticking plasters!

To keep clubs in good condition if carrying a lightweight bag or using one with no dividers, it pays to buy some plastic tubes at the pro's shop.

There are a number of practice devices for use at home or when traveling. There is one attachment, for instance, which can be fixed to the shaft of a club to tell you your exact swing speed, and another which clicks at the right moment if your timing is right.

Battery-operated putting cups return your ball to you if it is hit correctly. Some models can be fitted in a briefcase which may also contain a take-apart putter.

A 12-inch rule with some white tape on the middle of it is a useful do-it-yourself practice device. In idle moments one practices the "Moment of Truth," a three- or four-inch swing along the line with a squared clubface.

There is no end to the ingenuity of golfers. Nor any end to the need for it.

A selection of useful accessories: (**1**) practice putting cup; (**2**) new grips; (**3**) cushioned bag-strap; (**4**) scorecard carrier; (**5**) brush to keep the grooves clean on your irons and woods; (**6**) ball-marker; (**7**) pitchmark repairer; (**8**) teepegs; (**9**) variety of balls; (**10**) ball-cleaner; (**11**) iron headcovers; (**12**) iron head-and-shaft covers; and (**13**) towels. All these are essential equipment for any serious round and most even for a "friendly."

GOLF PRO SHOPS

The Professional's Shop, once a small shed beside an even smaller workshop, now is the game's Aladdin's Cave.

Usually there is almost nothing relevant to the game that cannot be obtained there: clubs; balls; headcovers; gloves; bags; trolleys and pull-carts, manual and electric; golf carts to rent; hats, caps and visors; shirts, pants, sweaters; shoes; rain wear and umbrellas; teepegs, ball markers, cards, charts, pencils, magazines, books, videos; and aide or tuition from professionals

In competition now with discount and mail-order houses with nationwide outlets the pro's shop has got to be good to survive.

Most will have the equipment to "customise" the clubs they sell, so that the lie is right, the weight is right, the flex is right and the grips are right for the particular individual. Most will also have trial sets of clubs which club members and interested would-be buyers can try out on the course.

In the old days of hickory clubs, golfers had to choose their clubs by feel alone. Now machines are available which determine the swing-weight so that sets can be matched on the spot. In many pro shops there are swing computers which can determine a player's normal clubhead speed and angle of attack so that suitable shafts and clubheads can be provided.

Because so many high-handi-

cap players slice the ball some manufacturers produce hook-faced clubs to help compensate for the error in their swing action. But the compensation does not always work, for the causes of the slice are several and varied. So such clubs may not be suitable for everyone. Only the pro and the swing machine can tell which type of club is likely to suit. And only the pro himself can eradicate the slice. The most valuable product is the professional.

Group lessons are much less expensive than individual tuition, and none the worse for that. Golf lessons in company may be more reassuring and less traumatic than solo lessons. However, when the time comes that a player ceases to

be a beginner and wants to hit real "golf shots," fine-tuning by the professional is essential.

The pro shop will also have cold soft drinks available, vital in hot climates.

Discount shops too have an important role in golf-life. They give the average guy or gal the chance to buy modern equipment which otherwise would be outside their money-range. But there is a product they do not sell – help.

To raise the Genie, Aladdin had to rub his magic lamp. All we have to do is walk in and ask.

Left: A section of a typical professional's shop at a typical golf club. Most of the essentials are to be found here: clubs, bags, bag-stands, trolleys, golf balls, tees, etc. The club pro and his assistants will help you select your equipment.

Below and opposite: A modern Golf Center where there is a much wider selection of equipment. Many different makes of club will be immediately available and there will be facilities for testing and checking them not only for length and lie but also for performance in relation to your individual swing.

"When a pro has the opportunity to introduce the game to a young person that he or she can enjoy for the rest of life, *That's Important!*

When a pro can give a family a common interest, *That's Important!*

When a pro can introduce a retired person to an activity that brings both exercise and companionship, *That's Important!*"

Michael Hebron, American PGA Master Professional.

HOW TO CHOOSE

With so many different clubs, shafts and clubheads to choose there is no reason why any individual should not get properly fitted. Old-time pros were constantly in their workshops tinkering with their clubs. These days it has to be done by computer. Most golf centers now employ computerised swing-testing machines. These can analyse the individualities in any swing and indicate the most suitable lie, loft, weight and set. Some manufacturers make spare sets available for an 18-holes trial before you choose.

It is important, too, to choose clubs with the right thickness of grip for a player's hands. The acid test is reckoned to be whether the third finger of the left hand (with righthanders) just touches the thumb-pad.

Care of Clubs

The heads of all woods – particularly wooden ones – should always be protected with headcovers during a round. After a round in wet weather the covers must be removed and the clubhead carefully dried. Special care should be taken with the inset on the face of a wood. Any scuffed areas should be cleaned and revarnished.

Headcovers can also be bought for irons but are not essential. What is essential is that the face of every iron club should be kept clean and the grooves brushed regularly. Regular use of metal polish is also advised.

Never dry wet clubs near a fire or close to a radiator. Dr.y them off with a towel and let natural warmth finish the job.

Shafts should be dried and polished, too, and grips kept in good condition. You should treat leather grips with a touch of castor oil or linseed, rubber ones with soap and water.

GROOVES

A series of straight grooves with diverging sides and a symmetrical cross-section may be used.
Any rounding of groove shoulders shall be in the form of a radius which does not exceed 0.020in (0.5mm).
The width of the grooves shall not exceed 0.035in (0.9mm) using the 30-degree method of measurement on file at the Royal & Ancient Golf Club of St Andrews. The depth must not exceed 0.020in (0.5mm). The distance between edges of adjacent grooves must be not less than three times the width of a groove and not less than 0.075in (1.9mm).

USUAL WEIGHT AND LOFT

1-wood	13¼oz (376g)	loft 12 degrees
2	13½oz (383g)	loft 14 degrees
3	13¾oz (390g)	loft 16 degrees
4	14oz (387g)	loft 20 degrees
5	14¼oz (404g)	loft 24 degrees
1-iron	13½oz (383g)	loft 15 degrees
2	14oz (387g)	loft 19 degrees
3	14¼oz (404g)	loft 23 degrees
4	14½oz (411g)	loft 27 degrees
5	14¾oz (418g)	loft 31 degrees
6	15oz (425g)	loft 35 degrees
7	15¼oz (432g)	loft 39 degrees
8	15½oz (439g)	loft 43 degrees
9	15¾oz (446g)	loft 47 degrees
Wedge	16oz (454g)	loft 52 degrees
Sand iron	16¼oz (461g)	loft 58-62 degrees

When using high-spin balls, players will often use clubs with less loft than average.

DESIGN RULES

1. The club shall be composed of a shaft and a head. All parts should be fixed so that the club is one unit. The club may not be adjustable except for weight. It should not be substantially different from the traditional and customary form and make.

2. The shaft shall be generally straight with the same bending and twisting properties in any direction. It must be attached to the clubhead at the heel either directly or through a single plain neck or socket. (The shaft of a putter may be attached at any point in the head).

3. The grip must be substantially straight and must not be moulded for any part of the hands.

4. Clubheads must be plain in shape and (except for putters) have only one face.

5. The face must not be concave and must be hard and rigid. No markings are allowed except the usual grooves. Metal clubfaces may not have insets or attachments.

6. During a round the playing characteristics of a club may not be changed, but a damaged club may be repaired during a round.

FLEX

Degrees of flexibility of different shafts are usually rated as follows:

X – Very stiff: for the strongest players
S – Stiff: for most pros
R – Regular: for most amateurs
A – More Flexible: for older men and young ladies
L – Most flexible: for slightly older ladies.

NOTE Different swings need different flexes: the above can only be a general guide.

TECHNIQUES INTRODUCTION

Jack Nicklaus, the top golfer of the modern age, if not all time, winds up for another powerful drive.

As the first of the great golf writers, Horace Hutchinson, noted nearly a century ago, in each generation a great golfer has appeared who was able to "to stamp his own authority on the golf club of his time."

Allan Robertson has been called the first true golf pro. With willowy clubs and the shafts held in the palm rather than the fingers he "played gently and swung quietly." He rarely strayed off the narrow fairways of his time. This set the mode for the early 1800s. But there followed Young Tom Morris, "a bold spirit," who hit the ball prodigious distances with rather heavier clubs. In the 1870 Open, which he eventually won by 12 shots from his nearest rival, he did the 578-yard first hole at Prestwick, Scotland, in just three shots.

Then came Harry Vardon. He was the first man to break the mold. His clubs were shorter and lighter than those of other great players of his day. He gripped the clubshaft more in the fingers than the palm, and used the overlapping grip pioneered by a top Scottish amateur Johnny Laidlay, in which the little finger of his right hand overlapped the index finger of his left. Whereas most others of his time swung very fully on a very flat plane, Vardon used a compact, upright swing. He was one of the first to use a "flying" right elbow and some of his contemporaries insisted that he violated all the known laws of swing. But the most obviously striking thing about the Vardon swing was its efficient elegance.

Vardon had an unusual wrist action. His own description of it has baffled later experts. He wrote that he started the downswing with his hands and that he threw the club to the right and a little behind the body at the start. But he did this with his wrists still cocked, almost as if he was hitting a stake into the ground with his clubhead. For a long time afterwards the general theory was that power in golf came from a snap of the wrists, although Vardon himself denied this.

Vardon, like most others of his time, employed a cupped left wrist throughout the stroke. That is, the wrist was concave, bent back, not only at the address but at the top of the backswing and even when the ball was struck. Bobby Jones, the greatest of all American amateurs, made a special note of this Vardon action. He saw it as the one great difference between himself and Vardon. Although he used the cupped left wrist at the top of the backswing he had it flat, in line with his forearm, at impact.

With the arrival of the steel shaft in the late 1920s less and less was heard of "wrist-snap" and the flat or even bowed-out leading wrist became the order of the day.

Bobby Jones, who won the United States and British Opens and the US and British Amateurs in the same year (1930), was a wonderfully graceful swinger. He too started his backswing in this order . . . left foot, body, arms and only then the clubhead. Dragging the clubhead away last gave a kind of whiplash element to the swing. Walter Hagen, among others, used the same method.

But times were changing. Byron Nelson, who in 1945 won 18 tournaments (11 of them in succession) in the United States and enjoyed a scoring average of 68.3 over the 120 rounds he played in all, developed a method of his own. He stood close to the ball. On the backswing he kept his left arm ramrod straight. He started clubhead, hands, arms and body back in one piece. And on the downswing he turned his left wrist "square" – "toward my objective" as he put it – some 30 inches before impact and then on into the follow through. Strangely very few people copied him.

It was Nelson's fellow-Texan Ben Hogan who became the role model for golfers all around the world. So far he is the only man to have won three "Majors" in a single year, the U.S. and British Opens and the Masters (1953). He stressed the chain-reaction downswing: hips, turning left, releasing the body, legs and arms in one cohesive movement. The hands then multiply the speed achieved, he said. And the left wrist comes into impact supinated; that is, square to the line and slightly bowed. Hogan also stressed the power added by the forearm.

In Britain Henry Cotton was the last of the great "hands" players. A different concept of the golf swing had taken hold. In America after the charismatic Arnold Palmer with his middle-weight boxer's forearms another truly masterly golfer rose to fame – Jack Nicklaus. He was to win the U.S. Masters six times, the U.S. PGA five times, the U.S. Open four times, the British Open three times – and some 70 other tournaments around the world as well.

Nicklaus has an upright swing and a flying right elbow – shades of Harry Vardon! – but a tremendously powerful lower body action. It is Vardon and Hogan combined in an even stronger physique.

There will never be another Nicklaus, but his swing has personified a major change which has come over the teaching and understanding of golf. The modern swing is powerfully based on lower body action with the hands used mostly in reflex, subconsiously. At the same time, we have acquired a deeper understanding of the science and mechanics of the swing. Now the greatest golfers are taking lessons. The day of the "guru" has arrived.

Above left: James Braid and his distinctive action. One of the Great Triumvirate, with Harry Vardon and J.H. Taylor, they ruled golf at the turn of the century.

Below: Henry Cotton, Britain's great post-war champion, was one of the last top "hands" players.

SCIENCE AND THE SWING

The science of the golf swing is almost as old as the hills. It was way back in the year 1581 that the young astronomer Galileo made the first notes on the basic elements of "swing." During an earthquake in Pisa he calmly timed the arcs made by the lamps swinging from the ceiling of a church. He found that a long swing took the same amount of time as a short swing. Therefore, he pointed out, its speed at the bottom of the arc was greater. He also noted that a true swing is always on-plane. Later in his career he laid it down that the path of any projectile is a parabola.

In 1673 the Dutch physicist Christaan Huygens worked out how to use this pendulum effect to operate a clock. He controlled and energised the swing.

Then at some time in the late 17th century a farmer invented the flail. He or she joined two sticks together with a leather thong. The "swingle" greatly multiplied the speed initiated by the handle and made threshing grain infinitely less tiring.

In the 1680s Isaac Newton established his Laws of Motion. The first – a vital one for golfers – lays down that once it is in motion a body will continue on its course in a straight line unless some outside force intervenes.

The second Law holds that any change in momentum is proportional to the force causing the change and operates in the direction in which the force is acting. The third law is that to every action there is an equal and opposite reaction – hence the need for what has been called "dynamic stability" in a golfer's stance and lower body action.

Kinetic energy – energy in motion – is defined mathematically as one half Mass times Velocity squared ... $M \times V^2/2$. In golf Mass is equated with Weight, in particular the weight of the clubhead.

So there, in essence, are the scientific fundamentals of the golf swing. The law of the pendulum. The effect of the flail. The necessary straight line of impact. The plane of the swing. The clubhead's speed at the bottom of its arc and its effective weight.

But there are other factors involved. For one thing there is the ball. This is compressed when struck and leaps off the clubface at a speed related to both that of the clubhead and its own "coefficient of restitution." Some balls fly faster than others. Then there are matters of ballistics – the resistance offered by the air and by gravity and the effects of different types and degrees of spin put on the ball at impact. A clubface not precisely at right-angles to the line of compression will cause sidespin.

Finally there is the purely human factor. The work that muscles do or can do. The coordination between hand and eye (or in the case of sightless golfers between hand and imagination). Differences in posture and the effect of habit upon that posture. For instance an American biochemist, Roger J. Williams, pointed out that the muscle people use to draw their shoulders down may be attached to the ribs in several different ways. And some 35 percent of people either have peculiarities in the way the muscle used to flex the wrists is attached or don't have that particular muscle at all.

These differences can make it difficult for individuals to translate the relatively simple laws of swing and of motion into competent action on the golf course. It's not helped by the fact that, unless they can see themselves in a mirror, most people do not know and cannot tell exactly what they are doing. But now, with movies, videos and computers, the possibilities for explaining science in terms of everyday experience have widened enormously.

In the past 20 years detailed analyses have been produced by the Golf Society of Great Britain, by the National Golf Foundation and the Centinela Medical Center in America, and by surgeons, physics professors, computer experts and engineers, notably Theo Luxton in England and Homer Kelley in the USA. Among the insights produced are these:

A golfer can generate up to 4 horsepower.

But the clubface is in contact with the ball for only ½-inch to ¾-inch.

The force applied on a full shot averages around 1,400 lbs and with big hitters among male professionals rises to 2,000 lbs.

The instant at which the ball *leaves* the clubface is the crucial

1

4

The Powered Flail

The golf swing is a powered flail. The power is stored in the body, from the feet up. The body coils and the potential energy produced is more electrical than mechanical. That is, there is plenty of power available yet no massive effort is needed. We can see this in the first three pictures (**1**, **2** and **3**). We can also see that the flail is being used

"on plane." The club shaft is parallel to the ground at three important phases of the swing.

The "on plane" swing, so vital for consistency, is shown from a different angle in the lower pictures, (**4**, **5** and **6**) as is the coil of the body. These pictures are worth a great deal of study.

one, not the moment of impact.

The swing center is in the spine below the shoulders. It moves forward some six inches on the throughswing, while the head stays back.

Muscle power comes mainly from the thighs and back. And the most notable difference between professionals and amateurs lies in the amount of trunk rotation used.

With all good golfers the hips initiate the movement toward the ball.

The precise set of the clubface

when it meets the ball must be pre-programd in the brain. Any attempt to control impact made during the swing is futile.

Most of the scientific analyses, however, deal only with full swings – and these are in fact less than half the game.

In a total sense it is the lines, arcs and angles of geometry that really matter most.

Ball Control

The ball leaves the clubface in a straight line both as regards direction and height. Every well struck ball has underspin; this is what keeps it in the air. Topspin will cause it to dive into the ground.

A glancing blow or one in which the clubface is not squarely at right angles to the line of strike will immediately cause sidespin to develop. The ball will then curve in the air. "Slice spin," which for right-handers produces a curve from left to right, is produced by cutting across the ball from right to left. One cannot slide the clubface across the ball from left to right in quite the same way, but compressing the ball more on the side nearest to you will cause right to left "hook spin" to develop. A sliced ball will gain height but lose distance. A hooked ball will tend to fly lower and run further on landing.

Extra height can be gained by "laying back" the clubface, thereby adding to its loft. A lower flight can be had by "hooding" the clubface, turning it down and taking off some of the loft.

The crucial factors, then are the direction in which the clubhead is moving when the ball leaves it and the angle of the clubface at that instant.

British scientists who contributed to a book called *The Search For The Perfect Swing* for the Golf Society of Great Britain concluded that at impact the clubhead is in contact with the ball for only half of one-thousandth of a second traveling at 100 mph, so it is almost true to say that it might as well be detached from the shaft. It is rather like an explosive charge

firing a shell from a gun. But not quite. Other scientists have claimed that some pressure-on-the-ball, or resistance to deceleration, between impact and separation will enable a slower swing to achieve the same launching speed as a faster one. Certainly it is clear that it is clubhead speed at separation, when the ball leaves, that determines how far the ball will actually fly.

The important thing therefore is to sustain the line-of-compression – the planned line, the programd line, the straight line. The one half of one-thousandth-of-a-second when the ball is in contact with the clubface is the real moment of truth.

The flailing action of the golf swing, mainly activated by the release of the wristcock, requires no

The Accurate Approach
Above: Approach shot to a well-guarded green. Note the stance (**1**) and the line of aim. He starts back with the triangle formed by his arms and the club shaft intact (**2**). He swings back on-plane (**3** and **4**). On the downswing his hips and legs drag the club down and through (**5**) and as he finishes with his chest toward the target the ball sails off in the exact direction he had planned.

conscious effort. Additional force to sustain the line-of-compression is provided, the scientists say, by the big muscles of the back and of the thighs *dragging* the clubhead through Impact to Separation and (for right-handers) by the release and extension of the right fore-arm.

The Vital Plane

In the geometry of the swing the two most important elements are the Plane and the Plane Line. Ben Hogan's original concept of the swing-plane has in the course of time been redefined more precisely by engineer-golfer Homer

The Full Swing
Below: Here we see a full swing from the front. Note the stance (**1**) and the triangle formed by the arms and the club shaft. In (**2**) the player's weight has very definitely shifted to the right although his hips have not swayed to the right. In (**4**) he has coiled his body, his shoulders fully turned and his hips half turned. The club shaft is parallel to the ground. On the down-swing (**5**) the wristcock has been maintained until the hands are waist-high.

Kelley. Hogan pictured the plane as a pane of glass sloping down from the golfer's shoulders to the ball. The golfer had to keep the club below the glass. But the modern idea is slightly different and more precise. The clubshaft (or the club's "sweet spot") lies upon the surface of the plane. This is an imaginary flat surface lying at an angle which stretches to the horizon in both directions. It may be raised or lowered or aimed left or right, but still the club stays on the surface.

The clubshaft obeys "The Law of the Parallels." Whenever the shaft is parallel to the ground it is also parallel to the plane-line, the baseline of the plane. At any other time one end of the club or the other points down to the baseline – or to a faraway extension of it.

If this plane is visualised as an oblong pane of glass the Law of the Parallels still holds good; but at other times one end of the club-shaft or the other will point to one of the sides of the glass. The law holds whether the plane is flat or upright; whether it is changed in mid-swing, as it may be; and whether it is aimed left or right or straight.

The Law of the Parallels is as vital to a consistent golf swing as is "the Moment of Truth," that instant between impact with the clubface and separation as the ball flies off.

If the golfer is visualising the shaft of the club lying on the plane, the plane-line (the bottom edge of the imaginary pane of glass) will come through parallel to the line-of-strike but about two inches on the player's side of that line. It does so because the club-head or blade is offset from the

DOCTORS

Medical men make these points:

Muscles do not work like pieces of elastic. They contract. At the top of the backswing they must be relaxed. Only the right foot feels ready for action.

The pelvis needs to feel "tucked in."

The head should be in strict alignment with the neck, with the chin neither tucked down nor raised up.

The swing axis is not central but rises perpendicularly from a spot, in a right-handed player, a couple of inches inside the left heel.

The most active muscle in most golf swings is the left *flexor carpi ulnaris*. This works the third finger of the left hand.

SWING THROUGH THE BALL

On every good shot the leading edge of the clubface goes under the ball and *along* for one half to three-quarters of an inch, depending on the speed or force of the strike.
The ball then leaves practically at right angles to the set of the clubface at that time, its loft and its direction.
This is the reason why players are told to swing *through* the ball —
And why the wrists should be firm during the "impact interval."

shaft. Only if the player is visualising a "sweet-spot plane" does the plane-line coincide with the line-of-strike.

Visualisation is vital because in golf most of the game is played in the mind. The golfer programs the swing first in the computer of the mind, and just before the swing begins he or she "sees" the target and the flight of the ball toward it in the mind's eye. He or she is conscious of that "moment of truth" detected by science.

POWER SOURCES

The main source of power in golf is simply clubhead speed. But it is supported by "thrust." For it is not the speed of the clubhead at impact that matters most but rather its speed at separation – that is, when the ball leaves the clubface.

First, centrifugal force is generated by the swing and by the whip-like action produced by the uncocking of the wrists. This is reinforced by the action of the lower body – feet, legs and hips – by the release of the bent right elbow (with right-handers) and by the forceful extension of the right fore-arm in the follow-through.

Both power sources are in use in any full swing, but the accent placed upon them differs. Golfers can usually be divided into "hitters" and "swingers." Jack Nicklaus wrote that "the speed of my forward-swing leg and hip action is the main determinant of how far I'll hit the ball." He added, "I *do* hit through the ball – and think of hitting through the ball – very hard." The English old-timer Ted Ray, when asked how a pupil could hit the ball farther, took his ever-present pipe out of his mouth and said succinctly, "Hit it a bloody sight harder."

But old Harry Vardon, Bobby Jones, Henry Cotton and Sam Snead were all essentially swingers. Bobby Jones said he "free-wheeled through the ball." Cotton added a definite hit with the right hand to this free-wheeling feel, but he was not a power player. Sam Snead perhaps is best characterised as a "swinging hitter," the power of his strike disguised by the unsurpassed beauty of his swing.

If speed and thrust are the sources of power, the body has five power accumulators. They are (in a right-hander) the right elbow, the wrists, the right hand, the left shoulder and upper arm and the thighs or hips.

Maximum power from the elbow comes from its late release and the automatic forward thrust of the fore-arm. The release comes as the elbow passes the right hip. Similarly, much clubhead speed comes from a late release (or uncocking) of the wrists.

Some additional power derives from a roll of the fore-arms as the clubhead nears the ball – the famous "hit with the right hand."

Then again, clubhead speed can be assisted by late release of the upper left arm which stays "attached" to the left chest until the last moment. The feeling is of swinging from the left shoulder.

Finally there is the lower-body action referred to by Nicklaus, a powerful forward thrust with the feet and thighs (or, some would say, the hips).

In a full-power swing all these elements are naturally in full use. But in less-than-full-power swings, or as a general "feel" in the swing, only one or two may be used.

A true swing – "the pendulum

Here are three main power sources. In (**1**) we see the upper body coiled and the club shaft beyond the parallel, giving this professional his greatest width of arc. A long swing, taking the same time as a shorter swing, naturally produces higher club head speed. In (**2**) we see a full wristcock. The straightening of this wristcock — its release — will obviously add to this club head speed. In (**3**) note the position of the right elbow. Releasing this adds thrust. And the later the better.   1

plus the flail" – produces adequate power on its own. The Kent golfer Ernest Jones, returning from World War I minus a leg, found he could continue to play par golf as long as he just "swung the clubhead." He founded a famous school on this principle after emigrating to the United States in 1920. A true swing will tend to follow strictly the First Law of Motion: a body set in motion will tend to hold its course in a straight line unless some outside force intervenes.

The feeling of a true swing, Ernest Jones said, can be obtained by attaching a weight to a string and swinging this along with, and in time with, a golf club. If they keep time with one another, that's swinging. But, for obvious reasons, this can only be a mini-swing. In the real game the golfer has to *make* the clubhead swing, not *let* it swing, Jones added. He

DRAG

For many good players the feeling of *drag* at the start of the downswing is crucial.
It is the feeling of dragging the clubhead down and through with the leading shoulder or upper arm, or with the cocked wrists, or with the right forearm, or with the hips or legs. There is no law about it. However it is done, drag provides a launching ramp for the release of power into the swing.

or she must use this weight-on-a-string feel. The clubhead then will find its own arc and plane and stick to both of them without the golfer having to provide any leverage or hand action whatsoever.

The trouble with such simplicity, however, is that it is incomplete. In making the clubhead swing a golfer will use the big muscles of the back and thighs but probably will not use them fully. So the later teachers

have adopted different methods.

One may be characterised in this way: turn the body and swing the arms. In other words, turn and swing on the backswing, turn and swing on the throughswing. The great English golfer Henry Cotton, the archetypal "hands" player, had much correspondence with both Ernest Jones and Bobby Jones, insisting there must be a definite *hit* within the swing. His feeling was of a hit with the right hand *past* the left, as was that

2

3

of the Scottish-American champion Tommy Armor.

More recently the emphasis has been on swinging with the legs or hips (although "legs and pelvis" may be more anatomically accurate). The feeling of true swing is then maintained but the awareness of an inner power is added.

The individual has to choose for himself or herself which method or which "feel" is best for them. The sources of power remain the same for everyone; but which is used or felt to be used will differ from person to person. Every year a World Championship is held for disabled golfers. Some have only one arm, some only one leg. One or two will have no legs. Some may even be in wheelchairs. They still play good golf. They use whichever power source suits them. More important even than power, however, is accuracy.

Sources of Accuracy

The source of accuracy is that "Moment of Truth" when the clubface is in contact with the ball.

The contact must then be with the sweet spot on the clubface.

The clubface must be moving fast along the appropriate line.

It must be appropriately angled.

The speed of the clubhead must be appropriate to the moment.

One says "appropriate" because, in the first place, the line-of-strike may be straight or to the left or right. It depends on how the player wants the ball to behave. Secondly the clubface may be angled differently for a draw or a fade, a high shot or a low runner. Finally the clubhead speed may be full or at half or quarter speed depending on the distance involved in the shot.

So control of the "Moment of Truth" is control of the swing. Control of the swing is control of the game.

Striking the ball with the sweet spot is one of the most elusive talents in golf. The clubhead may be traveling at 100 mph. The shaft will be flexing and twisting very slightly. And the whole assembly, shoulders, arms and clubshaft will be stretched outward by centrifugal force. The problem is, how do you achieve consistency?

In part it will, again, be a matter of feel, practice and intent. But there are certain steps a golfer can take to counteract the outward pull of centrifugal force during a full swing. One may be to address the ball with the toe of the club. Another step may be to stretch away from the ball as the final movement before starting the backswing. A third may be to establish the weight of the body over your heels.

Establishing a fixed relationship between the hands and the sweet spot at the address can be crucial. In particular, the set of the leading or top hand (left hand for right-handers) can be related to the set of the clubface so that the one is, so to speak, the mirror image of the other. Then if the particular "set" of the hand is maintained through the impact area the "set" of the clubface will also be maintained. Hence the importance of a consistent and individual top-hand grip.

Finally repeated practice of the "Moment of Truth" alone – a

This player uses a long, wide swing. He *extends* his arms fully on the backswing and the weight of his upper body coming back beyond his right foot gives the impression of a sway. But it is the hips which shouldn't sway to the right (**2**). At the top of his backswing his body is fully coiled (**3**). The legs and hips now bring the club, the arms and the upper body down toward impact (**4**). The wrists are still cocked. The right elbow is close to the side. Release of both wrists and elbow give great power without effort (**5**). The wrists add speed and the right forearm, extending after the ball add punch or thrust. This happens automatically when there is the intention to *extend*.

JACK

Jack Nicklaus, the longest accurate driver of his day (and perhaps of all time), once made an interesting comparison between himself and two of his colleagues.
He himself had strong legs and used them, he said. Arnold Palmer had strong arms, shoulders and back. He used them. Chi Chi Rodriguez, a small and wiry man but extremely long off the tee, could move very fast. So he used speed of movement for power. In other words, exploit your particular physical assets to develop and improve your game.

---

miniature swing along a six-inch line without a ball – can be invaluable. This exercise will also feed the concept of a consistent line of strike into the computer of the brain. Then it is valuable to hit a series of very short shots when practicing with a ball, concentrating on actually *seeing* the clubface hit the ball.

Probably the easiest way to learn to swing at the appropriate speed is to familiarise yourself with quarter-shots, half-shots and three-quarter shots as well as full ones. *It is easier to control clubhead speed with the length of swing than with changes of rhythm* (although full swings at a more leisurely pace also need to be used occasionally).

Power in the Mind

It goes without saying – although from appearances it seems often to be forgotten – that a player needs to have clearly in mind both the distance the ball is to be hit and its intended trajectory when he or she hits a shot. There must be a clear *intention* to hit the ball to a specific place in a specific manner. Most psychologists would add that a player should always conjure up a *mental picture* of the target he or she is aiming at, the flight of the ball to that target, and the kind of swing that is going to be used.

Details of technique need to be "fed into the computer" on the practice ground or in very friendly friendly matches. Particular details can be brought on to the screen of the mind in competitions if necessary.

But in general it would seem best to aim for a reflex swing, a subconscious swing, powered by the appreciation of just what one wants the ball to do on each shot. In other words, once you have programed your computer, just relax and trust that it will feed the necessary instructions to your muscles.

1

4

SETTING-UP STANCE

The straight line is vital to good golf. It is the basic element in Newton's Laws of Motion. It is the loadstone for the perfect swing, the benchmark for the facing of the clubhead. It is to the straight line to the target that golfers must relate their aim, their stance, their grip, and the arc of their swings.

The first vital necessity, therefore, is to note and mark in your mind's eye that line before playing any shot, from drive to putt, and then to set yourself up in precise relationship to it, depending on the type of shot to be played.

A major difference between most professional and most amateur golfers is the fact that the former do this punctiliously, whereas the latter for the most part do not. Nor are most amateurs aware of the reason why this seemingly easy skill is in fact very difficult to acquire and needs to be practiced relentlessly.

The reason for the difficulty is the phenomenon of *parallax*, the apparent displacement of an object, or the difference in its apparent direction, when observed from two different points. In golf these two points are (a) behind the ball, while you look at the target, and (b) beside the ball but two feet or so away from it when you take up your stance. "I check my alignment at least once a week by laying a couple of clubs on the ground parallel to my target line," Curtis Strange has said. "The set-up is the single most important maneuver in golf," insists Jack Nicklaus. "I once considered aim, alignment and stance excruciatingly boring," Severiano Ballesteros once admitted. Then, he says, he "faced up to one of golf's hardest facts": they are vital. Nick Faldo, Greg Norman and the rest

of the top professionals never play any shot without carefully checking their alignment.

The line to the target is the crucial one. When standing behind the ball, most pros note a mark on the turf a foot or so in front of the ball precisely on a straight line to their target. On the practice ground they will place a club on the ground just beyond the ball with the shaft aiming along an exactly parallel line. Then they will place another club close to the line of their toes and parallel to the first. Then, before they try anything else, they will set their bodies – shoulders, hips, knees – parallel as well.

Only when that can be done without the aid of the clubs can a player alter his set-up with precision for different shots. He will now, perhaps, stand a bit open or a bit closed in order to fade or draw the ball. But only when the parallel lines have been established can a truly square stance be taken and accurate adjustments made to it.

To some players the line of the shoulders seem the most important; to others it is the line of the hips or of the knees. The finest precision in lining-up, however, will be attained if to being with shoulder, hips and feet are all parallel to the target line.

The width of the stance varies from player to player although the general advice is to have the feet about shoulder-width apart on long shots and to narrow the stance progressively as shots get shorter. Those who find it difficult to judge what shoulder-width means are sometimes advised to imagine they are about to catch a heavy sack being thrown down to them from a high platform. The

1

4

Testing The Stance

Lining up correctly is a fundamental necessity. If you are not lined up right you can't swing right. The basic stance is with the shoulders square to the line of aim (**2**). In (**1**) the professional has "closed" his shoulders. In (**3**) he has "opened" them. The use of a club across the front of the shoulders makes it fairly obvious whether those shoulders

are "square," "open" or "closed." To make this more obvious the professional in the lower sequence has opened and closed her shoulders more fully (**4** and **6**).

It is sometimes necessary to open or close one's set-up. Many players find it easier to insure an in-to-out swing if the shoulders are slightly closed or open them to play a fade. But first learn to be square.

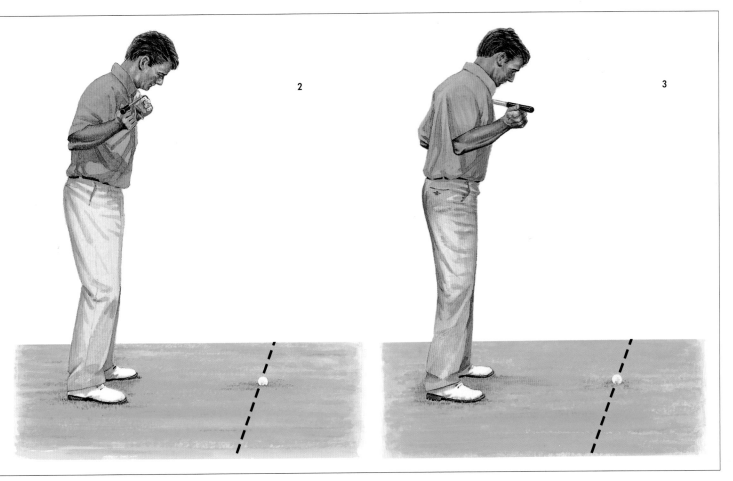

theory is that they will immediately adopt a strong, well-balanced stance.

The knees should be lightly flexed, the exact amount of flex being dependent on the length of a player's legs in relation of the length of the club. It should be the minimum necessary to establish and maintain what has been called "dynamic balance."

Many teachers advise pupils to bend from the waist when about to address the ball, but this can lead to a bent spine and to faulty distribution of weight. "Bend from the hips" is probably better

advice. If the knees are flexed at the same time the buttocks should go back behind the line to the heels, and with the head forward the body-weight will be properly centerd. The spine will be relatively straight up to the point just below the shoulders where the upper spine, the "neck spine" begins. This upper spine will be angled forward. Muscles should feel ready-for-action but completely relaxed.

Some players stand with the toes of both feet turned outwards, believing this facilitates the proper hip turn either way. Ben

BALLESTEROS

Here is one of the great iron players of today — Severiano Ballesteros. He says he starts the clubhead back with his right hand, not his left. At the top of the backswing it is his right hand he feels to be fully cocked. He braces his right leg but *maintains his knee-bend* and cocks the knee a little toward the target. He bends his left arm. Just before he completes his backswing, Ballesteros says, the lower half of his body begins to pull him forward. When he senses this *tugging* his right side "fires" automatically. After that he feels nothing. What are we to conclude from this? Surely only that "feels" differ and methods differ. But the strike does not differ.
The good player keeps a good rhythm going. He or she then sees that the clubface meets the back of the ball and launches it forward squarely aligned to the target. The action is firm and the head stays back until the ball has gone.

1

Hogan advised turning the left foot out "a quarter of a turn" (about 22 degrees), but to have the right foot square since this would control the amount of hip turn taken while at the same time setting the muscles up for the along-the-line drive in the throughswing. England's Henry Cotton said you should stand as you walk; he walked a bit pigeon-toed so he took his stance that way. The acid test is whether the set of the feet encourages a player's natural feeling of "swing" or not.

The arms hang vertically from the shoulders with the hands usually below the eyes. The leading arm (the left with right-handers) is slightly stretched at the address and the other arm slightly bent with the point of the elbow pointing to the waist. That arm is usually slightly behind or "inside" the leading arm.

Viewed from the front the leading arm and the club are usually more or less in line (though much depends on the grip and the set of the wrists) but from behind the player, looking up the line-of-aim, there is a distinct angle between arms and clubshaft.

Left: A man and a woman both set up perfectly in relation to their build. In both cases the seat is behind the heels. This balances the head, the heaviest single item in the body, which is directly above the end of the club shaft. The knees are flexed rather than bent so that the muscles are relaxed and both players are ready to swing in a relaxed but active manner.

Below: The man is setting-up in a simple and straight forward fashion. He starts by standing upright with the club held out in front of him and his arms straight (**1**). Then he bends from the hips (**2**), automatically lowering the club down toward the ball. By flexing his knees and allowing his seat to go back behind his heels (**3**) he grounds the club correctly behind the ball.

2

3

GRIPS

There are three main ways of gripping the club and two unusual ones.

1. The overlapping grip, in which the little finger of the lower hand (right for right-handers) overlaps the index finger of the higher.
2. The interlocking grip, in which these two fingers are firmly interlocked.
3. The two-handed or baseball grip, in which the two hands are separately on the shaft but close together.

A reverse overlap is often used for putting and sometimes for chipping. With this grip the index finger of the top hand overlaps one, two or three fingers of the lower. Very occasionally a cross-handed grip may be used with the usual higher hand below the other. A black golfer from South Africa, Sewsunker Sewgolum, won the Dutch Open three times using this rather eccentric grip.

Which grip is used depends to some exent on the musculature of the hands and their size. The

trous; some are distinctly right-handed; some are basically left-handed but play golf right-handed, like Ben Hogan. There is a school of thought that those who are distinctly right-handed should use the two-handed grip and then train the left hand in the ways of the right. Whichever grip is used the important thing is that the top hand should be firm when the ball is struck and for several inches after it has gone.

The Set of the Grip

The set of the hands at the address is usually defined by the number of knuckles of the top hand the player can see. One knuckle is too "weak." Two knuckles is standard, or neutral. Three knuckles is reckoned fairly "strong"; all four is very "strong." A two-knuckle grip with the palms of the hands parallel and square to the target line is the one most recommended, even though many of the most successful golfers do not use it.

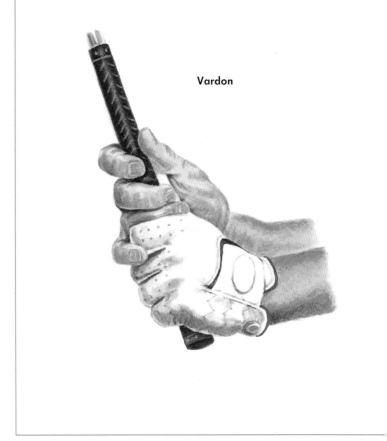

Vardon

JUDY'S PUNCH

When Judy Rankin (5ft 3in) first set out on the US women's tour she was told by a famous teacher, Bob Toski, that she would have to change her grip. It was too strong, he insisted. It showed four knuckles. If she carried on using it, he said, she would get nowhere, only out.

She replied, in effect, "Nuts!" only more politely and stuck with what she had got. What she got very soon was $150,000 in a single season and the Presidency of the US LPGA. Her "karate" grip allowed her to draw the ball and she became the longest driver, pound-for-pound, in America. [A drawn or hooked ball runs furthest on landing.]

Gripping Story
In the pictures above we see the three main types of grip on the club. The first is called the Vardon grip because the great Harry Vardon was the first to popularise it, although not the first to use it. The little finger of the right hand rests on the index finger of the left and when necessary presses on it. Vardon had very big hands and felt that in this way he bound his hands together in one unit. The second is the interlocking grip, used by Jack Nicklaus for one (Jack has small hands). The third is the two-handed grip, often called the "baseball grip" although batters do not grip quite like that. Right handers may find this the most natural grip to use.

---

hands, it is said, should work together as a unit; as if made of a single plastic moulding. They must not turn or twist one against the other during a swing.

Old-timer Harry Vardon who popularised the overlapping grip (even today its often called the Vardon grip), had very big hands. Jack Nicklaus, who has always used the interlocking grip has relatively small hands. The "Welsh wizard" Dai Rees, a small man, used the two-handed grip. It is impossible to say which grip is best. It is a matter of individuality – but also, perhaps, of "handedness." Some people are ambidex-

A complication arises when it is realised that the number of knuckles visible varies with the set of the wrists and the extent to which the top wrist is bent and whether the hands are ahead of the club, level with it or behind it. If the hands are behind the club head at the address and the top wrist is very bent, all four knuckles may be visible, even though basically the grip is "weak." If the hands are well ahead of the club, only one knuckle may be visible although the grip is perfectly neutral.

A better yardstick might be the set of the wrists and the fore-arms.

If both are square to the line-of-aim, then the grip is neutral. If the wrist and forearm of the top hand are turned so that the edge faces the line of aim then the grip is very strong. It is often said that the palms of the hands should be parallel, but what is really meant is that the insides of the wrists and forearms should face each other.

There is no natural law about these things. Several Open champions in Great Britain and the

United States – and in other countries, too – have used very strong grips, with the top wrist turned virtually at right-angles to the lower and all knuckles visible. The only law is that the two hands should bring the clubhead through impact firmly at the desired speed and along the desired line.

With a neutral grip and the forearms facing each other, the hands, wrists and arms naturally turn or roll clockwise on the backswing. They then turn the same amount anti-clockwise on the downswing and another 90 degrees or so on the follow through. If the turn does not happen for any reason, the player has to make it happen, ensuring that the clubface is correctly angled when the ball leaves. You can test it in practice, without a ball. Swing back with an iron club to the point where the blade is chest-high. The leading edge of the clubhead should be "up-and-down" (vertical). Now swing back and through to where the blade is again chest-high. The leading edge should once again be vertical.

With a strong grip, in which the

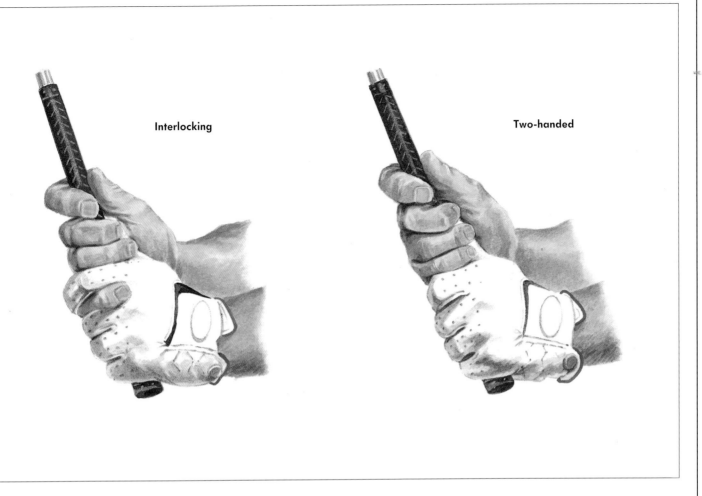

Interlocking

Two-handed

thumb of the upper hand is on the right side of the shaft as you look down at it, there will be less roll of the forearms on the backswing, and on the through swing the edge of the upper wrist and forearm gives a kind of karate chop through the point of impact. This is where the "strength" of the grip comes in. Its virtue lies in this powerful action. Its drawback is that nature causes a reverse roll at times, bringing the hands almost to the neutral position at impact; and since this will also have the effect of "turning in" the clubface, the result is likely to be a big pulled hook.

Most teachers would probably agree that the lower hand should normally be held square to the line-of-aim, with the palm and wrist facing directly forward whatever the set of the upper hand. With a strong grip in which both the upper and lower hands are turned so that their palms face each other, a straight hit becomes virtually impossible.

There is one further element in the "set" which needs to be considered: the extent to which the upper wrist is cupped or bent

PLAYER'S WEAKNESS

When Gary Player first arrived in Britain he too was told that he would never get anywhere with his very strong grip. So he weakened it. He made it, some said, much too weak. But a year later he won the British Masters and an invitation to the US Masters, which he has since won three times. [His grip is now more neutral].

With him the very strong grip caused a big, big hook occasionally. That's why he had to change. To compensate for any loss of length he built up his muscles. The fact is that it is the grip that is personally effective that counts.

back at the address and during the stroke. A century ago almost every golfer cupped the left wrist, then dragged the clubhead away in the backswing – hands, arms and body first, clubhead last. At the top of the backswing the left wrist was under the shaft and the clubface angled almost vertically down toward the ground – thoroughly "open." This action helped to whip the clubhead through the ball and it also insured that during the impact interval – the ¾-inch moment of truth – the left wrist would be flat, in line with the forearm. With any other "set," the

thought of whipping the club through would cause the left wrist to flap – that is, to bend forward too soon – ruining the stroke.

The cupped-wrist action was still being used in Bobby Jones" and Walter Hagen's heyday in the 1920s; but as steel shafts became universal there was felt to be less of a need to whip the ball and the action which later became known as "square-to-square" began to take precedence. In this action the left wrist is flat, in line with the shaft, at the address and at the top of the backswing. The clubface at the top is neutral, not up-and-

down and not facing skyward.

Some players have the top wrist right on top, bowed-out, at the top of the backswing and bring it through bowed out, giving the clubhead extra clout that way. But this action can be risky, inviting an occasional hook. Lee Trevino, who has always markedly bowed-out his left wrist, stands wide open to avoid the hook and plays a power-fade instead. Ben Hogan, who when young was plagued with a wild hook, eventually used his own version of the cupped-left-wrist action on the backswing and considered it one of the secrets of his consistency. As in all golf, the action that works consistently for you is the action to use best.

Taking the Grip

Players should take their grip on the club with the clubface precisely square and upper hand first (the left hand for right-handers). The shaft should lie half in the fingers, half in the palm. That is it runs from the crook of the index finger diagonally across the hand

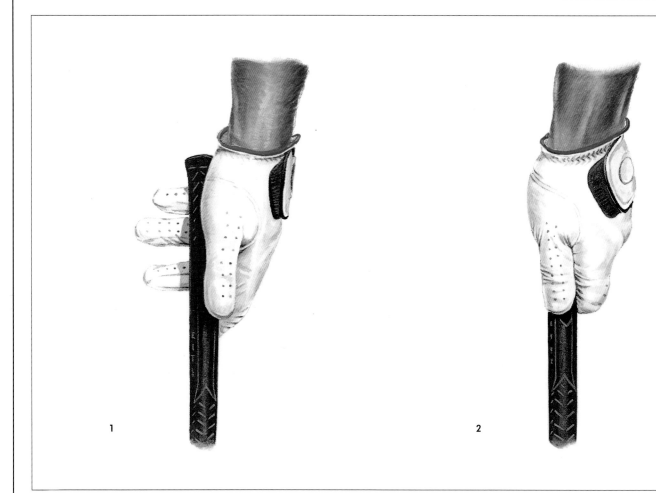

1

2

Taking the Grip

Above: A right-handed player takes his grip. First the fingers of the top hand, in this case the left, are placed under the shaft (**1**). Then the thumb is placed on the top of the shaft and slightly to the right (**2**). The thumb is pulled up rather than stretched down the shaft. The lower hand, the right, is now added (**3**), the center of the palm pressing on the thumb of the left. The fingers are wrapped round the shaft (**4**). The thumb is to the left.

Setting The Grip

Right: Here we have three different settings for the grip. The first is called "weak," the second "neutral" and the third "strong." In the first only one knuckle of the top hand is visible to the player. In the neutral grip two knuckles are visible. In the strong grip, three or sometimes four knuckles become visible. Most players use the neutral one. But some use the strong grip which gives a power feel.

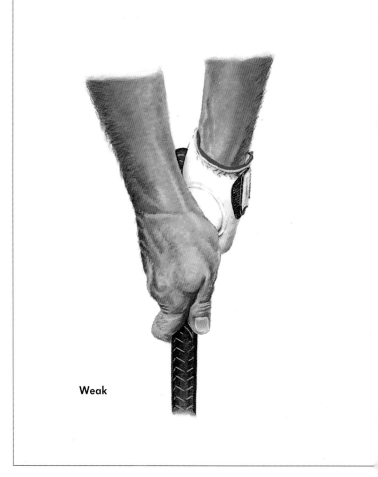

Weak

to the heel of the palm or thumb-pad. An inch or so of the clubshaft should show beyond the closed hand. Hogan's test for the left hand grip was whether or not the club could be held, balanced, just by the crook of the index finger and the heel alone, with the other fingers off the club.

The lower hand (the right with right-handers) holds the shaft mainly in the fingers, the two middle ones supplying most of the grip.

Research suggests that the two most active fingers in the grip in a muscular sense are the third finger of each hand. Opinions differ as to whether the grip should be firm or light. Possibly it depends on which type of wrist action is used. With a very cupped top-hand grip and "open" action a light grip, almost a touch-it grip, may be better. With the square-to-square method and the bowed-out left wrist action a firm top-hand grip is probably advisable. The main essential is to avoid a flip of the wrists, certainly before impact. With a cupped top-hand wrist such a flip is almost impossible for the swing itself will straighten the wrist. But with a bowed-out wrist a flip is almost inevitable unless the grip is firm.

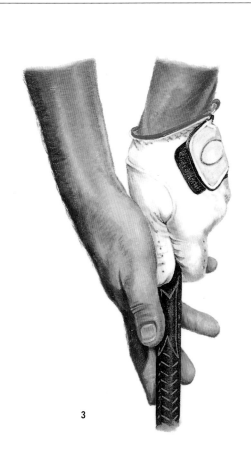

3

4

Neutral

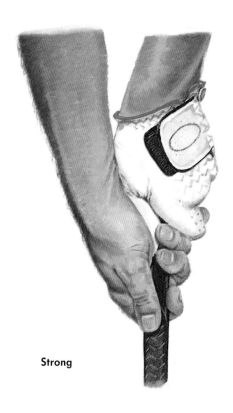

Strong

SET-UP ROUTINE

Every player should adopt a set-up routine of his or her own and to stick to it religiously. The basic elements of it are of course the target line, the grip and the stance.

Here is a 10-point plan:

1. Stand behind the ball and select a target: an area of fairway in the distance with, say, a tree or a house or the flag behind it; the green or a particular spot on the green; or the hole itself.
2. Note a mark on the turf a foot or so in front of the ball which is precisely on that line.
3. With the clubhead on the ground and the toe pointing at the mark on the turf, take your grip.

slowly, gracefully start the backswing.

How the stance will be related to the target line depends on your individual method and the kind of shot to be played. For a straight shot it will usually be square to the line. For a fade it may be open with the leading foot drawn back an inch or two from the line; for a draw, with the back foot drawn back.

Many top professionals advise players to keep the ball in the same position relative to the feet with every club unless they want to do a special shot of some kind – a low runner, perhaps, or a very high ball, or a drastic curve of

---

HEAD

The head may move, rotating a few degrees to the rear on the backswing, but the hub of the swing in the neck-spine must remain still until you are well into your follow through.
To keep the hub still, imagine that there is a straight line, a distance-piece, down from the adam's apple to the back of the ball. It must never move.
In deep rough or in a sand bunker, lengthen the imaginary line. Then you can be sure of swinging the leading edge of the clubface well under the ball, and of keeping the hub still.

AMERICAN TAKEAWAY

When starting the swing the takeaway should be as slow as the start of a pendulum and low to the ground, just brushing the turf.
The start-down should also be as slow and as smooth as a pendulum changing direction.

---

4. Raise the club to eye level and aim the leading edge at the target or along the target line, with the edge vertical.
5. Now step around and place the clubhead directly behind the ball using (if right-handed) the right hand.
6. Make sure the clubface is precisely square to the target line and regrip the club.
7. Place your feet together opposite the ball.
8. Widen the stance, making sure that you relate it to the target line and that the ball is in the correct position for the particular club you are using.
9. Look along the target line and back up again.
10. Now waggle along the line, make a slight forward "press," and

some kind. Others prefer to have the ball opposite the instep of the leading foot for a drive, nearer the center of the stance for a mid-iron, and closer to the back foot for a wedge. Again, what works best is what is right.

For many players the "waggle" during setting up is the coming stroke in miniature. It is a rehearsal of the type and strength of the stroke. And the forward "press" is almost a rehearsal of the position of hands and clubhead they want to achieve at impact – a reminder, too, of the shift of weight and the correct angle of the clubface. (It is often said that the position at impact is a mirror image of that at the address. But this is not so. The feet are moving the hips left. The head is back, the shoulder behind it

down. And the hands are probably ahead of the ball). It is well worth rehearsing impact, at least in the mind.

And what of a practice swing or two? Do it by all means, but do it *before* you step up to address the ball. Practice swings are useful to bring up the graphics of the swing, the elementary geometry, on the screen of your mind to the best of your favorite rhythm. The essential geometry concerns the target line, the plane and the line of strike. This last comes from in-

side the target line, just slightly outside, then in again. But the feeling is that it comes in and then *along* the target line and up.

It is advisable always to take a practice swing to a full finish. One should never practice the backswing on its own (even without a ball indoors), but swing through to the finish every time.

To Sum Up

Always aim at a precise target. If the shot is blind the target will

---

BE AWARE

Most great players train themselves to be aware of the arc and position of the clubface throughout the swing. They know where it is and where it is going.

have to be in your mind's eye. Either way you must note a mark on the turf precisely on the line to the target.

Having done this take your stance parallel to that line. Only then, if adjustment is necessary for any reason, should you stand "open" or "closed."

Make your stance wide enough to feel "ready for action" on long shots and narrow enough to feel elegant on short ones.

The buttocks should be behind the heels. Then you should bend forward from the hips, flexing rather than bending the knees unless you are very tall.

Your arms should hang almost vertically from the shoulders. The leading arm (left for right-handers) should feel lightly stretched; the other arm should be bent slightly at the elbow and positioned slightly "inside" the leading arm.

Whichever grip is used, your hands should feel like a single moulding: two hands that act as one. The grip should be finalised with the clubhead on the ground and the clubface precisely square to the target lie.

Develop a regular set-up routine to suit the particular tempo of your game. And, if possible, keep a slight motion going from the time you take your stance to the very moment of the takeaway.

Above left: The player is carefully assessing the shot he has to make and is equally taking precise aim from directly behind the ball. Never be casual about this. Don't take any time over it, but always do it. Note a mark on the turf a foot or two ahead of the ball which is exactly on the line so that you can aim precisely and align yourself accurately.

Above and right: The player is about to take his stance squarely parallel to his line of aim. His intention is to hit a straight shot and so his stance is "square" and his club head is placed squarely behind the ball. It is close behind the ball but not, of course, touching it. Once again it is important not to be too casual about this. Golf is a game requiring what might be called "relaxed precision."

DRIVERS

For the accomplished golfer the driver is perhaps the most important club in the bag after the putter. For the average golfer it is a puzzle, the club for the wishful thinker. And the duffer should leave it at home.

It is the longest club, usually 43 inches in the shaft. It has the least loft, 10 degrees or even less. This makes it harder to put the necessary backspin on the ball – but easier to give it unwanted sidespin. The first priority, then, when using the driver is to deliver the clubface to the ball with perfect accuracy. Only if this is done will the extra distance the club provides prove of any value at all. So the problem is how to combine maximum clubhead speed with great accuracy of strike.

The first step in solving this problem, as all great golfers past and present would agree, is to select the right driver for you. The swing-weight has to be right; the flex has to be right; the length has to be right; the "feel" has to be right. Sam Snead, whose driving combined long distance with amazing accuracy for 50 years or more in competition, owned a favorite driver he had been given by fellow pro Henry Picard in 1936 which he used well into the

vital, great attention should be paid to your alignment. A slightly closed stance is usually recommended. The takeaway should be low, smooth and wide. The turn of the torso must be full. And the clubshaft must be on-plane at the top of the backswing. That is, when it is parallel to the ground it must also be parallel to the intended line-of-strike (usually the target line). The start of the down swing must be as slow and smooth as a pendulum.

As a general rule players are advised to tee up so that 50 per cent of the ball is above the top of the clubhead and to have the ball well forward in the stance. With the driver the ball is hit on the upswing. This is important if a very long shot is desired. The legendary Bobby Jones, who had a degree in engineering and an enquiring technical mind, had the theory tested with a driving machine. A number of balls were contacted before the clubhead reached the lowest point of its arc and an equal number after it had reached that point. The "afters" won hands down.

"Where extreme length is desired the aim should be to impart as little underspin as possible," Jones remarked. So he teed

1

4

OPPOSITES

Golf is a game of opposites. You aim left to curve the ball right, right to curve the ball left.
You hit down to make the ball rise, hit up to make the ball run. Short shots are hit firmly, long shots in a lazy fashion. There is one major exception: you hit straight to make the ball fly straight.

1960s. In the end it had more nuts and bolts in it, he admitted, than any club he had ever seen and was even wired together here and there. But Sam felt it kept his swing in the groove better than any of his other drivers.

It is impossible to describe "feel." But most top professionals seem to agree that a driver's clubhead should feel light and manageable – yet with just enough weight to transmit the feeling of "drag" at the start of the downswing. It should nourish the appreciation of "good tempo."

Because accuracy of strike is so

the ball for his drives high and well forward.

All top golfers throughout the game's recorded history have agreed that for full power a full body turn is needed, particularly of the hips or lower back. Interestingly, Harry Vardon advised turning from the waist. "It is the only way to success at golf," he insisted. These days England's Nick Faldo says "Turn the stomach," and his coach David Leadbetter, "Turn the navel." Jack Nicklaus has described the idea of a big shoulder turn over a restricted hip turn as "hogwash," insisting

SWINGWEIGHT

Swingweight is a scale of measurement combining balance, weight and shaft flex of a golf club. It represents science applied to "feel." Recommended swingweights for men range from D0 (light) to D5 (heavy) and for ladies from C0 to C9.
The concept of swingweight allows manufacturers to offer sets of clubs from driver to wedge which all, theoretically have the same feel.

that every good driver needs the fullest hip turn he or she can manage while staying well balanced.

The hips or legs, then, lead the downswing, and as they approach

"the hitting area" Bobby Jones discerned in all his best contemporaries "a powerful wrench of the body."

All agree that the downswing

starts with a smooth pulling action, and that for accuracy's sake the player should have the intended line-of-strike in mind.

The only latitude allowed in all these agreed techniques for the average player is in the question of the height of the tee-peg. If you are by nature a low-hitter, they say, never tee the ball low when you drive off. If you are naturally a high-ball hitter be careful not to tee too high. Tee the ball at the height appropriate to your own individul game.

Another useful piece of advice is: "Go with the shot you"'ve got."

In other words, if you tend to fade or to hook the ball, you should consistently allow for that in your overall game plan. The first truly great South African golfer, Bobby Locke, hooked virtually every drive he hit. He had grooved that hook so he knew to a yard where the ball would finish. Jack Nicklaus plays a power-fade. When on the tee a player must always relate the shape of the hole and the distances of the hazards to the individual characteristics of his own game. When the driver is used, maximum length must be combined with maximum accuracy.

In Short

Pick a Driver that feels good

Align yourself very carefully

Tee the ball high and forward

Turn smoothly and fully on the backswing

Drag the club down and through with the lower body on the downswing

And keep your head back and down until the ball is long gone in the distance.

Using the Driver
The ball is opposite the left heel in (1). The stance is as wide as the shoulders. In (2) the player has started the takeaway. His shoulders have turned. His weight is over his right foot. But there is no wristcock yet. His wrists cocked naturally on the way to the top, pictured in (3). Now his turn is complete and his left heel has been raised off the ground.

In (4) the down-swing has started and the weight has gone back on to the left heel. The hips have turned before the shoulders which are lagging back. By (5) the hit is done. The head is back, counter balancing the force of the hit, leading to a full finish (6).

FAIRWAY WOODS

Fairway woods are used when the lie is good and the distance required is long. The shafts are longer than those of irons, the soles broader, the heads bigger.

In the old days the clubs were named brassie, *spoon* and *baffy*; they were the equivalent of the modern 2-, 3- and 5-woods. The most famous fairway wood shot of all time was the 4-wood struck by Gene Sarazen at the 15th hole at Augusta National in the second U.S. Masters tournament in 1935. It sailed 235 yards over the pond, on to the green and into the hole for an albatross (3 under par). Sarazen went on to win a 36-holes play-off against Craig Wood. The 4-wood was always one of Sarazen's favorite clubs, yet nowadays it is little used by the tournament professionals. Most pros can get the same distance with a long-iron, and with a greater feeling of security. Most amateurs now use only the 3- and 5-woods for fairway shots; and many take 7- and 9-woods with them for shots out of the short rough. The 2-wood also seems in decline, though

The shafts of fairway woods are usually shorter by half an inch as the loft increases. The 3-wood will probably have a 42-inch shaft and 18 to 24 degrees of loft. But 3- and 5-irons will have shafts perhaps four inches shorter and lofts six or seven degrees higher. The types of swing needed will therefore differ.

With the fairway woods the ball is swept away. Because of the longer shaft the swing is wider and the swing-plane less upright than with iron clubs. The advice is often given: "Swing, don't hit." The stroke should be smooth, long and unhurried.

Most players "bring the ball back in the stance" as the number of the club and the loft increase. (The phrase is in quotes because in fact it is the set of the feet that is altered, not that of the ball.) With a 3-wood the ball might be opposite the left heel if the player is right-handed; with a 5-wood it will be two inches or so further to the right. But the player must always remember that with a wooden club the ball is best swept

SPOON-FED

The 3-wood — once called the Spoon — is a club of infinite resource. So said Roger Wethered, last amateur to get within a shot of winning the British Open (in 1921). Cynics then called it "the duffer's comfort." But, said Wethered, "it is also a brilliant companion to lovers of fancy shots."

It has just enough loft to deal with cuppy lies and just enough strength for a good long hit. And as one David Douglas said a century ago: "You must use it like a scythe . . . Must sweep, not strike." In today's terms that makes it user-friendly.

Nick Faldo's use of a metal one in winning the 1990 Open may bring it back into favor.

These changes in club use have come about mainly because of the technical improvements made to shafts and clubheads and the great widening of choice. It is even possible to buy an all-woods set of clubs. Such a set would suit a player who feels easier when playing a sweeping type of stroke, brushing the turf rather than hitting down on it and taking a divot. Also one in which the broader sole and larger head of a wood instils a little extra confidence.

away, rather than thumped away.

Whether a wood should be used rather than an iron thus depends largely on the lie. There should be a clear, uninterrupted path for the clubhead. No bump in the way. No divot to be dealt with.

The natural action of the player concerned will also affect the choice of club. If he or she is a high-ball hitter by nature fairway woods may be easier to hit than irons, the reverse being true for low-ball hitters. Use the club that suits the swing may be the best advice.

WOODLOFT

These are the usual degrees of loft on fairway woods:

2-wood 12 degrees	5-wood 24 degrees
3-wood 16 degrees	7-wood 32 degrees
4-wood 20 degrees	9-wood 40 degrees

Bobby Jones once remarked that the inexperienced player is always likely to choose a club because of the number on it not because of what he or she can do with it. So every golfer should make themselves aware of what

they can and cannot do with their fairway woods. Also the distance that they can usually achieve with each one. Another piece of wisdom from Bobby Jones was this: "The desire for length at any cost more often than not causes the

player to exceed his limit.''

The essence of the swing is smoothness – one flowing, continuous motion. The wood is swept away, actually perhaps brushing the grass at the start of the backswing. There should be a definite feeling of width on the backswing. The whole torso turns as fully as is consistent with good balance. At the top the clubshaft in a full swing will be parallel to the line-of-aim.

Action shots of the top golfers show that, with right-handers, the left side actually starts to move forward toward the ball and the line-of-aim before the clubshaft reaches the top of the backswing. But this appears to be an unconscious movement and probably should not be started deliberately. The intention to *sweep* the clubhead smoothly "through" the ball is possibly enough to make the early lower-body movement happen.

Practice in brushing the turf (or even brushing the carpet if you are indoors) can be invaluable to those who want to play their fairway woods well. After a dozen or so swings without a ball most people should become aware of the lower body action that is necessary for an effective shot.

Lofted clubs like the 7- and 9-woods can be effectively used off the fairway for shorter approach shots. But their real role is in playing out of light rough or fairly long grass. Special woods with "bump soles" are available for use in the rough and with these you need to hit "down and through" to get the ball up in the air more quickly.

But the essential recipe for the successful use of normal fairway woods are a good lie and a full, clean sweep with the clubhead.

On the Fairway
With fairway woods the swing is similar to that with the driver but as the ball is not teed-up it is not quite so far forward in the stance (**1**). The backswing is the same — all in one piece (**2**). The swing is full; in this case very full (**3**). On the downswing the player is preparing to sweep the ball away. The butt end of the club is pointing down to the ball and the weight is centerd (**4**). On the follow through the head is back but quite still. The weight has gone left and the right foot has come up on to the toes (**5**). Once again there is a full finish (**6**) and the player has maintained a perfect balance.

Long Irons

The long irons are those numbered 1, 2, 3 and 4. The lengths of the shafts for men are usually 39 inches, 38½in, 38in and 37½in respectively. The degrees of loft, which determine how high the ball can be hit, are usually 15, 19, 23 and 27 respectively. The clubs are intended for fairway shots from distances of from, say, 160 to 210 yards. The 1-iron however is used mostly by professionals as a surrogate driver when fairways are tight and the second shot will not be of extreme length. Few week-end players use the club at all these days. Their 2- and 3-irons do them well enough.

Although it is true that all players should use the same basic swing with all clubs, there are some small but significant differences in the way irons are used as compared with woods. As the shafts are shorter the swing plane tends to be more upright. The strike, while still a sweep is a more downward sweep. The blade clips the turf instead of brushing along it. And as the blades of the irons are so much smaller than the heads of woods and cannot be rounded-off like woods to forgive the slight mishits, even greater accuracy of strike is required.

For that reason, as players waggle the clubhead before starting to swing, they are well advised to relate the sweetspot to the center of the back of the ball, seeing the relationship both in the mind's eye and in their normal vision.

The stance is usually square. The feet are not quite as wide apart as the shoulders. The left arm (if you are right-handed) is straight, the left shoulder is higher than the right, and the left hip is slightly foward toward the target. With most players the ball is an inch or so to the right of where it would be if using a fairway wood.

Once again the "take-away" is wide, giving a feeling of full extension to the backswing. The body weight goes round on the right and the head is almost directly over the flexed right knee. Most players allow the head to turn slightly to the right while keeping the "hub" between the shoulder blades steady. With most top players the hands cock as they reach waist height.

There is a feeling of the body being coiled ready for action when the backswing is completed. But it is here that most long-iron shots can go wrong. For this feeling of a power-coil can lead to an effort to hit the ball hard which is deceptive and even dangerous. The long-iron swing, they tell us, should be smooth and elegant. It is still a swing, not a hit.

One of the greatest difficulties teachers experience in getting pupils to use their long-irons

Using The Irons

Below: As can be seen in picture (**1**) with all the irons the ball is usually more central in the stance. The takeaway is wide and the arms extend away from the body as fully as is possible without causing a sway to the right (**2**). The swing is full so that maximum club head speed can be generated with minimum effort (**3**). The hips turn ahead of the shoulders on the down-swing (**4**). The weight naturally shifts to the left. The wrists are then released, also quite naturally, and although there has clearly been a forceful hit the player has kept perfect balance (**5**). This leads to a perfect finish as we see in picture (**6**).

1

2

3

Left: The address position for both the man and the woman is virtually identical, although each has a slightly different grip. The weight is slightly to the right because in each case the head is to the right "behind the ball." Both are ready to swing.

The arms are as close together as Nature permits and in each case the right elbow is pointing to the right hip. The heads are in what might be called a "neutral" position with the chins neither pressed down nor lifted up.

simple and effective formula.

As the downswing starts you should have in mind the inside line of strike. As it comes toward the ball the blade of the club should be swinging in at a narrow angle toward the target line. It should meet the ball squarely, collect it and for an inch or so cut slightly across the target line – in-to-out – then return in once again and up. The feeling, however, is that of swinging the club in to the target line and then along that line.

After the strike there should be a feeling of wide and decisive *extension* after the ball. The swing should then be allowed to come through naturally, inevitably to a full finish.

Each individual will hit different distances with different clubs in varying conditions. But as a general guide here are the ranges a good male amateur might expect from his long irons:

1-iron .... 190 to 220 yards
2-iron .... 180 to 200 yards
3-iron .... 170 to 185 yards
4-iron .... 160 to 175 yards

It goes without saying that every serious golfer must make himself or herself familiar with the usual distance he or she hits every club in the bag.

properly is to convince them that the club will do the work – that the loft on the clubface will automatically send the ball up to the required height, and that a wide, smooth unhurried swing will itself provide the necessary clubhead speed for the shot. At the top of the backswing the feeling should be of an intention to swing quietly but fully *along* the line-of-aim.

The downswing begins in the same way that any other full swing begins – with a feeling of *dragging* the club down, through and along. The drag may be felt to be with the legs, the hips, the forward shoulder or even the arms. It is the drag that is crucial: drag, release and swing through is the

THE HUB OF THE SWING

The "hub" of the swing is at the base of the neck between the shoulder blades, so to speak. One swings around this "hub" and it is this rather than the head which one has to keep as still as humanly possible. This is naturally important on all shots of course, but particularly important with the long irons which demand absolute precision.

4

5

6

MIDDLE IRONS

The middle irons are the 5-, 6- and 7-irons. They are for the middle-distance shots to the greens. For the average player this probably means shots of from 120 to 160 yards.

For many people these are their favorite clubs. They are easier to use than the woods and the long-irons. The shafts are shorter and the lofts are greater. Not only does the swing feel easier and the plane more upright, but the worst effects of sidespin are much reduced if the strike is not exactly square and central. (Greater loft gives greater

"three-quarter" backswing is usually adequate. The ball will fly higher than with the longer irons and run less far on landing.

Perhaps because these clubs feel easier to use there is always temptation to use a higher-numbered one than is actually needed – a 7-iron, say, when the distance calls for a 6 or even a 5. With these clubs one should be aiming to hit the center of the greens (unless the greens are exceptionally dry and hard), and the commonest fault among amateurs is to come up short. The best advice is almost certainly to take a higher-num-

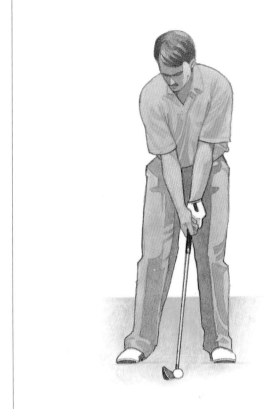

SHAFTS

Middle Irons	Shaft Length	Loft
5-iron	37 inches	31 degrees
6-iron	36½ inches	35 degree
7-iron	36 inches	39 degrees

Always remember the golden rule of loft: The ball will always leave the clubface at right-angles to the tilt of the clubface at the instant the ball leaves.

---

underspin, reducing the effects of any sidespin).

When playing the middle-irons the stance is narrowed a little. The ball is near the center of the stance. There is less of a sweeping action through the ball.

While players make a full turn of the torso on the backswing the swing itself need not be as full as it must be with longer clubs. A

bered club than you think you need and then to swing easily.

There are many true stories of golfers who have reduced their handicaps dramatically after resolving never to be short of the hole again with any shot that is in their range, from mid-iron to putt, and then to have kept that resolution always firmly in mind. The only times when it might be folly

The Favorites

Below: The middle irons are most people's favorites for a variety of reasons. They are shorter than the long distance clubs and feel more manageable. The swing is more upright. And the "hit impulse" which wrecks so many distance swings is usually absent. This is clearly visible in this sequence in which there is a manifest absence of effort.

The ball is very slightly to the right

of the center of the stance. Although the shoulders turn as fully as ever the swing is shorter than it was with the long irons, as evidenced in pictures (**1**), (**2**) and (**3**). Because the swing is more upright it becomes natural to hit down on the ball instead of sweeping it off the ground; (**4**) shows the player about to release the wristcock, swinging to (**5**).

1

2

3

Left: In both these pictures the players have the ball back in the stance. This helps achieve the feeling of swinging "down and through." The player's heads are well back, almost opposite their right knees. In both cases the club heads are close behind the ball. This is important because if one grounds the club head any distance behind the ball one tends to hit the ground at that spot when one makes the swing. This is a frequent cause of hitting the ground before the ball and muffing the shot. One must not touch the ball, of course, just have the club face close behind it.

SILVER SCOT

Tommy Armor, "the Silver Scot," was considered one of the greatest iron players of the inter-war years. Writing in the magazine *American Golfer* in 1934, Armor made these particular points:

1. His left hand was in full control. And he moved it back at least two inches before the clubhead moved at all.
2. Only then did his left shoulder, left hip and left knee work together smoothly to make the backswing turn.
3. His left arm at the top felt firm and straight, the left wrist well cocked and his weight "planted firmly on *a straight right leg.*"
4. The straight left arm and the straight right leg were, he said, as essential for a mid-iron shot as for one with a long-iron.
5. At impact his weight moved forward to a straight left leg, his right shoulder coming under, not around.
6. His right arm and hand came in to add clubhead speed, the right arm extending fully in the follow through.
7. His head and chin stayed firmly anchored well into this extended follow through.

---

to stick to it are when the hole and any greenside trouble are both near the very back of the green.

Mid-irons are often used at close range out of the light rough or if there is no trouble between the ball and the flag. And if the ground is firm.

There is a fine art in "chipping," as this type of shot is called. First you have to judge how far the ball is likely to run once it has landed (it will obviously fly lower and run farther with a 5-iron than with a 7 for the same weight of shot). Then you must pick the exact spot on which to land it. And then loft it to that spot.

When taking the stance the weight should be positioned mainly on the forward foot (left for right-handers and vice versa). The strike should be downwards, any divot taken being in front of the ball. To make the ball run on farther than it usually would the player can strike the ball from in-to-out, at the same time turning the clubface slightly from "open" to "closed." To bring the ball to a halt after only a couple of bounces the player makes a definite downward strike, with hands ahead of the clubface at the point of impact.

These are "touch" shots and require considerable practice with each of the mid-irons. Only when they become second-nature to the player will they pay-off in competition.

In short, when playing with the middle-irons swing easily and have confidence in what you are doing.

4   5   6

SHORT IRONS

The short-irons are the "scoring clubs." they are the 8-iron, the 9-iron, the wedge and the sand-iron. They are the ones that put you close to the hole – or in the hole – if you have missed the green or come up short.

They have the shortest shafts, the most loft, the greatest opportunity for control. The ridges in their clubfaces grip the ball strongly, providing maximum underspin and, when necessary, backspin. The 8-iron has a loft of around 43 degrees, the 9 has 47, the pitching wedge 52 degrees or more and the sand-iron 58, 60 or even 62.

With all these clubs the player

ciate that the club gets the ball into the air, not them. The loft of the club does the work. All they have to do is to swing firmly *down* and *through*.

For most players except professionals the 8-iron has a range of from 75 to 100 yards, the 9-iron from 70 to 90, the wedge from 60-80 and the sand-iron, if used from the fairway or the rough, probably a maximum of 50. But all golfers differ in physique, technique and age and the important thing for everyone is to know just what their ranges are. This is true for all shots, of course. But it is particularly true for the "scoring irons."

WOOSNAM

Welshman Ian Woosnam shot a course record 62 in the final round of the 1990 German Open. How come? Well, he returned to some old short irons, sending some new ones back to Japan for fine tuning. Moral? Well, the shorter the club the more vital it is to make sure it suits you exactly.

---

stands close to the ball. He or she normally has the ball just to the right of the middle of the stance. The swing is upright and the clubhead is swung downward and under the ball, creating a divot *in front* of where the ball was. The shot is firm and so is the follow through.

It is vital for beginners and long-handicap players to appre-

Although the shots with these irons are firmly done it is necessary to relax all one's muscles before playing them. Muscles work well only when relaxed. Stiffness, don't forget, is a complaint.

The stance should be quite narrow. And because there will be very little hip action it should also be open with the leading foot

The Short Iron Swing
Below: This sequence shows the player has made a full swing with his wedge. The ball is well back in the stance. The turn away from the ball is full and the club shaft follows "The Law Of The Parallels." That is, when parallel to the ground it is also parallel to the player's line-of-aim (**1**), (**2**) and (**3**). The player's weight has shifted to the right foot without him swaying.

On the through swing there is a shallow angle of attack. The leading edge of the club face goes down, under the ball and up, throwing it forward. But it is the loft on the club face that makes the ball fly high, not any action on the player's part (**4**), (**5**) and (**6**). The swing is the same as with longer clubs.

1

2

3

The Scoring Clubs

Left: With both players the ball is central in the stance. The hands are ahead of the ball. Their heads are back and turned slightly right and the arms are straight but relaxed. As with the other clubs their right elbows point to the right hip. Both club faces are close to the back of both the balls and both players are clearly aiming to take a divot in front of the ball. Both stances are "open," that is with the left foot drawn back an inch or two and the shoulders turned very slightly to the left. The hit when it comes will be firm but not furious, particularly through the ball.

PITCH

For little pitches I can recommend nothing better than a long, leisurely stroke with the face of the club laid off slightly, and the attempt being made – I hope successfully – to nip sharply at the very bottom of the ball as it rests upon the turf. When it comes off, it is the loveliest shot in the game.

Bobby Jones.

---

drawn back a couple of inches from the line. There should however be *some* hip action as the club is swung smoothly back on a slightly inside line; some, but not much. Some players like to feel they are swinging everything gently from the knees, with the body, arms and hands working unconsciously in reflex.

But technique may be less important than common sense. We are well advised not to try the difficult shot if the simple is available. Don't use a sand-iron if a wedge will do. Don't put backspin on the ball unless you have to – say, because the hole is just on the other side of a sand bunker. For most players a pitch-and-run is easier than a pitch-and-stop. It is a matter of knowing well one's own strengths and weaknesses.

The top teachers advise us not to try to play pitch shots with the hands and arms alone and certainly not with the hands and wrists alone. The turning of the body should simply be proportionate to the length of the shot. There is however one unusual technique used long ago, but rarely now, which could be of interest. At the address have the hands *behind* the ball. Consider only the leading edge of the clubface. Swing this back along an inside line – the rest will come too, of course! – until it feels far enough back. Now swing the leading edge down, under the back of the ball and up. The grip at the address should be very light, by the way, and the whole thing is done by magic; that is, by swinging the leading edge of the clubface.

Visualising the shot to be played is important on all shots but on none more so than with the short-irons. One picks a precise target, the exact spot for the ball to land on, and marks the line to the spot by noting a mark on the turf. The target and the spot will rarely be on the same line, for every green will have slopes on it. Now as one plays the shot one "sees" the ball rising in the air to the required height, dropping on the spot and either running on or backing-up into the hole.

Golf is not *quite* all in the mind – but most of it is.

4

5

6

AROUND THE GREEN

Imagine a green sloping from left to right and back to front, with a ridge in it. There's a pond to the left of it and sand traps to the right. The entrance between them is narrow. Behind the green and on each side there's long grass. What's the best way to play it? The simplest way you can.

You Are on the Fairway in the Gap

You''ve been lucky. You have a clear line to the hole and all you have to contend with is that ridge and the slope of the green. The flag is toward the back on top of the ridge. Your ball is about 25 yards out. This is almost certainly what your professional would say: "First, put that sand-wedge away. Take your hands off that wedge. Pick the short iron in which you have the greatest confidence and prepare to do a pitch-and-run or a chip-and-run."

Because of the slope of the green you will have to aim left and because of the ridge, further left than otherwise. Imagine how the ball will run from three particular spots on the green if hit at the right speed. (The right speed will be that which is guaranteed to get the ball up the ridge). Now having done that, select the spot where you intend to land the ball. Be ex-tremely positive about this aspect.

Picture a line from your ball to the landing spot. Note a mark on the grass just ahead of your ball which is definitely, precisely, on that line. Stand to that line. Your stance will be narrow, your back as straight as possible yet quite relaxed. Your shoulders are parallel to the line to the landing spot, but your front foot (left if you are right-handed) is drawn back an inch or so from the line. Look down at the ball with your neck-spine almost level and your head properly balanced on it; that is, the chin should be neither tucked in, nor held up so that the back of the head is angled backwards toward the neck. Just relax.

Now just make the shot your professional has taught you – and that you should have practiced dozens of times. No wrist action: just brush the ball off the turf and let the loft of the club do the work. Don't look up until after the count of three. Hit the ball hard enough to be sure of getting up that slope.

If you need a lot of run, practice what used to be called "the Musselburgh Run-Up." Have the face of the chipping club slightly open. Look at the spot on the nearside back of the ball. Swing along an in-to-out line and as you hit the ball close the clubface slightly, as if playing for a hook.

1

2

4

5

You Are on the Left Behind the Pond

You have been unlucky. You haven't much green to work with. You have got to get over the pond. Now is probably the moment when you will have to take your sand-wedge and hit the highest shot you are capable of. Make it a full shot. Although there's not much green, aim to go beyond the hole. And aim left of the hole.

As your professional has certainly told you, in these circumstances do *not* open the face of the club and try to slice the ball. Hit it as a straight shot. And hit firmly down on the ball. Hit, too, so that you make a full follow through.

You Are on the Right Behind a Sand Trap

There's more green to work with here, so you can take either your wedge or your nine iron, whichever gives you most confidence. Have your weight to the left with shoulders square to the line you have chosen but stance slightly open. Hit firmly down on the ball.

You Are Behind the Green in the Long Grass

In this situation you should probably take either your wedge or

the time you hear the ball land.

Don't make a big thing of it. Pretend it's easy.

You Are 80 Yards from the Green on the Right

Now you have quite a distance to the hole and only a narrow opening at the front of the green. The safe thing would be to aim to drop the ball in the center of that opening and *beyond the edges of both the pond and the sand trap*. Don't be short – you might get a bad bounce. Don't be cute and hit a high pitch – you'll probably be short. Plan to hit the opening

your sand-iron, whichever you are more confident with. You are not going to get much stop on the ball because of the effect of the grass. Aim to drop the ball over the light rough on to the green short of the hole. Because of the slope of the green aim well to the right.

Think of it as a perfectly normal shot – but use your imagination. Imagine the leading edge of the clubface going into the grass one inch *under* the ball. See yourself following through well after lobbing the ball right on to your chosen spot. And as you make the stroke *keep your head and neck perfectly still*. It may help you to turn your head to the rear (toward the right shoulder if right-handed) and keep it there until

beyond the hazards and take what comes.

With this kind of shot it is vital to be lined-up correctly. Locate the exact spot where you want the ball to land. Mentally draw a straight line to it. Note a mark on the grass a foot or so in front of the ball and align yourself squarely to it. Align shoulders, hips, knees, feet . . . the lot. Prepare to hit a shot straight to the spot and to be long rather than short.

Take a Different Green

This green is raised on one side as if it was on a mound. Your ball is on the low side, under the mound and all you can see is the top of the flag. On the way to the green you will have noted the position of

What is being played here looks like the trickiest shot in the game, running the ball up a slope between two bunkers and on to the green. The player is using his 7-iron. As you can see he does it to perfection. It is a short, simple swing and all that is required is a perfectly square club face swinging under the ball and along the line-of-aim.

Above: Sometimes it is necessary to get down on one's knees (and not to pray!). The shot is quite easy. Grip the shaft further down and use a simple hand-and-arms swing.

Professionals when they give clinics often use their drivers for an off-the-knees shot and hit the ball 200 yards. For the rest of us 100 will do.

Below: If you've got no room for a backswing, grip the club down near the hosel and flip the ball out. It's all wrist, and very effective.

of the green, just make sure you do not go so far beyond the hole that your ball falls over the edge. That's just common sense. Use a lofted club. A wedge would probably be best. And for once aim to be a foot *short* of the hole.

What about the Texas Wedge?

The "Texas wedge" is the putter used from just off the green. It is a favorite weapon with some people, and can be effective as long as there is no visible trouble in the way. But it does have its drawbacks. One drawback could be that repeated use of the putter from off the green, over rather rough terrain or tufty grass, can influence your putting stroke when you are on the green, particularly if the green is slick. Another danger is that some trouble may not be visible – like a couple of small bumps and a hollow.

Unless you are absolutely sure of the surface on the way to the green it is always safest to loft the ball on to it. This is why you should practice different lofts from different distances. If you have missed the green, your first priority is to get on to it, even if you can't get close to the hole.

that flag. It looks rather close to the slope. What do you do?

If you are an expert you can take your sand-wedge and aim for the top of the flag, giving the ball as much backspin as you can. But nine players out of 10 would be better advised to take a middle-iron and run the ball firmly up the slope. If it is steep you might even use a long-iron, say a 4. If it is quite a gentle slope you might use a 7-iron. Hit to go about twice as far on the flat as the distance you've actually got to go up the slope. Hit to make the ball run rather than to get it up in the air.

If your ball is on the other side

The Art of Visualisation

Every great player runs a video in his or her mind which pictures the perfect shot to come: the way the ball rises into the air . . . its flight . . . its descent on to the chosen spot . . . its run from there to the hole. What's more, he or she can then create a mental picture of the exact swing which is going to produce the shot. Each watches the clubface strike the ball.

For some it is like having a third eye. The two normal eyes watch the ball and the strike, while the third eye sees the approach to the hole, the slope of the green and the flagstick in the hole. This is a talent worth acquiring and, once acquired, worth cherishing. It makes golf much simpler, particularly around the green.

Water Hazards

Pitching the ball over a pond and onto the green. In the first picture (**1**) the player is taking the club back low and slow. In the second (**2**) his shoulders turn. In the third (**3**) he has finished his backswing. It is only a three-quarters swing. His shoulders however are well turned. As he starts his downswing (**4**) his knees come naturally into a "sit down" position. His wristcock is retained until the last instant. The shot is really finished in (**5**) and his head is just beginning to come up. He has hit down under the ball with a short, firm swing. And the ball has sailed to the pin.

TROUBLE SHOTS/BUNKERS

1

2

The places which give most players most trouble are the bunkers (or sand traps, as the Americans call them). Yet for professionals sand shots are among the easiest of all. Why?

The first reason, one supposes, is that professionals practice endlessly in the sand and the average golfer doesn't. Indeed he or she has little chance and less time for bunker practice. Gary Player, the South African reckoned by most of his peers to be the finest sand-shot player of all time, as a young man used to rise at six o"clock and put in two hours sand practice before breakfast. Later he might stay most of the day in a bunker, or at least until he had holed-out five times. Which computer programr, which business person, which mother-of-four can do that? The first time in the week that they see sand is when their ball is in it on the golf course.

But there are other reasons why most players find the sand so challenging. One perhaps is just that they are scared by it. Another could be that they do not believe they can use their normal swings, a third that they have not studied the minor adjustments needed to insure that their normal swings can get the ball out readily enough.

As former Ryder Cup player and present TV commentator Peter Alliss once remarked to a frustrated amateur, "If I gave you a

Watch The Sand

Above: Here we have an excellent sequence showing the "moment of truth" in an explosion shot from the sand. The sand-wedge comes down into the sand behind the ball, swings through the sand and comes out of it a couple of inches beyond where the ball was. The player has taken the sand, not the ball. The ball actually follows the club head, as we see here.

It is a fact that professionals find the sand shot easier to play than most other shots. This is partly because it is actually easier to take a scoop of sand than it is to hit behind

shovel you would get the ball out all right." Possibly the main cause of frustration is that so many golfers have been taught to think in terms of the clubhead at impact. But it is *separation* – the moment the ball leaves the club head – that matters more. Nowhere is this more obviously true than when the ball is in a bunker.

Other things being equal, the ball will pop out at right angles to the loft on the clubface at separation and at a speed proportionate to the speed of the clubhead at that moment. The sand iron, which is a lofted wedge with a flange behind the leading edge, was invented by Gene Sarazen specially to insure that there always was the required clubhead speed on separation. The flange insures that the clubhead does not slow down too much or even come to a dead stop in the sand. It

the ball with absolute precision.

This sequence also shows the golfer's feet screwed well down into the sand. This has a dual purpose. First he can tell the depth of the sand and whether it is soft or fluffy or whatever. Then he can be pretty sure of swinging through the sand well under where the ball is. One has to remember all the time that it is a sand shot, not a ball shot.

Only if there is little sand or it is very wet or hard should one hit *down* on the ball instead of under it.

Below: The player has drawn a circle in the sand to show the entry

and exit points of the club. This is useful to picture in your mind, especially if the ball is sitting down low.

It is important also in all bunker shots to follow through fully. The sand itself will tend to slow the shot down and the temptation is to cut the swing short. This temptation and the braking effect of the sand both have to be resisted.

Right: Greg Norman plays a sand shot in a tournament in Australia. Note the still head, the firm wrists, and the explosion of sand.

3

4

will often do so in certain types of sand if you use an ordinary wedge.

The first rule of bunker play, the experts agree, is to swing right through the sand. *Not* through the ball. Forget the ball: swing through the *sand*. How big a slice of sand you take will depend on the nature of the lie and the distance the ball has to go. The second basic rule, the experts say, is to use your normal swing with the following relatively slight adjustments.

From Greenside Bunkers

First, as you take your stance you should wriggle your feet in the sand so that the stance is firm. But there is a second purpose in this foot action: to feel the texture of the sand, whether it is dry, wet, soft, very soft, firm or whatever. The texture will make a difference

THE WIZARD

Gene Sarazen invented the sand-wedge, perfecting the magic flanged club in 1932. In that year and the next he won the British Open, the US Open and the US PGA championship. Used well, it's a winner.

1

2

to the speed of the shot to be played and the size of the slice of sand to be taken.

If the lie is good aim slightly to the left of the hole with the stance (both the feet and the shoulders) and slightly to the right of the hole with the open clubface. Feel that the knees are going to swing the clubhead. Break the wrists early on the backswing. Then on the downswing hit through the sand behind and under the ball and straight up.

It will help if you note a mark in the sand not only the distance *behind* the ball where you want the clubface to enter the sand but also *beyond* the ball where you

want it to come up for air. Place both shots on the "graphics" in the brain: just be aware of them. Now swing as usual.

If the ball is very close to the front of the bunker increase the openness of the stance and the clubface, and shorten the swing. *But always play right through the sand.*

Many players are too flippy in the wrists when playing a sand shot. If you have this problem, try the straightforward "shovel" technique. Forget the early wrist-break. Have the right elbow not close to your side but pointing to the rear, as you would when using a shovel. Then, having done this,

Under A Bank
Above: Here we see the player dealing with a difficult problem. The lie of the ball is not good and he has to get it up quickly over a steep bank (**1**). He breaks his wrists quickly on the backswing (**2**) and uses a steep shoulder turn. Note the still head.

His shoulders having turned fully and his wrists cocked fully (**3**) he is

prepared to explode the ball up and out. He hits down into the sand and through under the ball (**4**), ensuring that the loft on the club face lifts it upwards. Without having to think about it, he is aware that it is the loft angle on the club face at the moment the ball leaves it that really matters. To increase this loft he has laid the club face at the address, opening the face.

just hit through the sand and up.

To hit a particularly high shot, have the ball forward in the stance and your weight over the back foot. If it is a fairly long shot use a longer swing, but at the same pace as usual. Don't take quite as large

a slice of sand. Hit through the sand as usual.

If the ball is in a buried lie do not open the clubface, keep it square. Have the weight on the left foot rather than the right. Use a steep swing. Hit firmly, deeply,

1

2

3

4

down into the sand behind the ball and THROUGH. Be determined not to leave the clubhead in the sand. Use the right forearm to make sure it doesn't stay there.

If the sand is very firm *hood* the clubface of an ordinary wedge.

Hit DOWN as if to drive the ball into the bottom of the bunker. It will pop out neatly, probably to one's great surprise. If the lie is downhill take a much bigger slice of sand than usual. If it is uphill, take less of a slice. With the ball

below the feet, you must bend the knees more than usual, hold the club at the top of the grip, aim well left, hit down-and-through – and pray!

Fairway Traps

Obviously the first rule for a golfer who hits his ball into a fairway trap is to make sure that he gets it out and back on to the fairway. So, he should always use a club with enough loft, even though this may prevent him hitting the ball very far toward the hole. A good principle is to think of a number and add one. If you

think a 5-iron will do the job, use a 6. If the lie is good, a master like Gary Player will have most of his weight on his *left* foot; he will widen his stance and plan to strike the ball cleanly, taking as little sand as possible. His advice to others is to play the ball well back in the stance, and add two rather than one to the number of the club they would normally use to hit the ball the required distance. They should make a special note of a mark in front of the ball and look at the mark when playing the shot. If using a fairway wood from a very shallow trap, they should open the stance wide and aim left, expecting a big fade.

The Scoring Shot

Below: In this sequence we see the player doing a more normal sand shot – the scoring shot. He has opened his stance, opened the club face and prepared to loft the ball directly toward the pin. The ball will take off along the line through which the club face is moving. The line of the swing may be to the left but the club face is aiming to the

right and the result is a straight shot.

Note the total action: the still head; the quick wristcock; the full turn of the shoulders; the three-quarters backswing; the hit right through the sand; and the full finish.

3

4

IN THE ROUGH

In the rough to err is human, to succeed is divine. But, as in the sand, the golden rule is to get back on the fairway. If the ball is in thick grass expect a "flyer": the grass will get between clubface and ball, eliminating backspin, and so causing the ball to run farther than you would expect. Therefore you can use a higher-numbered club than you would normally select for the distance. Which is sensible, anyway: the worse the lie the higher the number on the club which should be

used. It is better to keep the ball back in the stance, and play down and under it.

If the grass is tough as well as rough expect to pull the ball left (if you are right-handed), so hold the clubface open to compensate.

One should not have to say this but the vital thing is to *get out on to the fairway*. It does not matter much how far up the fairway you hit the ball so long as it is there, somewhere, on the mown grass. Often one sees golfers trying to

hit the ball a country mile out of the rough and finishing in a worse place than where they began. The only place and time to be clever is when one is close to the green. Then it is important to be not only clever but sensible, as below.

Below: A player in the rough grass. He has taken his wedge, opened his stance and very slightly opened the blade of his club. He is going to hit *down*, under the ball and *along* before the club head comes up.

In the main sequence the player is

playing out of the rough on to the green. He knows that it is quite a simple shot. It is the club head, indeed the club face, that does the work. All he has to do is to aim correctly and then to swing correctly, generating just the right

amount of club head speed.

Study the set-up, the takeaway, the three-quarter backswing, the steady head as the club comes down and "through" the ball. The player knows the club head does the work.

1

4

5

If playing out of heather, rather than grass, hit down firmly. Just concentrate on getting back on to the fairway – by playing out sideways, if need be. Play all these shots with your strong hand (right if right-handed) dominant.

If it is possible to go for the green, plan to hit a high ball because (as we have seen) the ball will tend to run. Grip the club lightly, steepen the plane of the swing and place most of your weight over the rear foot. Keep your head absolutely still. In tiger country (really fierce rough) close the clubface, keep the hands ahead of the ball, use a steep plane, and swing with the legs. If the ball is in a divot hole, play it as if it was in the rough: use a more lofted club than normal, play the ball back in the stance, and *watch the strike*.

Sometimes you will get a "teed-up" lie in the rough, with the ball sitting up on a tuft of grass. In this case, do *not* swing under the ball. Flatten the plane of your swing and think of hitting *along* and through. If the ball stops in water but is not hopelessly submerged and you can get a club to it, do so. Use a wedge. Hit down and through – and expect to get covered in mud. Keep your head down regardless.

In the Woods

Let common sense prevail. If there is a good gap between the trees – but only if there is a *good* gap between the trees – be meticulous in the matter of alignment. To play straight through the gap take a stance that is definitely, positively, absolutely square. Use a lower-numbered club than usual (to keep the ball low and running) and use a half swing instead of a full one. Aim to hit it straight. To play under the branches, use a driver if you have one with you, a 1-, 2- or 3-iron. If they are low branches, as on a bush, try kneeling down and hitting a low shot that way. Close the clubface and *watch the strike*.

2

3

6

7

ON THE SLOPES

One of the trickiest shots in golf is one when the ball is below your feet. The best advice is not to expect too much from it, so don't try anything too ambitious. The ball will tend to fade (or even slice) and then bounce farther away on landing.

Since the ball is further away from you than normal, hold the club at the end of the shaft, and at address bend the knees more and, widen the stance. Then, since too much body action could upset the balance, you should shorten the swing and make full use of the arms, and also arch the wrists a little more, than usual. If (as a right-hander) you aim left to counter the slope it is vital to adjust the stance so that it is still precisely square to the line-of-aim, otherwise any slice will be even more pronounced.

When the ball is above the feet, keep the body weight over the heels and hold the club well down the grip. The knees should be flexed rather than bent. Take one club longer than usual. And aim to the right of the green, as the ball will normally draw.

On a downhill slope, take a more lofted club, (the ball will fly lower and run farther than on the flat). Have the body more or less perpendicular to the slope, but feel the weight on the back foot. Play the ball back in the stance and make sure to swing well through, the feeling being "under and along down the slope."

On uphill lies the ball usually flies higher and less far than usual. Take at least one more club than the distance suggests. Stand perpendicular to the slope, bracing the rear leg to maintain your balance. Use less body but more arm action. *Be prepared for a draw*.

In the Winds

When playing against the wind, any spin that you put on the ball is likely to have a greater effect than usual. So swing more gently than usual, *not* harder. Sweep the ball off the tee or the fairway with a straight-faced club and with a full follow through along the line.

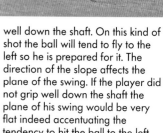

Here we have a variety of lies on sloping ground and in every case the professional is making sure that he stays centerd and balanced.

Above: In the first two photographs the player is faced with a downslope. Note the position of his feet in relation to the ball. And also his hands, which are ahead of the ball. On the downslope he is using a more lofted club than he would normally use considering the distance he has to go as the ball will tend to fly lower and run further.

Above right: The player is playing across an upslope with the ball above his feet. Study his stance. Note how he has gripped the club well down the shaft. On this kind of shot the ball will tend to fly to the left so he is prepared for it. The direction of the slope affects the plane of the swing. If the player did not grip well down the shaft the plane of his swing would be very flat indeed accentuating the tendency to hit the ball to the left.

Below: The player is coping with an upslope and, in the right-hand photographs he has the ball well below his feet. These call for very different actions. In the close-up note the stance and the position of the ball in relation to it. The pro has taken a stronger club than usual for the distance as the ball will tend to fly higher than usual and to run less far on landing. It will also tend to draw, that is to curve to the left. With the ball below his feet he has lengthened his grip on the club and is standing closer to the ball than he would on the flat. The swing will tend to be more upright and the ball will probably fade to the right. Knowing this he is prepared for it.

Slice spin against the wind can be fatal so the stance and the set of the clubface should favor a draw, if only slightly.

Near the green, however, a headwind can be helpful. You can hit more freely, take more club, and be pretty sure the ball won't run very far after it lands.

With the wind behind you, the ball will tend to fly lower than usual and will run a bit further (the wind takes some of the backspin off the ball). Have the ball forward in your stance. Take a full swing. Favor a 3-wood rather than a driver. Swing easily.

In crosswinds do not try to be too clever. If the wind is at right angles to the line of flight it may not have much effect on the shot except to push the ball left or right. But if it is coming toward you from half left or half right, so to speak, it will have rather more effect, and any spin, particularly slice spin, will be greatly exaggerated. *Be prepared*.

Up Against It

If your ball finishes close to an obstruction you may have to invent a shot. If it is a wall or a stout tree, maybe you can bounce the ball off it. If it's a wire fence, perhaps you can turn your back on the line and hit the ball on to the fairway from between your legs.

If the ball is near a gorse-bush or thicket and your backswing is almost impossibly restricted, a shot-saver can be to grip an iron right down by the hosel and "flip" the ball out with the wrists alone. It is surprising how far the ball will travel. If you are right-handed but a right-handed shot is clearly impossible, you can turn the club upside-down and play a left-handed shot. With all trouble shots it is important to remember one's addition. If the green is 200 yards away and you can get the ball out only 50 yards up the fairway, your next shot is just a middle-iron. Get it out a bit further and you may just have a wedge to the green. Either way, it's just two shots to the green. On the other hand, if you get too ambitious and try to get to the green in one shot from a really bad lie, you are just as likely to end up in worse trouble than before – and that's where double and triple bogeys come from!

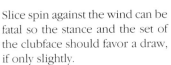

SPIN

To control the ball the golfer needs to have a thorough understanding of the concept of spin. Scientifically it is quite a complex subject; golfwise it is relatively simple.

One starts with the line-of-aim. Cause the clubface to cut across this line from "outside" (the side away from the player) to "in" (the player's side) and slice spin will be put on the ball. It will then curve away from the player, to the right if he is right-handed, to the left if left-handed. Slice spin can also be put on the ball if one swings correctly in relation to the line-of-aim but has the clubface "open" (angled away from one).

It is not humanly possible to cut across the ball the other way, from "in" to "out." But if the line of the swing is in that direction but the face of the club is square (at right-angles) to the initial line-of-aim, the ball will be compressed more on the nearside than in the center. This hook-compression will turn to hook-spin and the ball will curve in the air in the opposite direction to the slice.

Slice spin will cause the ball to fly higher and stop more quickly on landing. Hook spin will usually cause the ball to fly lower and to run farther on landing.

Every ball will have underspin (backspin) at least to start with. If it did not it would dive into the ground just ahead of the player. This underspin causes the ball to rise in the air. A shallow or narrow arc to the swing – hitting quite sharply down on the ball – will maximise underspin. A wide, sweeping arc will minimise it.

The ball will normally set off at right angles to the loft (tilt) of the clubface at separation – that is, when the ball leaves it, not at impact, when it is first hit. (This is why you should hit "through" the ball). It will also separate at right angles to the set of the clubface in relation to the line-of-aim – straight, to the left, or to the right.

So if he can control the clubface the golfer can hit a slice, a hook, a fade, a draw, a high ball or a low ball . . . at will. A shot that flies straight to right or left of the line without curving at all – a push or a pull – is caused by a swing which

is not related properly to the line-of-aim. They are just straight shots that are going in the wrong direction.

Variations in a player's alignment at the address, in the arc of the swing, in the use of the wrists and hands and in movements of the body can all be causes of variations in the flight pattern of the ball. This is why the line-of-aim is so fundamentally important. Players who do not appreciate this

or who are casual about establishing the line before every shot are likely to be plagued with inconsistency.

A stance which is "open" (aimed to the left of the line with right-handers) will tend to put slice spin on the ball. A stance which is "closed" (aimed to the right of the line) will tend to put hook spin on the ball. (The line across the shoulders is the main, though not the only, determinant

of the direction in which the stance is aimed). If the plane of the swing is not "square" (parallel to the line-of-aim), that will also cause variations in the flight pattern. Imagine the plane as a pane of glass with the player's head and shoulders sticking out through a circular hole in it. For straight hitting the glass pane must be aimed straight. The bottom edge must run down the line-of-aim, or be closely parallel to it.

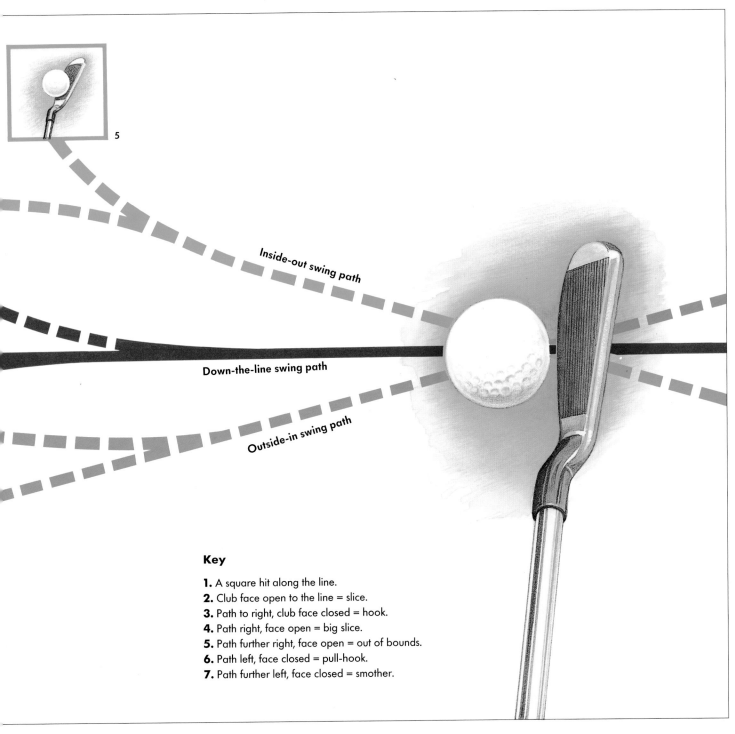

Inside-out swing path

Down-the-line swing path

Outside-in swing path

5

Key

1. A square hit along the line.
2. Club face open to the line = slice.
3. Path to right, club face closed = hook.
4. Path right, face open = big slice.
5. Path further right, face open = out of bounds.
6. Path left, face closed = pull-hook.
7. Path further left, face closed = smother.

Aim the swing-plane left or right of the line and hooks and slices may result even though the original alignment was correct.

Wrist action is a complex subject, and individuals differ slightly in their musculature. But in general three actions are involved: flexion and dorsiflexion (hinging back and forth); radial and ulnar deviation (cocking and uncocking); and pronation and supination (the turning of the wrists and forearms). For straight hitting the wrists should come through the brief impact interval – the "Moment of Truth" – square to the line and either neutral or with the top wrist slightly bowed-out. Neutral would see the top wrist flat, in line with the forearm and the lower hand bent back a shade.

A lot of flexion-dorsiflexion produces a kind of "flip" in the swing which will usually add

To control the ball one needs to understand the principles of spin. These are set out clearly in the pictures above. The two main elements are the direction in which the club head is moving and the angle of the club face at impact.

height to the shot. But if the top hand is well bowed-out at impact a lower shot should result.

Swinging the shoulders round too soon, instead of starting down

Slice spin is caused by cutting across the ball from beyond the line of aim to one's own side of that line. Hook spin starts from compression of the ball on its near side which causes an anti-clockwise spin to develop.

with a sort of rocking motion (rear shoulder DOWN) will cause a slice. At separation the shoulders should be parallel with the line-of-aim.

For control of the ball everything must be related to the line-of-aim, and the movement of the club, the arms and the body must be angled with precision. Where the ball is placed in the stance will also influence its behaviour in flight.

How to Fade and Slice

Aim the stance to the left if right-handed. Take a relatively "weak" grip, seeing one or two knuckles only of the left hand. (If you can see more, turn the hands anti-clockwise on the grip.) Have the ball well forward in the stance. Cause the swing to cut across the line from out-to-in.

If the clubface is square to the line-of-aim at impact, and therefore "open" to the line of the swing, the ball will start out fairly straight and then curve off to the right. If the clubface is open the ball will start out on a line to the right and then curve more severely to the right.

A fade is a controlled slice. The stance need be only slightly open.

The clubface should usually be square to the line-of-aim. The swing-line should be only slightly across the line.

A draw is a controlled hook.

How to Draw the Ball

Close the stance. Take a "stronger" than usual grip, hands turned clockwise on the shaft if right-handed. Have the ball back in the stance. Aim the plane or swing-line to the right. The club-face should be square to the line-

Above: On the left the player is preparing to hit the ball high. On the right he is intending to hit it low. In the picture on the left as we can see the ball is well forward in the stance and the weight favors his right side. He is using a lofted club. On the right the ball is well back in his stance, the hands are ahead of the ball, the weight is more central and he is using a less-lofted club.

of-aim at impact, and therefore closed to the line of swing. If these actions are exaggerated a big hook will result. If they are defi-

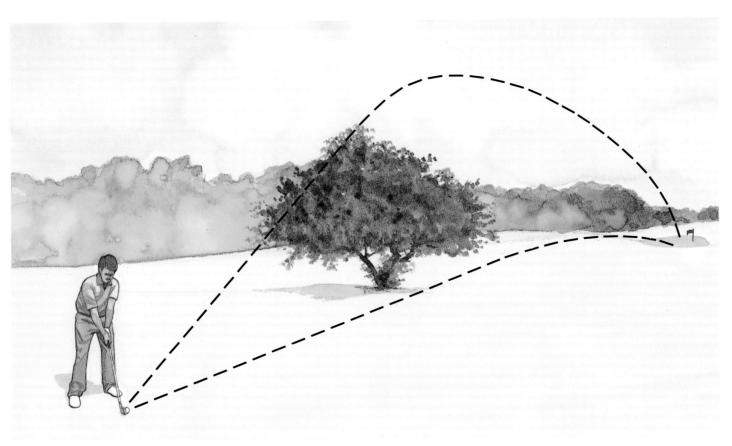

Two Shots in One
Here the professional has a tree right in his line to the flag and he has a choice of two shots. He can hit the ball over the tree with his wedge, or maybe a 9-iron, or he can run it under the tree, perhaps with a mid-iron. Which route he chooses will depend on which shot he is most confident about. The pro will almost certainly take the high road, the amateur the low.

nite but minimal the ball will curve left in a controlled manner. It will also run on after landing, giving the player a little extra distance.

How Not to Slice

This is easier said than done. The reason, usually, is that the habitual way of swinging feels right, so that the right way feels wrong. Either because of body action – probably the right shoulder coming round instead of swinging down and through – or because of incorrect hand action the clubhead comes through with its face wide open or on an out-to-in path.

The cure in the longer term is to practice the downswing and throughswing in slow motion concentrating on the correct angle of approach to the straight line-of-aim and the truly square clubface at impact. An immediate remedy, is to close the stance and clubface and use a "stronger" grip.

HANDS

There are three different normal hand actions and one eccentric one.

1. The left wrist is cupped on the backswing and the clubface is opened. At the top, the clubface is wide open with the leading edge vertical. On the throughswing the hands and clubface must be deliberately rolled back square.
2. The left wrist is flat, in line with the forearm, at the address and at the top of the backswing. The clubface is neutral, half way between being fully open and fully closed. On the throughswing the hands and clubface turn square at impact without conscious effort.
3. On the backswing the left wrist is bowed-out. The clubface at the top aims at the sky. On the downswing any roll through impact will be certain to cause a hook
4. A variation of (3) is to turn the left wrist under on the backswing and keep it square to the arc of the swing for as long as humanly possible. On the throughswing the left wrist stays square to the arc all the way from chest-high to chest-high. There is no roll, no slice, no hook.

How Not to Hook

The great American professional, Ben Hogan, when young was plagued with a big, and often extremely destructive, hook. He cured it when he was older – from 1946 through to his greatest year 1953 at the age of 41 – by opening the clubface on the backswing and slightly cupping his left wrist at the top. It took him a great deal of practice to groove into the new action.

The immediate remedy he and others would recommend is for the player to weaken the grip a little, draw the front foot back (thereby slightly opening the stance), and feel rather as if swinging the clubhead a shade out-to-in.

How to Hit It High

Have the weight favoring the rear leg. Use a lofted club. Lay the clubface back a little to increase the loft. Use an upright swing and a relaxed wrist action. If it is a long high shot do not take a divot. If it is a shot near the green take a divot in front of the ball.

For a lob shot at short range play the ball a bit forward in the stance. Use minimum wrist action. Swing the clubface lazily under the ball using a brushing or sweeping action. The ball should rise easily with little backspin. On landing it will roll forward.

How to Hit It Low

Have the ball forward in the stance. Hands ahead of the ball. Clubface hooded. Weight forward. Wrists firm. Use a wide, sweeping swing. Take no divot.

PUTTING

Putting is the artless art, the game within the game, a purely personal thing. So far as we know there has only been one great putter who never faltered, who remained as consistent in old age as he was in his youth – the South African Bobby Locke. In his very last game before he died he took only 27 putts! Yet nobody has ever copied him exactly. Locke took a narrow stance, a normal grip, an inside-out stroke with a closed clubface – and appeared to hook his putts. He said this enabled him to put "true topspin" on his putts straight away. Scientists say that is impossible. But the method worked for him.

Every day one reads stories of professionals who have done wonders with a new putter, or a very old one, or a borrowed one, sometimes for a day, sometimes for a month; but never, it seems, forever. One theory is that a fresh putter works because the player watches the putter face hit the ball. Later he or she forgets to do that. They soon think more of the mechanics of the stroke or the state of the green or something else. And then the subconscious element in putting – the simple intention to roll the ball into the hole – is reduced. It may even vanish.

Certainly this *intention* should be kept in the front of the mind on the putting green, whatever club, whatever stroke and whatever technique one is using. For this reason the question of one's handedness may be crucial. Ambidexters probably putt better two-handed, left-handers should emphasise the left hand (even if they putt right-handed) and dexters should roll the ball toward the hole with the palm of the right hand. But to insure the retention of the subconscious element, it may be that establishing a set routine in putting is even more important than technique because it helps to cut out extraneous thoughts. Always approach the putt in the same way; grip the putter the same way; take the same number of practice swings and the same number of sightings between ball and hole, before rolling the ball away.

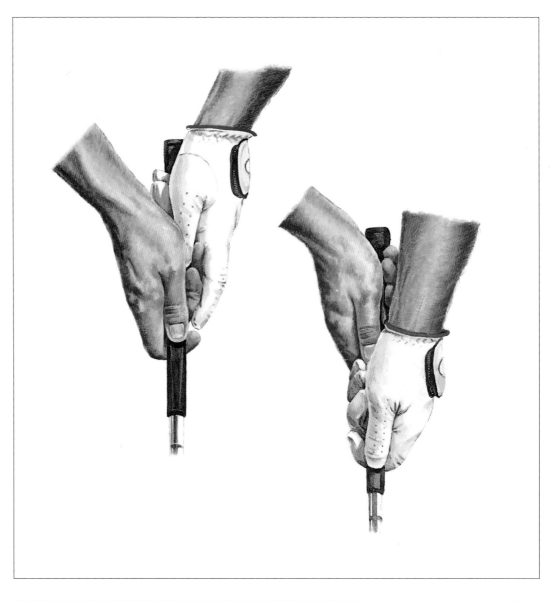

TREATING THE TWITCH

The "Twitch," also called the "Yips," is the worst known disease to affect a golfer. It is believed by many that once you have got it you"ve got it for good. As you stand over a putt some gremlin causes your hands to twitch or flip and whatever you do you cannot strike the ball truly.

The old master Harry Vardon caught the disease in later life and had to be given any putt of four feet or less, just out of sympathy. Walter Hagen got it too but called it a "whiskey jerk."

But Bernhard Langer has shown us the cure — change your grip.

Above: Two particular types of grip are pictured here. The grip on the left has become the norm, although there are many variations of it. The right palm (with right-handers) is placed on the club squarely facing the intended line. The index finger of the left hand covers the fingers of the right. Sometimes the index finger of the right is placed directly down the shaft. The picture on the right shows an "upside-down" grip, used by Bernhard Langer to overcome the yips.

Most professionals today use the "reverse overlap" putting grip. The index finger of the upper hand covers the last three fingers of the lower. Some occasionally use the "upside-down" grip. The hands are then reversed. The two-handed grip, in which the hands are not linked in any way, is also popular. There is no law about it.

Stance

The usual advice is to stand square to the line-of-aim with the eyes directly over the ball. But since the shaft of a putter must slope at least 10 degrees from the vertical, some players find they get a better response if their eyes are slightly "inside" the line.

Note: It is the line-of-aim that is of crucial importance, not the visual line going straight to the hole.

There is nothing against an open or closed stance, as long as the blade of the putter comes through precisely square to the chosen line. What works is what matters. And what works depends on your judgement of the line or curve of the putt.

Line

Conditions around the hole are crucial. Are there any hidden bumps or slopes near the hole? If you were three feet away, what would be the correct line? A good putter always considers these questions. Then he determines what will be the correct line for the ball to travel *in order to get to the point where it will curve into the hole.*

Having made a decision, a good putter then picks out a spot on the turf a short way in front of his ball at the beginning of the line he has just noted. He does not aim for the hole. He rolls the ball over the spot with what he judges to be the correct force.

Force

The force used may be applied by touch or mechanics. By touch I mean that the player leaves the

decision largely to his subconscious. One clubmaker invented the idea of "putt ergs" – the amount of force needed to be applied for each foot of distance: 1 putt-erg for one foot, 2 putt-ergs for two feet and so on. The player learnt to acquire the "feel" of the basic putt-erg.

The mechanical system is based on the use of the same apparent *strength* of stroke on all putts while varying the *length* of the stroke. On the practice green

Above: In the left-hand picture above the player has his eyes slightly "inside" the ball, that is on his side of it. In the right-hand picture his eyes are directly over the ball. The "eyes over the ball" method is the recommended one, but several top professionals have found that the "inside" method works best for them. The reason probably is that the putter shaft slopes down to the ball at at angle of at least 10 degrees. It has to do so under the rules of golf. Determine which is best for you.

Below: Here we see the player making a putt. He has taken note of a mark on the turf ahead of the ball which is exactly on the line he has chosen. Then he swings the putter back with his arms alone (**1**). There is no wrist break. In (**2**) he hits the ball. Again there is no wrist movement. In (**3**) he follows through along the line. His follow-through is longer than his backswing. This is not mandatory but most good putters make their follow-through at least as long as their backswings, if not longer.

1

2

3

before a game the player tests how long a swing, backwards and forwards, is needed that day to send the ball, say, six feet. A swing twice as long will send it 12 feet, half as long three feet, and so on. Some players using this system progressively widen their stance the longer the putt, in every case taking the backswing back exactly as far as the toe of the rear shoe.

Methods

There seem to be two different basic methods of striking the ball and a number of variants of each. The basic two are the *rap* putt and the *stroked* putt. In the first, the ball is rapped with the putter head, with little follow through. In the other, the ball is stroked and the follow through is usually longer than the backswing.

A variation of the rap putt is one using wrist action virtually alone. The left hand (for right-handers) is touching the left thigh and its wrist is used as a vertical hinge. The player hinges back a relatively short distance then swings through straight-along-and-up, hingeing the left wrist vertically forward.

With the stroked putt there is little or no wrist action. The arms, the hands and the putter grip form a triangular assembly which swings back and forth in one piece. Using a similar system, some players rock the shoulders.

The "pendulum putt" used by players who have adopted the long-shafted putter can also be adapted for use with more orthodox weapons. Other players use the Sam Snead method. They face the hole instead of standing square to the line, hold the putter with one hand well down the shaft, then use a croquet-mallet stroke to roll the ball to the hole. A variation of this last method is to swing from the knees, using the trunk, arms and hands in reflex, subconsciously.

Mechanics

British scientists running a series of tests with a putting machine concluded that all putts slide for

Take A Break
Above and above right: The player is obeying the First Law of Putting. He is on a very sloping green and so he has taken great care to assess the point where the ball will start turning (dotted line) and to note a mark on the turf or blade of grass which is precisely on the line. After

that he has taken his stance squarely parallel to that short line, not parallel to the direct line to the hole. And he has not looked up at the hole again last thing before striking the ball. His last look has been at the mark on the line of the putt, that short line it starts out on.

Off the Green
Below: The player is attempting a putt from just off the green, known as the "apron." The putt should be lined up like any other one, with the line being assessed as the pictures above, but the flag has to remain in the hole or be taken out — it cannot be held .

But the question is: do you always want the putt to start rolling at once, even on slick downhill greens? Some players say no and use a bit of slice spin or even underspin. Walter J. Travis, U.S. and British Amateur Champion in the first years of the century, preferred using a putting cleek because it has a bit of loft on it.

Last Thoughts

On level putts Locke putted to let the ball just drop into the hole. On uphill putts he putted to go from six inches to a foot beyond the hole if the ball didn't drop in. On downhill putts he imagined a hole six inches in front of where it actually was. Many older players and even some younger ones suddenly suffer from the "yips" – a nervous and uncontrollable twitching of the hands. Bernard Langer has repeatedly suffered from the condition and has defeated it with intense practice and the use of different grips and different clubs. Others have never overcome the condition.

the first few millimeters or centimeters of their travel. The New Zealand physicist and inventor Minden Blake argued that this is not necessarily so. He pointed out that the ball's center of rotation is five-sevenths of its diameter up from the ground and that if you strike it there on the upswing the ball will start rolling straightaway. Homer Kelley in *The Golfing Machine* agreed.

South African Bobby Locke believed he did this. He closed the clubface slightly going back on an inside line, then topped the ball while swinging through in-to-out with the blade square to his line-of-aim. All his putts seemed destined to die before reaching the hole, but very few did. His putting averages suggest he could have outputted the British machine.

It is possible that the yips result from repeated, but unnoticed, postural stress. Most players crouch when putting. They bend their spines in unusual ways. The set of their heads on the neck-spine in particular is distorted. Can this cause a twitch? Very probably. Players are therefore advised to stand for some seconds, upright but relaxed, immediately on leaving the green, with the head properly level. Relaxation is one of the keys to good golf and a straight spine is one key to good health.

Finally, when putting keep the hub of the swing (between the shoulders) absolutely still. Listen for the putt to drop.

Left: Every golf club has a practice putting green. And every sensible golfer uses it before setting out to play, or when he has time to spare. Putting is half the game and usually the most rewarding half. On the practice green the two most valuable things to practice are these: the short putts and the sloping ones. And always putt out.

PRACTICE

Practice makes perfect, so they say. Well, it should do. And perhaps it will if we go back to basics.

Basic Exercise 1

Attach a light weight to a length of string. Take a mid-iron and swing it and the weighted string together from hip-high to hip-high. This gives you the essential feeling of swinging rather than hitting.

Basic Exercise 2

Indoors or outdoors, using your favorite iron club, practice brushing the turf or the carpet squarely along a target line for three or four inches (not more), using a mini-swing. Do this for about a minute.

You may find that the club may bump on the ground. Take another minute to smooth out this three- or four-inch brushing action. Make sure the clubface is square.

Now brush the ground using, first, a half-swing, then a three-quarter swing. Get the feel of it. If outdoors, shut your eyes and still brush the turf. In 1934 the American pro Olin Dutra, who was off form, was advised to go back to this drill by his coach, J. Victor East. It must have worked: he won that year's U.S. Open.

On the Range

Leading pros are unanimous about the proper way to practice on the practice ground or at the driving range:

Make all practice absorbing.

Always practice to a target.

If ironing out a kink in the swing, hit some "opposite" shots – hooks if working on a slice, low balls if you have been hitting high ones.

If the kink doesn't go, leave it and come back another day. *Don't make failure habitual.*

Try picking out a short-iron target and hitting balls to it with a driver, a 3-wood and a 5-iron. Take out

There are practice ranges now in every golfing country in the world. They are usually called Driving Ranges, which is or ought to be a misnomer. For when we go there we really ought to practice all the shots, not only the long ones. Or we should practice the particular club which is giving us a bit of a problem at the time. And a little at a time, not a lot.

the appropriate short iron only when you have established a quiet, smooth rhythm with these other clubs.

Hit shots one-handed, right as well as left.

Play a "round" by imagining the holes at a favorite course and using the appropriate clubs.

Take a friend to the range and have a practice match, seeing who can hit the balls nearest the various targets.

Use the practice bunker.

At Home

The pros say everyone should have a weighted club and regularly practice full swings with it. Attach lead tape to an old club or even put a weight in a sock and tie the sock to the clubhead. Also use slow-motion swings.

With the weighted club "play statues" in the six basic positions. At the top of the back swing, with the club shaft parallel to the ground, torso fully turned. Approaching "release," hands hip-high, club shaft again parallel.

Swing is a simple word but a difficult concept. To get the basic feel of a true swing it is a good idea to attach a weight to a length of string and then to swing both it and a golf club at the same time, using a very short swing. When the club and the weight swing in unison you are truly swinging. If they don't, you"re not. The trick then is to recall this feel when making a full golf swing. It will help if you swing with your eyes closed sometimes. For some reason "sight" seems to get in the way of "feel." One must get the feel of the club head swinging truly just as the weight-on-a-string did.

At impact, with the body shifted left, club pressing into the ground. At separation, with the club a few inches farther forward, after "brushing" the turf. At follow through, with the club shaft again parallel to the ground, clubface pointing vertically upward, body turning. At the finish, with the club behind the back, hands shoulder high. Hold each position for about five seconds.

There is another valuable exercise which can be done with either a weighted club or an ordinary one:

1. Stand upright, completely relaxed.

2. Raise the club and place the shaft on the right shoulder (if right-handed).

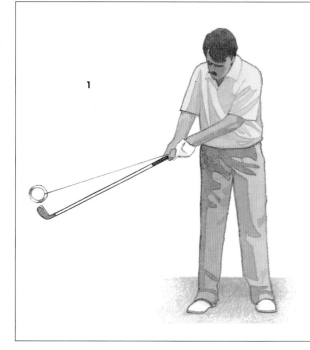

Hit several balls to a hole about 12 feet away without looking up at the result. After hitting all of them see how close some of them have come.

Putt three balls with a closed (hooking) clubface and three with an open (slicing) face. Note what happens.

In the Bunker

Throw down half a dozen balls. Hit a series of shots so that you take sand from one inch behind the ball to two inches in front of it. Look at the sand, not the ball. If there is a bare patch, use a wedge, hood the clubface and hit *down* on the ball. See what you can do.

Most important of all

Indoors or out, make a habit of regularly practicing the "Moment of Truth" – that three-inch swing with the clubface exactly square to the line-of-shot. If there are lino tiles in your kitchen, use them as guides to alignment and square-ness. Or just put some white tape in the middle of a foot-rule and swing squarely over the tape. When outdoors combine this sometimes with Basic Exercise 2 – brushing the turf. Control of the "Moment of Truth" is the secret of enjoyable golf.

3. Turn shoulders and hips fully with the club still there.

4. Bend over toward the ball. Stop and think.

5. Raise the hands, lifting the club off the shoulder, transfer your weight to the left and swing down to hip-height, so that the club is parallel to the ground. Hold it there for a few seconds.

6. Swing through to a full finish. Practice the grip, set-up, alignment and the plane using a full-length mirror.

If there's no net in the back-yard, hit shots with "aerated" plastic practice balls. Indoors, if allowable, pitch real golf balls off an old rug into an armchair. Hit *along* the line and see the ball go *up*.

On the Putting Green

Put several balls in a circle about three feet from one of the holes. Hole them all.

Go to where there are slopes on the green and practice "reading the line." Don't worry about holing the putts – the important thing is to see how accurately you can judge the line.

2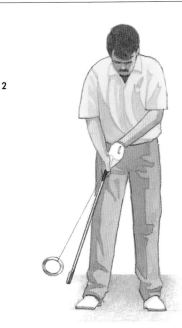

3

EXERCISES

The exercises a golfer needs are not hard. Although they demand some stretching and perhaps some muscle building, they should always be done in a relaxed manner. The three requirements for a good golf swing are rhythm, some wrist-speed and a bit of forward thrust.

The main muscles concerned are those of the legs and the lower back, the triceps (which extend the arms), the fingers and the feet. Apart from the muscles, one needs to be concerned with the mobility of the joints. For the legs a good place to start would be China – that is, to adopt some of the stances and exercises of *Chi*, the basis of the martial arts. Try the Horse Stance, for instance. Feet apart, knees bent, seat down as if sitting in a saddle. Hands at the sides as if pulling back on the reins. Back straight. Neck straight. Sit well down and hold the position for as long as can comfortably be done. As you get used to this exercise, you should sit lower and lower.

A useful variation of this stance is the Kick. Adopt a moderate Horse Stance. Put the weight on the right leg and kick gently with the left. Then put the weight on the left leg and kick gently with the right. Do this six or seven times with each leg.

Now stand straight, arms relaxed, head up. Roll the head to the left, then in a semi-circle to the right. Pause. Roll the head the other way. To begin with you will hear the neck creak. Relax. After a while the creaking will cease and your head and neck will be mobile.

On the floor

Lie on your back on the floor with your head on a fairly hard pillow or even a book to keep it level. Raise both legs toward the ceiling several times, flattening the back. Then wave one leg at a time, rotating each hip. Finally, describe a circle with each leg, clockwise and then anti-clockwise.

At the finish of this series bring the knees up as close to your chest

as possible, with arms relaxed at the sides. Now simply relax everything, just for a few minutes. (This anti-exercise will probably help considerably if you feel any slight back pain coming on).

With a club

Stand with a club behind your back grasped in both hands. Lift the club up vertically without strain. Now stretch the arms, pulling down first with one hand and then, having reversed the club, with the other. Exercise each arm several times.

With the club still behind the back, exercise the trunk by turning to the right as fully as possible; then to the left. Then raise the club so that it is behind the shoulders; as you turn, dip down with the shoulders. Make the forward turn steeper than the backswing turn. To encourage the proper posture, with the club still behind the back, place it vertically along the spine with one hand holding the club's grip, the other just above the hosel. Have your weight over the heels. Now bend forward from the hips. Stop when the club comes off the back. Stand up straight. Relax. Breathe deeply. Now do it again several times.

Without a club

Pick an imaginary (or real) target. Note a straight line between you and it. Stand parallel to that line, with your trunk bent as at the address, arms hanging loose. Now swing the arms back, causing them to turn the body. Stop when your back is toward the target. Then swing the arms down and through "along the line," then up until they bring the body round to face the target.

Do a similar arm swing but this time swinging from the knees. Swing back so that the forward knee touches the rear knee, then forward so that the rear knee touches the forward knee. Allow the arms to swing naturally.

Finally, starting almost from the address position with a slight swing back of the arms, swing

fully forward so that the hands swing up behind the head. Repeat several times.

Fingers, Wrists and Forearms

Do isometric exercises. Use a grip-spring, or squeeze a tennis

ball or a squash ball; stress the grip especially with the third finger of each hand.

Place the palms together as in prayer, and press one firmly against the other for about seven seconds. Relax. Repeat seven times – or any number of times you like.

2

3

2

3

Again with a Golf Club

Slip a strap or tie a cord around your upper arms, bringing them close together. Now practice full golf swings.

Next tie the strap or cord around the legs just above the knees. Again practice full swings.

With or without the strap, stand to a line and practice continuous swinging, back and forth, back and forth. Feel the rhythm. Think of keeping your head still. Then think of watching the strike. Keep swinging. Visualize the plane of your swing. Work on anything in your swing that is bothering you.

For instance it could be you are not effectively:
– Pushing off with the right foot
– Leading the downswing with the left hip
– Swinging the clubhead in-to-out
– Widening the arc of the swing.
It is entirely up to you.

Two of the most useful exercises are pictured above. In the upper sequence the player is swinging two clubs together. This gives the feeling of weight and helps to keep the tempo slow. In the lower sequence the man is exercising the body turn. It is more than just the "shoulder turn" we so often talk about.

THE COURSES
INTRODUCTION

One of the most scenic and most photographed golf holes in the world - the 16th at Cypress Point, on the Californian coast.

A famous American teacher, Alex J. Morrison, reckoned he could teach anyone to swing in 10 minutes. Yes, he could, agreed England's Henry Cotton – but not how to play golf. For golf is not just a matter of swinging correctly. It is not just a game against other players. It is always also, and primarily, a game against the golf course. And golf courses exist in almost infinite variety.

There is a golf course in Saudi Arabia where players have to take their own piece of carpet or astroturf with them, from which they may play any shot. There are courses in the mountains of Kashmir where the record is claimed, they say, by a Yeti. There are courses on farmland, wetlands,

heathland – country of heather, gorse, pine, birch and sand, and often hills. A rather different type of game was needed. Heather clings. Pines, if you get amongst them, block the view. Accuracy of strike became even more important and trouble shots more frequently required.

The first known golf club in the United States began in 1888 with a three-hole course in a cow pasture – the St Andrew Club at Yonkers, New York – and later moved to an apple orchard. Many of the early American courses were rather similar to the pine-and-heather country of England's first. But with the spread of the game more and more parkland and farmland had to be brought into use. What the rains did not do to

that the best courses tend to be regularly "updated" to meet the challenge.

Every tee shot should demand accuracy and most should require length as well. But whereas even only 20 years ago a drive of 250 yards was a very long one, these days shots of more than 300 yards are not uncommon and in tournaments the longest hitters *average* more than 275 yards. To cope with this, either tees have to be put back or hazards relocated.

In the past it was the approach to the green that was likely to contain the most subtleties. Cunning slopes, humps and hollows would make a successful chip a matter of the nicest judgement. The placing of sand bunkers would encourage (or enforce) the bold shot. But today it tends to be on the greens themselves that most of the subtleties are found (or are not found), and for most good players the fear of bunkers has disappeared. They would rather be in the sand than in the long rough grass around the green.

This has led, particularly in the United States, to the "tricking up" of courses used for the major professional tournaments. Narrower fairways. Tougher rough. Tremendously fast greens. But it has also led to much greater use of water as a hazard – to island greens and sometimes long lake carries off the tee. At the same time as adding to the difficulties of courses, this use of ponds and lakes has added to their visual beauty.

Golf is an art form, not just a walk in the country (or, in these days, a drive). Art is defined as "skill in performance, acquired by experience, study or observation; knack . . . human contrivance or ingenuity, as in adapting natural things to man's use . . . systematic application of skill or knowledge . . . the production of beauty."

The purpose of a golf course is to draw out from every player his or her share of this skill, this knack, this contrivance and ingenuity in what is after all only a game. Every course, every new day, will have its challenges and the meeting of them always pro-

vides a kind of beauty of its own.

It is amazing how well the original linksland courses still fulfill the main purposes and the principal challenges of the game. But it is refreshing to have at one's disposal so many different types of golf course all around the world. There isn't a golfer in existence who, given the chance, would not love to play them all.

Left: The 8th hole at Shoal Creek, in Alabama. It is a sparkling inland course designed by Jack Nicklaus, and has been host to a number of major championships including the 1984 and 1990 US PGA.

Above: Carnoustie, one of the longest and toughest courses in Scotland.

deserts, heathland, linksland, parkland, lakeland; courses designed and planted by Nature, and others fashioned and manicured by great designers. Each presents its own unique challenge to the golfer, whatever his or her degree of skill – and each its own beauty.

The first courses were on the links, the land behind and between dunes of Scotland and later England, bare of cover, open to the sea winds, and flecked with the sandy hollows where centuries of sheep had sheltered. Often with brick-hard greens, these courses favored the low-flying, fast-running ball, and the luck of the bounce had to be accepted with good grace.

The first inland courses, almost all in England, were laid out on

soften the soil the hoses of the head greenkeepers and course superintendents began to do instead. Target golf was being born.

Already a new profession had arisen, that of golf course architect – Willie Park, Jr, Dr. Alister Mackenzie, Harry Colt, Donald Ross and many others of equal distinction.

The objective of every architect is to make the best use of the available land to produce a course which is a delight for even the rankest amateur to play, yet provides a stern test of the shot-making abilities of the very finest players. In meeting this objective architects fight a constant battle against improvements in the performance of clubs and balls and in the understanding of technique, so

THE SEVEN FACES OF GOLF

Golf is now played all around the world in every season and on every type of land.

Here are the bare bones of seven totally different courses, from the Atlantic to the Pacific, from the North Sea to the South Seas that make the point in picture-book fashion.

ST ANDREWS

St Andrews is a small, gray-stone Scottish town devoted to golf and to learning, home to one of the very oldest universities in the United Kingdom and one of the very oldest golf courses in the world. The Old Course, in all its structural essentials, is something fashioned by nature, not by man, over hundreds of years. In this flat and windy stretch of Fife linksland there are few obvious landmarks to aim at off the tees. The treeless fairways roll and tilt toward the greens, several of which have two flagsticks on them and are shared between different holes. There are swales, bumps and hollows everywhere and most of the bunkers (especially the horrendous little pot-bunkers) are hidden from the eyes until you reach them. These are the sands of history: – Hell bunker, Student's bunker, Ginger Beer bunker, The Beardies, Scholars'' bunker, the Principal's Nose, Deacon Sime, Mrs Kruger, and many others.

The first time he played the course in the 1921 Open, the immortal Bobby Jones tore up his card after taking 6 at the formidable short 11th hole in the third round. The first time the American professional Tony Lema played it, he won the 1964 Open. When Sam Snead first saw it he is reported to have remarked, "Hey, that looks like an old abandoned golf course. What do they call it?" But the thoughtful Australian Peter Thomson, five times an Open winner, gave this verdict: "It finds you out. If there is one part of your game not quite right, no matter how you try to hide it, the Old Course will find it during the championship."

You have to learn the course. As one old caddie told one old professor, "When ye're learning the laddies Latin and Greek 'tis easy work, but to play golf you maun

use yeer heid!" The safe way round would seem to be to draw every long shot slightly to the left; that way, it looks as if you can avoid most of the trouble. But, in fact, the way to score is to fade the ball to the right. After a few rounds the best tournament professionals find the course easy enough if the day is calm; but when the sea winds blow, as they so often do, it is a different story.

During the 1988 Dunhill Cup, an international stroke-match-play tournament, Australian Rodger Davis shot a 63 to hold the record for one day. Next day American Curtis Strange shot 62. In 1970 Tony Jacklin went round the first nine holes in 29 shots. Then the heavens opened to a tremendous storm; play was abandoned, and on the following day it was a different course – and a different Jacklin.

In 1888 a violent arctic wind scoured the course. Defending champion Willie Park Jr. took 90 shots in the morning and 92 in the afternoon; "Old Tom" Morris took 94. The "Old Lady" won, as so often before and since.

The first hole on the Old Course – there are the Eden, New Course, and Jubilee close by – looks pretty easy. The fairway must be one of the widest in the world. The green is only 370 yards away – a 3-wood or long iron and a wedge for the top pros. All that stands in the way is the narrow Swilcan Burn which, winding its way to the sea, cuts right in front of the green. The green, however, slopes imperceptibly down toward the burn, and too much backspin on the pitch can see the ball rundown backwards into the burn. It doesn't happen often; but that was the fate of Australian Ian Baker-Finch in the final round of the 1984 Open, when he was leading.

The 2nd and 3rd holes are not too difficult, provided you keep to the right of the fairway. You keep

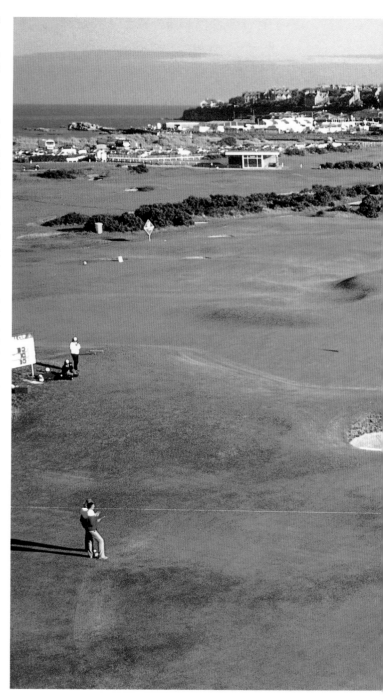

The Old Course at St Andrews remains as nature made it. Unaltered for 600 years, it remains also a great test of every golfer's talents.

right on the 463-yards 4th hole, too, unless you can drive 275 yards over the trouble or draw the ball out on to the 15th fairway. There is an awkward mound in front of the green, too, which may throw the ball off in almost any direction. The 5th is a par-5, of 564 yards, and whether or not it is dif-

ficult often depends on the wind. In 1933, with a gale behind him, the American Craig Wood drove into bunkers more than 400 yards away. (Later, he lost to his compatriot Denny Shute in a play-off.)

The 10th hole is named "Bobby Jones" in memory of a great golfer and perfect gentleman, who was made a Freeman of the town of St Andrews. It is only 342 yards in length and these days, if the wind is not against the players, some may even drive the green. But very great accuracy is demanded. A drive to the left may find the

heather or one of the many whin (gorse) bushes, while there's sand on the right.

On first acquaintance the 316-yards 12th looks straightforward. But in fact straight ahead is a hidden family of bunkers, invisible from the tee.

To the right on the 567-yards 14th is an out-of-bounds wall. To the left are the frightening bunkers called The Beardies. In the path of most second shots is the huge Hell bunker. A safe shot left, on to the 5th fairway, is often the preferred route, but it leaves

a tricky approach to the green.

But it is the 17th, 461 yards and one of the greatest par-4s in golf, which so often settles championships. In the old days players had to drive over the corner of some railway sheds encroaching on the fairway from the right. Today these have been replaced by other buildings of similar shape. A long fade to the right is the best shot, so long as it does not curve into a hotel's garden. A safe drive to the left often puts the infamous road bunker into play for the second shot. Safety says "Hit

short"; boldness says "Go for the green," but that risks running it through and on to a road (which is in play) and, possibly, up against a wall. The bunker is quite small but very deep; moreover, it not only bites into the left front of the green, but has a deceptively large "catchment area" for balls pitched or putted near it.

The 18th, called "Tom Morris," is a relief after the 17th. The Royal and Ancient clubhouse stands invitingly behind the green, its clockface providing the best line for the tee shot. The fairway is

acres wide. The hole is 354 yards long and many players have driven the green, including Jack Nicklaus when winning in 1970. Anyone who doesn't has to be sure not to put his second shot into the Valley of Sin, a large swale at the left front of the green, whence it is all too easy to take three more. And then, if you are going to win, you will almost certainly need a single putt, wherever you are on a somewhat deceptive green.

It's an ancient course, full of mystery, but still a great one.

AUGUSTA NATIONAL

Like the Old Course at St Andrews, the Augusta National is unique. But it is as unlike St Andrews in every other respect as it is possible to imagine. Essentially it is golf for fun in a visual paradise. The fairways are wide. There is virtually no rough. The holes are named after the gorgeous flowering trees and shrubs of the balmy Georgia spring: Pink Dogwood, Flowering Peach, Magnolia, Yellow Jasmine, Carolina Cherry, Camelia, Azalea and so on. Every now and again there is blue water in the shade of the majestic Georgia pines.

Bobby Jones founded it, Dr. Alister Mackenzie, a Yorkshire-born Scot, one of the foremost course designers of his day, (he was also responsible for Cypress Point and Royal Melbourne), produced the original design; Robert Trent Jones is one of the great architects who have since improved on it. One of the most remarkable qualities of the course is that it is hugely enjoyable, and yet often immensely testing, for the average club member, the low handicap player and the tournament professional alike.

The greens are subtly and sometimes wickedly contoured. On tournament days holes are cut so as to demand a really fine shot to get close to them, and the greens are lightning quick. Every medium-length putt is difficult and, to use Bobby Jones' words, long putts are intended "to present a real problem if the player is to get down in par."

The second nine holes (originally the front nine, but Jones changed them round in the 1930s) make it hazardous for someone to protect a lead, yet at the same time they present opportunities for a very low score to someone throwing caution aside in a closing charge.

Holes 11, 12 and 13, where the course turns sharply round Rae's Creek, are now known throughout the world of golf as Amen Corner. If players do not say

The Augusta National is a golf course in a garden, a vast, rich, luxurious garden in the American South. Here Nick Faldo and Jack Nicklaus approach the beautiful but deceptive 16th green.

goodbye to their chances here they praise the Lord.

A round starts pleasantly enough. The 1st hole (Tea Olive) is 400 yards long and presents a gentle dogleg to the right. There is a deep bunker on the right to catch a poor tee shot, but otherwise no great difficulty about the

hole. The 2nd (Pink Dogwood) a par 5 of 555 yards, immediately causes players to think in terms of strategy. Long hitters can get on the green in two, but it is a big, sloping, rather treacherous green where you really must leave yourself with an uphill putt if you are thinking to get a birdie.

The 3rd (Flowering Peach) is a par-4 of only 360 yards. But the second shot; from whatever part of the fairway, can present problems. The green is very small and has downslopes on three sides. Some 30 flowering peach trees

frame the scene spectacularly.

The 5th hole (Magnolia) is a 435-yard par-4 with a severe dogleg left over roller-coaster land with a fast two-level green, the 6th (Juniper) a 180-yard par-3 from a very elevated tee. The 9th (Carolina Cherry), 435 yards, curves sharp left down the hill and around the corner. The green is near the top of another hill and a ball that does not reach it will roll left away and away and away from it.

So to Amen Corner. The 11th (White Dogwood) is a formidable

par-4 of 455 yards. It challenges the drive, which must have pin-point accuracy; the approach must avoid the pond at front and left. The 12th (Golden Bell) is only 155 yards but some reckon it the hardest hole on the course. There is nearly always an unpredictable wind swirling through the tree tops. Correct club selection is vital. The 13th (Azalea) a short dog-legged par-5 of 465 yards, demands a long, high draw over a hill, round and down to the left so that one can then be certain of clearing Rae's Creek (fronting

the green) with the second shot.

Hole 15 (Fire Thorn), is a 500-yard par-5. It was here in 1935 that Gene Sarazen scored an albatross 2 with his 4-wood to tie Craig Wood. He then beat him in the play-off. There's water in front of the green and behind it, the ground falls away sharply through trees – so once again course management is vital. The fairway of the par-3 16th (Red Bud) consists almost entirely of water and requires an accurate iron shot of 170 yards, for the player must hit the right part of the green,

depending on where the flag is.

The last two holes complete the picture. The 17th (Nandina), 400 yards long, looks easy. The fairway is generous. There's not a bunker in sight. It is the design of the approach to the green that presents the problems. If the second shot is left or right of the direct line there's trouble – a bunker each side of the green and wicked slopes fronting the bunkers. If you hit through the green it is almost impossible for you to get back near the hole in a single shot.

Then finally comes Holly, only

the second hole with a righthand dogleg. The tee shot is framed by the tall trees. There is a double fairway bunker to the left which will catch the tee shot if the player does not get enough fade on the ball, bunkers left and right of the green itself, and then a two-level green. Arnold Palmer lost to Gary Player in 1961 by finding both greenside bunkers. Scot Sandy Lyle won in 1988 by firing the perfect 7-iron out of the fairway bunker and then sinking his first putt.

That's golf. That's Augusta.

LAS BRISAS

Las Brisas, near Marbella on the southern coast of Spain, is a Robert Trent Jones course set in a spectacular valley blessed by the western Mediterranean sun. There's water, water everywhere – and not a drop you don't have to think about when planning your shots. Ponds, streams, lateral water hazards – Las Brisas has them all. The greens are generous in size but not in their contours. You have to be a really good putter to fully enjoy this course. It challenges the best.

The bare and rumpled peak of the La Concha presents a theatrical backdrop to the lush green fairways. The course has a lovely open feeling – at least for most of the way. But the last half dozen holes can change the picture. You arrive at the short 16th after threading your way through tight avenues of trees, and there in front of you is perhaps the biggest challenge of the lot. From the back tees the 16th is 225 yards long, with the green above the level of the tee. It is waiting for the perfect shot. If you are short, there's water for you. If you push or pull the shot there are sand traps either side. And if you hit the green, unless the shot is absolutely right the ball is likely to run back toward you.

On the 1st hole, a little over 405 yards, there are bunkers on the right ready to gobble up a fade, and, for the second shot, a bunker and a wide stream on the left of the green to take a draw. The 2nd, a dog-leg right of 425 yards, has out-of-bounds to the right and at the distance of a powerful drive, which would open up the view of the green, a pond on the right and bunkers on the left. There is an uphill second shot to a sloping green that is an island in a sea of sand, or rather crushed marble. The 5th hole is a 590-yard par-5, dog-legging a bit right past a string of 10 bunkers to another awkwardly contoured green.

The 8th and the 12th are shorter par-5s, 530 yards and 520 respectively. They are both holes where water plays a challenging role. For each there is a relatively safe route and a trickier but more rewarding way over the water near the green. On the 12th a stream keeps biting into the fairway on the left, while on the right at driving range is a big bunker. Near the green the fairway takes a sharp left turn, once again over water. For the professionals a par-5 is easy here, but a birdie is sensational. Of Las Brisas' four par-3s, two are over water, the second of them being that impossible 16th.

This is not a course for the faint-hearted. But, then, who among the world's golfers is faint-hearted? It is not that kind of game.

At Las Brisas in Spain the architect, Robert Trent Jones, has painted the course in water colors.

SINGAPORE

On Singapore Island golf has been taken to the jungle. It provides vital breathing space in one of the world's smallest and most crowded independent states, a polyglot community bustling with immense energy and throbbing with advanced technology.

The Singapore Island Country Club boasts not one fine course but four, with more than 7,000 members. It all started in 1891 with a nine-hole layout near the racecourse. Thirty years later, when members demanded an 18-holer, the Singapore Golf Club, as it then was, had to move farther out of town. It bought the lease of a larger site out in the jungle near

a reservoir, hired the great Scots golfer James Braid to design the course and opened it – the Bukit Timah course – in 1924. (Braid did the designs entirely from maps they sent him at Walton Heath Golf Club in Surrey, England, where he was the professional until the end of his life in 1950.)

A second club, the Island Golf Club, was formed in 1932 and both prospered until the Japanese invasion and occupation in 1941-2. Much of the land was ploughed up and it was not until 1952 that both clubs were again functional. They merged in 1963, and both their courses were redesigned by Frank Pennink, a distinguished English amateur champion of the 1930s who became a successful golf course architect.

Bukit Timah was a sufficiently testing golf course to be chosen as the stage for the World Cup in 1969, when it was won by Lee Trevino and Orville Moody for the United States.

Bukit is 6,690 yards in length, the New Course 6,874. The two other courses – the Island and the Sime – are some 500 yards shorter and are less testing physically. The Bukit course has rolling fairways between the jungle trees, and two of its three par-5s are more than 530 yards long. The MacRitchie Reservoir provides no hazards but is scenically vital. And, of course, what it does provide in plenty is water.

Bermuda grass is used on both fairways and greens, since it is almost the only strain of grass

On Singapore Island there are four fine courses cut and molded from the jungle – this is Bukit.

which can thrive in the moist jungle heat. This presents no problem on the fairways but can do so on the greens. The lie of the grass after mowing becomes tremendously important, and against the grain the ball has to be struck with great firmness.

All the courses are most enjoyable to play and remain in a sense very British. The golfer needs to be able to play the bump-and-run as well as, or perhaps even more than, the pitch-and-stop. The artist does better than the power player on Singapore Island – although maybe only at golf.

KASUMIGASEKI

Kasumigaseki is the most honored course in Japan, a beautiful tree-lined course with frightening bunkers and with twin greens on almost every hole – one with summer grass, the other with the grasses of winter. And the flowers, shrubs and trees remind one that in Japan flower-arrangement is an acknowledged art.

It was here that in 1957 Japan won the Canada Cup, now the World Cup. Torakichi Nakamura and Koichi Ono simply outplayed the cream of the world's golfers on a course they understood so well. That "cream" included players of the quality of Sam Snead, Gary Player, Roberto de Vicenzo and Eric Brown.

The course was designed by a Japanese amateur, Kinya Fujita, and a British architect, Hugh Alison, who had set out the Tokyo Golf Club in 1914. Kasumigaseki opened in 1929 but was not finalised until around 1932.

One of the difficulties had been the effect of the Japanese climate on the traditional grasses used then in golf-course design. The rye grasses and the bent withered away in the Japanese summer. So the twin-green concept was introduced, with the local Korai grass covering the summer greens. Korai is like Bermuda grass, tough and spiky, and for those not accus-

tomed to it, it is extremely difficult to putt on.

Alison's bunkers, deep and cavernous, form another unusual aspect of this great Oriental course. It is 6,959 yards in length with a par of 72 and boasts 100 of these bunkers. The short 10th, 180 yards, has two greens, two lakes and six sand traps and is in effect two different holes in one, depending on which season one is playing it.

The long 14th, 593 yards, has an enormous bunker-in-the-woods to catch the pulled tee-shot, then rolls majestically along its tree-lined fairway to meet three vast bunkers short of the two greens and four more surrounding them.

In spite of its length and its difficulties, Kasumigaseki is marvelous to play. Its landscaping is breathtaking. The sad thing is that so few Japanese golfers can play the course. Of the 12 million or more golfers in the country, about 10 million "play" the game only at more than 4,000 driving ranges and on their TV screens. It is accepted as a fact-of-life. And it explains why the Japanese, the world's greatest exporters, are buying-up or laying-out golf courses all around the world within a reasonably airplane hop from their crowded native soil.

Kasumigaseki is a spectacular Japanese course where flowering shrubs frame deep oriental bunkers.

SUNNINGDALE

Sunningdale in Surrey is perhaps the most charming of English heathland courses. Heathland was where golf was first played in England, King James I (James VI of Scotland) introducing it to the English at Blackheath near his riverside palace at Greenwich in 1603. Heathland was the perfect substitute for the links of Scotland, for the soil is mainly sand, a great belt of which runs through the countryside from Kent,

through Surrey to Hampshire. Useless for agriculture – the natural vegetation is mainly heather, gorse and pine – heathland was made for golf.

Sunningdale, however, presents a perfect example of man improving on nature. When double Open Champion Willie Park Jr, was asked to design a course there at the turn of the century Sunningdale Heath was open country – moorland without trees – and it was only later, when Henry Colt was brought in, that the thousands of trees that give

the course so much of its flavour were planted. Colt improved the Old Course and designed Sunningdale New; but great as his New course is, it is the Old Course with which golfers fall in love.

One of the most famous rounds of golf was played there in 1926 by Bobby Jones when he was qualifying for the Open (which he went on to win at Royal Lytham).

Jones went round in 66, breaking the then course record by no less than six shots. But the great thing about the round was that he scored only 3s and 4s, hitting 33 shots and sinking 33 putts. It was known as "the perfect round." (In the afternoon, he scored a scarcely inferior 68). Jones said afterwards that he only wished he could take the golf course home.

Sunningdale Old, at 6,566 yards and with a par of 72, is short by modern standards. But it is lovely. Every time you play there you want to play it again. Virtually every hole is separated from its neighbours now by trees. It starts generously with a relatively flat par-5, followed by a slightly shorter par-5 of 484 yards. But the second shot there must contend with a leftward slope alongside the green. Then follows an up-and-down, right-sloping par-4 of less than 300 yards. And the 4th is 160-odd yards uphill to a fiendishly sloping green with bunkers waiting in front and at left and right.

At the 10th – a short par 5- you can look over or through the trees to London, drive downhill and play your second uphill – but you will need to hit it more than 200 yards if you want to get home in two. The 13th is a short down-hiller of some 185 yards, with bunkers in front of the green and a ditch beside and behind it. And then you come home between the trees to a demanding final approach shot to a seemingly simple but actually demanding green. It is a course that will never defeat you – just charm you, into error, maybe, but also into playing above yourself.

A favorite course for golfers in southern England, Sunningdale is all heather, sand, trees and challenges.

BALLYBUNION

They call it "the best golf course in the world." Who are "they"? Some of the best golfers in the world, like Tom Watson; the best golf writers in the world, like Herbert Warren Wind; the devoted club golfers who have been to this magical place in the far west of Ireland on the south side of the estuary of the river Shannon:

Ballybunion. And today, moreover, one is not at all sure which Ballybunion course they are talking about, the Old or the New. Each represents the best of its kind – the New Course having been fashioned by Robert Trent Jones, the Old Course mainly by Nature with the assistance of a golf magazine Editor, a consultant to an English firm of seedsmen, and finally, in the mid-1930s, an English golf architect.

Much of the magic is in the setting. Visiting the west of Ireland for the first time one sometimes gets the feeling that this is how the world began. It's remote, wild. Inshore from the white beaches, on the crumbling cliffs, are huge granite boulders, washed up perhaps like pebbles in gigantic early storms. It is a land that feels empty, but never lonely. There's real Irish warmth in the winds from the Atlantic ocean.

The great green dunes roll away from you invitingly but defiantly. The 1st hole is downhill. The fairway looks wide. But there's a bunker to catch the drive on the left and wild dunes on the right and the 392 yards seem longer. "Sure," says your companion, "and are they not Irish yards!" On the 2nd hole you must avoid not only bunkers left and right but the rough slopes of two huge sand dunes.

On the 220-yard par-3 3rd hole not only must you keep away from the dunes and out of the bunkers right and left but you must cope with a slope that looks as if it will run your ball down on to the highway just beyond the green. It calls for a tee shot blending power and precision in equal parts.

The 7th, at 423-yards, is many people's favorite. It runs along the clifftop with the sea to one's right. There are hills and valleys, curves, bumps and hollows to negotiate. The green is guarded not only by bunkers but by a mound in front of it and a chasm behind it. Then you turn your back on the sea and play downhill to an 8th green that is only 150 yards or so below you but looks to be entirely surrounded by unpredictable slopes and hollows.

The 10th, 359 yards takes you back to the cliffs again. From there on it's drama all the way. Sand-hills, slopes, doglegs, mounds and green, green valleys.

Herbert Warren Wind, after walking the course, noted that he could remember all the 18 holes. "To put it bluntly" he wrote in 1971, "Ballybunion revealed itself to be nothing less than the finest seaside course I have ever seen." And Wind noted something else significant: it is perhaps the *only* such links course where you *must* hit your approach shot to the pin.

It's target golf on a links. On most holes the bump-and-run is just too dangerous.

In golf, every day is a different day, every shot a different shot and every course a different challenge.

Sited on the very edge of the west coast of Ireland, Ballybunion has a wild, exciting and yet most inviting feel to it. Here you breathe the very air of golf.

COURSES IN NORTH AMERICA

Early in this century one of the great golf-course architects, Dr. Alister Mackenzie, set out his ideas on the basic concepts of good design.

He said there should be little walking between greens and tees. Every hole should have a different character. There should be few blind holes. Along the way an infinite variety of different strokes should be required. Players should not have to suffer the annoyance caused by long searches for lost balls. And, finally, there should always be an advantage in placing tee shots in a particular area or on a particular spot.

Except for the fact that motorised golf carts have removed the need for walking on many modern courses, these criteria still hold good today. When panels of experts get together to select the 10 best courses, or even the 100 best courses, in any area they ask themselves questions such as the following:

How well does the course test accuracy? To what extent does it demand length of shot and to what extent finesse? How varied is it? How memorable are its holes? How much does the scenic value add to the pleasure of a round? How well does it accord with tradition?

Here are some of the many great courses of North America which, in fulfillling these criteria, have had a powerful influence on the game, and on the art of golf course architecture. In addition to this they have given enormous pleasure to those lucky enough to play them.

The several thousands of courses in North America range from the majestic summer splendour of Banff in Canada, laid out under the backdrop of the northern Rocky Mountains, to the many holiday courses of Florida in their almost perpetual warm sunshine. And from East to West from the almost English atmosphere of The Country Club at Brookline, a suburb of Boston, to the Californian glamour of Pebble Beach, Cypress Point and the Olympic. Then near the center is Medinah, boasting all the toughness associated with Chicago, the windy city.

Banff

Banff Springs is a holiday resort set in the Canadian Rockies in Alberta. The course will take your breath away, and not only because of the scenic splendour of the foothills of the mountains. It lies at an altitude of 4,000 feet. The air is crystal clear, and the ball flies farther than at sea level. This makes the 6,626 yards of the course seem shorter than they are. As if to make up for this, there are 144 sand bunkers to be negotiated. And along one side of the course runs the cold Bow River, its banks lined with conifers.

The old clubhouse is situated where the Bow meets the Spray river and the first tee shot has to cross the river and thread its way between the trees to the crest of a small hill.

The 4th hole is a long par-5 (578 yards) which doglegs twice to the right; there should be a "Keep Left" sign on the tee. The short 8th they call "The Devil's Cauldron." It is only 171 yards from tee to green, but the tee is high above a lake, the green, on the other side of the lake, is small, hemmed in by trees, and has bunkers to the right, to the left and straight behind.

Holes 12 and 14 are also short and at each the Bow River plays a part. At both you need to be able to hit an accurate length, 130 to 140 yards on the 12th and 210 to 230 on the 14th. And now the river and Mount Rumble are always in your view as you make for home and the famous, or infamous, 18th. This is a 429-yard par-4 with a twist in its tail – if by then you have managed to avoid 20 of the 28 bunkers. These bunkers are strategically placed, confounding all but the best players.

Banff is made up of three nine-hole courses and of course the palatial Banff Springs Hotel. When the winter ice and the mountain snows melt, it's wonderland.

Royal Montreal

The oldest known golf club in the Americas is the Royal Montreal, founded in 1873. Originally sited in a public park, the Royal Montreal Golf Club has had to move twice since then as the city of Montreal expanded. The club now owns a wooded and well watered property at Ile Bizard, large enough to house two 18-hole courses and a nine-holer. The Blue course, completed in the 1950s, is the current championship course, 6,738 yards with a par of 70.

The architect was a civil engineer, Dick Wilson, who had already produced courses in difficult country in the southern United States. Now he had to drain swamp and lift boulders and excavate hard ground to produce a beautiful tree-lined course good enough to host the Canadian Open.

There are few fairway bunkers on the course (only 11 to be precise) but the greens are enormous and very heavily guarded. On most of the holes it is the second or third shot that really counts. Not on all, for the final four holes play over water. The 16th, indeed, needs two shots over the water. An American pro, Pat Fitzsimmons, playing in the 1975 Canadian Open hit his tee shot on to the only island in that water, waded across to it, hit an iron to the green and, taking two putts, scored his par-4.

The Royal Montreal plays an annual match against The Country Club at Brookline, Massachusetts, which was the first international match in North America and indeed is the oldest in the world between sides from different countries.

The Country Club

The Country Club, Brookline, founded in 1860, was the first club of this kind in America. But golf was not played there until six holes were laid out in 1893. Today

Here we see two courses of very different types: Banff (*above*) is a course in the northern Rockies, while the Country Club (*left*) at Brookline, Mass., is a course with an English parkland air about it. One represents golf on holiday, the other tournament golf.

there are 27 holes, divided into three nines, the Clyde, the Squirrel and the Primrose. Customarily the first two are combined to make the main 18-hole course with the Primrose nine ear-marked for ladies, children and beginners. But usually now in major tournaments holes taken from each of the three nines are combined to make a champion-ship course.

The Country Club is strong on tradition and has a very English air about it – except for the heat and humidity, which in a Massachu-setts summer can become quite oppressive.

The course is tree-lined with two fine lakes; but on the most famous day in its history much more open. That day was in the summer of 1913 when a young local amateur Francis Ouimet defeated the two great British pro-fessionals, Harry Vardon and Ted

Ray, in a play-off to take the U.S. Open Championship. This victory marked the beginning of a new era in the game in which, until the mid-1980s, Americans would be totally dominant.

For the 1988 Open Robert Trent Jones' younger son, Rees Jones, revised the course. In the Open which followed, England's Nick Faldo tied with America's Curtis Strange over the 72 holes and Strange went on to win the play-off.

Brae Burn

Not far from The Country Club, in West Newton, Mass., is another old rather English-style country club, Brae Burn. It's history dates back to the 1890s and it might be called the Sunningdale of New England. It has hosted the U.S. Women's Amateur, the Curtis Cup, the U.S. Women's Open and

the U.S. men's Amateur – the last, in 1928, was won by Bobby Jones.

Brae Burn was designed, and later remodeled by Donald Ross, a Scot from Dornoch in the High-lands who emigrated to the United States and designed more than 600 courses in his adopted country. Among these were the original layouts for such super-lative courses as Seminole, Pine-hurst No. 3, Oak Hill, Scioto and Inverness.

Donald Ross

Most of the famous Ross courses have been recast to some extent (though not always improved), mainly because of the irreversible North American trend toward tar-get golf. Ross himself produced very subtle strategic courses with generous fairways that required more and more thought as the golfer approached the greens.

At Shinnecock Hills on Long Island, New York, you play golf on a true American links: rolling fairways; sandy soil; tough seaside grass. And, often, a strong salty seawind to contend with.

Many of the greens were on little plateaus (like those at Royal Dor-nock) and encouraged finely judged chipping rather than pitching. There would be bunkers on the approach to these greens, but rarely bunkers behind them. Ross's view was that bunkers in front of a green made accurate judgement of distances more test-ing but that a bunker behind a green discouraged the bold shot.

A genuine Ross bunker would have a curved rather than a straight face, so that the ball would tend to roll back, leaving the golfer with a reasonable though still difficult shot.

There are still many "genuine" Ross courses in America. There's the Country Club in Asheville, North Carolina, for instance (Asheville is a Shangri-la hidden in the midst of mountain country); there is the Winnapaug Golf Club in Rhode Island; the Wampanoag in Hartford, Conn.; the Penobscot Valley in Maine; the Burlington in Vermont; the Holston Hills in Tennessee; the Beverley in Chicago. And of course there is the Brae Burn, and also the Charles River Country Club nearby.

Brae Burn actually has two courses, No. 1 being 6,516 yards long and No. 2 rather shorter. The notable 11th on No. 1 is a par-4 of 445 yards, with out-of-bounds on the left and bunkers in the driving zone on the right. Trees overhang the green, discouraging the conventional high approach shot of target golf, and the crafty golfer, plays his second to the front of the green and chips up for the par. Like all Ross courses, it is a real pleasure to play.

Shinnecock Hills

Shinnecock Hills is one of the oldest and possibly the most unusual golf course in the United States. It takes its name from a Red Indian reservation which once occupied the tip of Long Island, about 100 miles east of the city of New York. The story is that three wealthy Americans, William K. Vanderbilt, Edward S. Mead and Duncan Dr.yder, were enjoying the winter in the south of France in 1890-1 when they saw the makings of Biarritz Golf Club, which the Scottish professional and architect Willie Dunn was laying out. "Gentlemen, this beats rifle-shooting!" Vanderbilt is said to have proclaimed; and the three agreed to finance a visit by Dunn to Long Island in the spring of 1891. Dunn found what to a Scot seemed the only really suitable site, a large open area of sandy scrubland near the resort of Southampton.

By summer's end a 12-hole course was completed and 41 other wealthy Long Islanders joined the original three as debenture holders in an incorporated club, the first of its kind in the United States. The following year another six holes were added and a palatial clubhouse erected. The game of golf took off with a bang and in 1894 Shinnecock joined with the St Andrews Club of New York, the Newport of Rhode Island and the Chicago Golf Club to form the U.S. Golf Association.

The course was modernised and lengthened by Dick Wilson in 1931, but he cleverly retained its original characteristics – rolling, undulating fairways on sandy soil, tough seaside rough, and the general atmosphere of a links course in a warmer climate.

Shinnecock was further lengthened to 6,900 yards for the 1986 U.S. Open (the length on the card is 6,697 yards), and only one player broke par over 72 holes. That was Raymond Floyd, then aged 43, who in 1990 was to come so close to winning his second Masters at Augusta.

As on most courses close to the sea there is nearly always a wind to contend with. It usually blows across the par-3 holes and against the golfer on the shorter par-4s. The greens are protected in Scottish fashion with swales and hollows and deep sand bunkers. And the long grass in the rough is penal. Yes, it's a tough old course.

Medinah

Medinah 3, on which the 1990 U.S. Open was held (and remarkably won by veteran Hale Irwin), has always been rated about the toughest course in the Chicago area – and that was even before they altered it and lengthened it for the Open! Alteration was re-quired because the USGA did not consider that the 18th hole was suitable as a finishing hole for their Open Championship. It was a right-hand dogleg of 415 yards, which meant that everyone played short off the tee. Altering the 18th meant disposing of the 17th as well, and in the end virtually all the back nine were remodeled.

As a test, the U.S. Seniors Open was held at the new Medinah 3 in 1988. Although the Seniors played from forward tees, their course still measured 6,881 yards, which is considerable longer than most they play. Gary Player and Bob Charles tied on 288, and Player won the play-off by 68 to 70. For the 1990 Open the course measured 7,195 yards. It is an up-and-down course held tight between massive oaks, but it is the sloping greens that have evoked the most criticism. The new 17th is a 168-yard par-3 over Lake Kadijah, with a green that slopes down to the lake for the short shots and a bunker at the rear for the long ones. In the 1988 Seniors Walter

The course at Medinah, Chicago, was originally built for the Shriners in the 1920s. Lake Kadijah, seen here separating the par-3 17th, is named after the Prophet's wife.

Zembriski was leading until he took a 7 at this hole. Even Gary Player said it was a bad hole. But not a bad course: "Medinah is a Mecca of golf," he affirmed.

Oak Hill

Oak Hill is another fine championship course in New York state. Originally designed by Donald Ross it has been updated by Robert Trent Jones. It derives its name from the hill behind the clubhouse, and to fortify that name a Dr. John Williams is credited with planting 28 varieties of oak around the course: there are said now to be 30,000 such trees framing the beautifully lush green fairways.

As on many great courses, it is the closing holes that find out the winners. The 16th, 441 yards, runs down a left-sloping fairway between thick stands of oak, maple and pine. The 17th is a long par-4 of 463 yards; two bunkers narrow the entrance to its green, tempting the golfer to make sure of hitting his second beyond them and braving the danger of going over the back into jungle country. Ben Hogan did just that to lose the 1956 U.S. Open to fellow American Cary Middlecoff.

The 18th is 450 yards long, with a huge fairway bunker on the inside angle of the dogleg as it turns to the right. The fairway then slopes downhill and finally uphill to a raised green surrounded by more bunkers. Lee Trevino won in 1968 with a record total of 275. Steps were taken to toughen the course – but Jack Nicklaus won in 1980 with 274. If you play well you score well.

Above: Thirty thousand oaks of 28 varieties were planted round this course at Oak Hill, New York. The 13th hole seen here is just on 600 yards long and it's uphill. They call it "the King of Par-5s."

Left: Pine Valley, New Jersey, is rated about the most difficult course in the United States. Built from a forest in a swamp surrounded by sand, it challenges the best. This the 14th, one of their most demanding water holes.

Pine Valley

Pine Valley at Clementon, New Jersey, is considered by many to be the most difficult course in the world. It was the brainchild of a Philadelphia hotelier, George Crump, in about 1911. Henry Colt, the British architect, gave him a helping hand in 1913, but it was not until 1916 that as many as 14 holes were ready for play, and Crump died just before the full 18 were finished.

The land Crump had fallen in love with was a forest growing on sand. And sand and forest mark the course today. There are also two lakes to contend with. But it is the sand that most people remember. On many holes it feels like playing to green little islands in a sea of sand. On the longer holes the first island is in the fairway, the second or third is the green itself.

For 25 years nobody broke 70. The first to do so was Ryder Cup player Ed Dudley. His first round on that occasion was 68; his last was 85. A club president once took 44 shots on a single hole. And the only man so far who can claim to have thoroughly conquered the course is the young Arnold Palmer. Trying to raise cash for an engagement ring, Palmer accepted a bet that he could not break 72 on any course his boss cared to name. His boss named Pine Valley. Palmer bogeyed the very first hole, but went on the score a 68 and win himself and his future wife $800.

Oakland Hills

Oakland Hills, just outside Detroit, Michigan, is another formidable course, but in a different way from Pine Valley. It is long (7,054 yards) and it is punishing. "I'm glad I brought this course, this monster, to its knees," said Ben Hogan when he won the 1951 U.S. Open there.

It is another of those classic courses originated by Donald Ross and modernised by Robert Trent Jones. Jones moved Ross's fairway sand traps 30 and 40 yards further on, narrowed the fairways and put new bunkers around the greens. The course now demands consistent accuracy and superb course management.

During the 1951 Open some of the fairways were only 25 yards wide, and the rough was gruesome. For three rounds nobody broke 70. Hogan had started with a 76. In the second round he managed to bring this down to 73 and in the third to 71. Now the great man knew the course. In the final round he scored 67, one of the greatest rounds in the championship's history, signing off with a majestic birdie on the 460-yard 18th. It was true: he really had brought a monster to its knees.

Monterey

In California, some 100 miles south of San Francisco, the glorious Monterey peninsula runs down from the Santa Lucia mountains through forests of eucalyptus, pine and cypress to the Pacific Ocean. It ends abruptly in jagged yet beautiful cliffs, beneath which sealions bask on the rocks. And it is here that three of America's greatest courses have been built – Pebble Beach, Cypress Point and Spyglass Hill.

Pebble Beach came first. It was conjured up by Samuel A. Morse, a real-estate man working in the early part of the century for the Southern Pacific Railroad. Ordered by the railroad to sell off its property holdings on the peninsula, Morse formed the Del Monte Property Company and bought the land himself. In 1914 he contacted another real-estate man, Jack Neville, who was a champion amateur golfer, and together they staked out the positions for tees and greens on what was to become one of the world's most spectacular golf courses.

Eight of the holes run along the clifftops of Carmel Bay. The 7th at 120 yards is the shortest hole on any championship course, but one of the most scenic. The tiny green is set below the tee and is surrounded by sand, and not far away by rocks. When the wind blows, so does the salt sea spray. The 8th is a wild par-4 where, for the top players, the second shot has to be played over a wide precipitous ravine where the ocean bites into the land. On the 9th and 10th, longish par-4s of great subtlety, the narrow fairways slope toward the cliffs.

The finish at Pebble Beach is superb. The 17th is a nerve-testing par-3 of 218 yards; and then the 18th curves and rolls left along the jagged tops of the cliffs. There are bunkers and trees on the right, the beach and the ocean on the left and 540 yards to go. In winning the 1982 U.S. Open, Tom Watson birdied this immense hole with a 3-wood, a 7-iron, a 9-iron, and 1 putt!

Nearby Cypress Point, rated by many as the best course in the United States, was built in the 1920s and was largely the work of Dr. Alister Mackenzie, whose philosophy was that the landscape determines the design. This landscape had not only sand dunes and clifftops but hills and a forest as well.

The first dozen holes run inland among the hills, and then it is down to the most dramatic of seaside golf holes. The 231-yards 16th is celebrated clear around the world in print and photograph. The tee is on a cliff edge; the direct shot is across the sea. The safe shot is still across the sea but is only a medium iron to a fairway bending right around a bay. The second shot then is a pitch over rough, rocky ground to this isolated green. Bing Crosby, whose Pro-Am tournament was held on Monterey's three great courses, once got a hole-in-one here. But when, as often happens, the wind is howling around the headland, you can forget about par, never mind birdies or aces. But, then, that's golf on marvelous Monterey.

Nicklaus' Muirfield

Muirfield Village at Dublin, Ohio, was designed by Jack Nicklaus with the assistance of Desmond Muirhead and Pete Dye. It is a course that has everything – hills, slopes, trees, sand, water, fairways like carefully tended lawns, and generous spectator mounds. It is now regularly voted one of America's top 10 courses. It takes its name from the equally great but totally dissimilar Scottish links where in 1966 Nicklaus won The Open for the first time: its chief (and obvious) inspiration was the Augusta National, where earlier in the same year he had won the Masters.

Muirfield Village reflects Nicklaus's intense personal interest in the effects of nature on the way the game is played, the visual impact of trees and shrubs, and the shapes of the course itself. One of the Nicklaus prejudices is that golf is a much better game played downhill than up so that even when there is an uphill slope in front of you the teeing ground is raised so that the tee shot is downhill.

At this course the drive is downhill on holes 1, 2, 3, 4 and 5. On the 7th you drive over a valley, which gives the same effect. There are elevated tees or high tees on 11, 12, 13 and 14. Very few of the second shots are uphill either. But water comes into play on 11 of the 18 holes.

Creeks and streams cross the fairways and snake around the greens on several holes and on the 12th and 16th, both short holes, the carry is over water virtually all the way. On the 12th, 158 yards, there's nothing indeed between tee and green but water – which strongly recalls Augusta's 16th.

The final two holes are 430-yards par-4s which require absolute precision of strike if they are to deliver birdies, the 18th being a cleverly doglegged hole leading to a cunningly sloping green.

For the ordinary golfer the club tees are usually 50 yards ahead of the tournament tees, for another of Jack Nicklaus's firm prejudices is that golf is played for relaxation and enjoyment when it is not your profession. If you are a pro your relaxations are probably fishing and tennis.

But Muirfield Village is not an easy course for anyone. True, you can see exactly what you have got to do: there are no hidden hazards. But you have got to think. And to score well you must hone up your short game. Golf, says the great man, "is a game of precision, not power."

COURSES IN EUROPE AND AROUND

Golf is now played on every kind of surface in every kind of climate and variety of weather, except perhaps for conditions of snow and ice (although there is evidence that the Dutch played a similar game on ice in the 15th and 16th centuries). It is played on untamed links, manicured parkland, on moorland and heathland, in woodland and on farmland. It is even played on courses laid out in the desert.

And on every continent there are courses that seek to make the best of local land and local conditions so as to provide golfers with a game that tests their skill, their wits, their patience and sometimes their endurance.

Here are a few of the best of them that can be found in Britain, Europe and the rest of the world.

Muirfield

Of all the great Scottish links the two most famous after St Andrews are probably Muirfield and Carnoustie. Muirfield is a very, very private course, the home of the oldest golf club in the world, the Honorable Company of Edinburgh Golfers. This company was founded in 1744 and set out the very first Rules of Golf. Carnoustie, on the otherhand, is a municipal course and a long, rough, tough one at that.

Both have made famous Open Champions: at Muirfield, among others, Harry Vardon, James Braid, Walter Hagen, Henry Cotton, Gary Player, Jack Nicklaus, Lee Trevino, Tom Watson and Nick Faldo; and, at Carnoustie, Tommy Armor, Henry Cotton, Ben Hogan, Gary Player, Tom Watson.

Muirfield has no trees but it has a "softer" feel than most seaside links. Andrew Kirkaldy called it "an old water meadow" but then he had just been beaten by Vardon. However, one knows what he meant. It's a fair course with no blind holes and no water and no extremely long carries. What you get is what you see. And what you see are some narrow fairways, many frightening bunkers, tough rough and difficult greens.

THE WORLD

Carnoustie

Carnoustie, at a little over 7,100 yards, is a shade longer than Muirfield and a good deal tougher. There are records of golf being played in the parish over 400 years ago and the Carnoustie Golf Club was formed in 1839, so perhaps it is little wonder that the local concept of golf is toughly old-fashioned. The 16th hole is a 250-yards par-3, uphill to an elevated green with unforgiving bunkers all around it – one of the

Left: The 18th at Muirfield, one of the great Scottish links courses. No trees. No ponds. No hills. And yet it is a great test of golf.

Below: The 6th on the fine English links, St. George's at Sandwich in Kent. The only southern English venue to hold the British Open.

greatest (and longest) short holes in championship golf.

On the 455-yard 17th the Barry Burn cuts across the fairway twice at awkward distances. And then, on the 486-yards par-5 final hole, there it is again – not only just in front of the tee but just in front of the green as well.

Ben Hogan came here to win in 1953. It was the first and last time he entered The Open and the small British ball, with which he had never played before, was then compulsory. He played several practice rounds with several balls and had his caddie go ahead to tell him the exact results of the different shots he made to the greens: drawing some, fading some, hitting some high, running some low. In his first round Hogan returned a 73; in the second a 71; in the third a 70 and in the final a 68 – a flawless round.

Carnoustie has left its mark on the game of golf in other ways too. In the course of time scores, perhaps hundreds, of its golfers have emigrated abroad to become teachers and course designers. They had a profound influence on the way the game was played, and where it was played, in its formative international years between 1890 and 1920.

St. George's

Along the southern coast of England from the ancient town of Sandwich in Kent to the edge of the equally ancient town of Rye runs a wide strip of duneland which is unique to the country. Both towns were once flourishing ports, although both now are well inland of the sea. The great lagoons that separated them have turned to marshland and the sandbars to links. This is now a great golfing country and boasts some fine links courses, Royal St George's, Royal Cinque Ports, the Prince's, Deal, Littlestone and the strange wild links of Rye.

St George's, at Sandwich was founded in 1887 as the English answer to St Andrews: each name is that of its country's patron saint. And it was sufficiently good from the start for the Royal and Ancient Golf Club to select it as host for an

Open Championship as early as 1894. But it is a quite different kind of course to St Andrews. Its dunes are huge and the rolling fairways imitate a severe sea swell. Many of the bunkers are enormous too; one of them is deservedly named Hades.

The course has a feeling of splendid isolation, and indeed until a few years ago the only road to it was over a toll bridge across a stream to the south of the town proper. On the sands beyond the course one can often see lone naturalists patiently searching for rare seaside plants.

To score well at Sandwich one needs to be a consistently accurate player, or to be an inspired one. Championship winners have include Harry Vardon, Walter Hagen, Bobby Locke and Henry Cotton. And it is Henry Cotton's play in 1934 that has been most vividly remembered. In a qualifying round for The Open he shot a 66. In the first round of the tournament proper he shot 67. Then he followed that with an amazing round of 65 – so amazing that it gave its name to a brand of golf ball, the Dunlop 65. After three rounds Cotton was so far ahead of the field he was able to fluff his way nervously round the course in the fourth round for a 79 and yet still win.

More recent winners have been Bill Rogers of the United States (1981) and Scotland's Sandy Lyle (1985). Arnold Palmer won the British PGA at Sandwich, too, playing a great final round in appalling weather conditions, a gale of wind driving up the English Channel accompanied by freezing rain. His clinching hole was the 508 yards 14th where his 3-iron second defied the wind and the rain to give him a certain birdie 3.

Wentworth

The West Course at Wentworth, some 20 miles south-west of London, has long been considered one of the finest inland courses in England. Opened in 1924, it was later given the nickname "The Burma Road" because of its length (almost exactly 7,000 yards). On that score time has

rather overtaken it and by modern standards it is not over-long. Yet it is not over-easy, either.

The main features of Wentworth are sandy soil, tall trees, heather, rhodendron, sloping greens and the feeling of great wealth. It is set in the middle of an estate of grand houses, most now hidden by many thousand pines. Entrance fees and annual subscriptions are now enormous by British standards.

The first hole, once a short par-5, today has been made a long par-4 (471 yards). One drives to a wide plateau, then plays a second across a deep ravine-like dip in the fairway to an elevated and tilted green. On the second, 155 yards, there is no fairway: one drives from an elevated tee to an elevated and well-bunkered green. The third hole, another long par-4, once had a three-level green, but this has recently been made more civilised. The main requirement on this hole as on so many others on Wentworth West is a long and well-placed tee shot. This requirement becomes more and more obvious the further up the "Burma Road" one goes.

Hole 12 (485 yards) needs a long tee shot to the right so that the player has a chance to see the hole round the bend to the left and have a good chance of a birdie. On the par-4 13th one has to be even more accurate. Hit the drive left and there are trees bulging out into your path; hit it too far right and you may find the heather. The 14th is a short hole up a steep hill to a narrow two-level green. The 446-yard 15th needs a long drive that misses a fairway bunker on the left. And on the final two holes, both par-5s, the course reaches a splendid climax. The 17th (571 yards) has a long dogleg left with out-of-bounds on the left edge of the fairway. The green, which slopes strongly right, is close up to this left edge. The top player's second is always a bold shot. Finally, the 18th curves right and provides the chance of an eagle-3 if one hits the tee shot exactly right.

The Ryder Cup and the Canada Cup have both been held here. And for more than 25 years now Wentworth West has hosted the World Matchplay Championship. It is a fine course.

France

Across the English Channel in France more new golf courses are under construction than anywhere else in Europe. In the days before air travel, Deauville and Le Touquet, on the English Channel, were resorts of Britain's rich and famous. Then they suffered a decline as everyone who was anyone began to fly down to the Riviera. Today, British golfers are beginning to realise how close northern France is to southern

This picture, taken from the 15th tee at Chantilly, tells us much about the course. It is truly beautiful but hard to conquer. The 14th is on the right.

England – just a drive and a long iron, so to speak.

There are two excellent courses at Le Touquet now, one a sort of Wentworth and the other, called La Mer, is a genuine links. Not far away is Hardelot, another excellent course. And there are many others.

Chantilly, in the forests north of Paris, has for long been the main Championship course. Their Champions have included their own Arnaud Massy, George Duncan, Henry Cotton, Roberto de Vicenzo, Peter Oosterhuis and Nick Faldo. Chantilly, 6,713 yards and with a par of 71, is in feeling rather an English course – a French Sunningdale, perhaps.

Pau, down in the shadow of the Pyrenees, was the first French golf course of all. It is said that Scottish officers convalescing there after the Napoleonic wars introduced the game. The course is short and rather flat but there are plenty of pine trees around to add to the interest. Hossegor, near the resort of Biarritz to the west, is a newer and more challenging course.

But perhaps the most influential course in southern Europe has been Mont Agel, the mountain-top course above the principality of Monaco. In recent years a new watering system has refreshed and renewed the course and it has become a favorite among professionals as well as tourists. It is set 3,000 feet up above Monte Carlo in a glorious situation and the ball flies far in the light air there. In 1990 in the Monte Carlo Open Welshman Ian Woosnam looked set to break 60 in his final round when on the 500-yard 17th he hit his second shot to within 12 feet of the cup. Alas, he missed the putt and could only par the 18th in 4, finishing with a 60.

Today in nearby Haute Provence new courses are opening up in some of the loveliest scenery in the world. Barbaroux, designed by Peter and P.D. Dye, is in the high country between Brignoles and Le Luc. It not only offers golf in glorious surroundings but, for the wealthy, it even has a helicopter landing-pad a few hundred yards from the clubhouse.

Germany

As the game spreads in a united Germany the best-known club in the federal republic, the Club Zur Vahr, will undoubtedly exert a powerful influence. This is essentially a sportsman and sportswoman's club first and a golf club second, although it does now have two golf courses. But many other sports are played there, from hockey to shooting, and the concept of the multi-sports club is becoming widely popular.

Vahr is a forest suburb of Bremen. The first course the club had was just a nine-holer, although the game had been played in the area since the 1890s. During and after World War II the course was closed, in 1945 being commandeered by the U.S. Army, and it was not until 1953 that the building of an 18-hole course was decided on. New land was found and the German Amateur Champion of 30 years before, Dr. Bernard von Limburger, was asked to design it.

West Germany took some time to recover from the war and it was not until 1970 that the Vahr course was ready for serious competitive events. The following year it hosted the first German Open.

There was a true international field for this event, professionals coming from Britain, Argentina, Australia and France, as well as from West Germany itself. And they found themselves faced with a formidable course.

The par is 74, the length 7,265 yards, it has six par-5s of over 500 yards, and it lies in a deep forest. The first hole is deceptive. It is only 355 yards long and is fairly open. One can see the 9th fairway on one's left and the 2nd on one's right. There is a dogleg around some rough, but not much other trouble. But the 2nd hole is a 536-yarder with a stream, a pond and a lone tree guarding the green against the long second shot. The forest looms over the left side of the fairway but the long tee shot needs to be hit left to get a clear view of the green. A drive hit to the right, although it does indeed give a clear view of the green around the dogleg, will almost certainly put one out of range for the second shot; and a very long drive could put one among some more pine trees.

The par-5 4th is another long dogleg, this time to the right. Then on the 574-yard 6th a player wanting to cut the dogleg will have to hit over trees, the stream and another pond. And so it goes on. The second nine, with the other three par-5s, includes six more difficult doglegs.

Germany's Club Zur Vahr demands power, boldness and accuracy and will certainly be a model for future courses in a united Germany.

Spain

Sotogrande Golf Club, on Spain's Costa del Sol, has two courses, and was the first club to be founded in Spain as an essential part of a grandiose real-estate scheme. Robert Trent Jones was brought in to design it. The result has been an American-style golf course with lakes and mounds and big two-level greens. But to achieve this style Trent Jones had to make innovations which have had a crucial effect on the total development of golf in Spain.

The first problem was simply the bone-hard nature of the Andalusian soil. That was solved by organising an immense and constant supply of water, both for the lakes that were to be introduced and for an automatic watering system. The second problem was how to get the grass to grow consistently on both fairways and greens – indeed, what grass to grow at all. Trent decided on a variety of Bermuda grass for the fairways and bent grass for the greens; both have proved totally successful. The result is target-golf but it is hard to see how it could be otherwise. Bone-dry

Above: Monte Carlo's Mont Agel where the light air shortens the long carries off the tees.

Right: Sotogrande in Spain is a long course down by the Mediterranean sea.

courses may not be easy, but they always produce low scores unless the wind blows hard.

Sotogrande's setting is as spectacular as the course. Away to the south-west the great Rock of Gibraltar rises majestically out of the Mediterranean; beyond it, across the strait, the shores of North Africa shimmer in the haze.

Many other courses have been built in Spain since Sotogrande opened in 1965; and, although some of them have made less use of lakes, all have to be heavily watered. All need to be long and heavily bunkered, too: the ball flies far in the heat and on the still-hard fairways.

The main course at Sotogrande is almost 7,000 yards long and has a par of 72. In the traditional manner it has four par-5 holes and four par-3s, none of them easy. The tees are long, allowing a lot of latitude for residents and holiday golfers, and the greens are large and in many cases weirdly shaped, allowing for many different pin placements.

Scenically, Spain is superb. Cork and olive trees make a pleasant change from the traditional oak, silver birch and pine of British inland courses. The Las Brisas course near Marbella lies in a valley of the Sierra Blanca, and Trent Jones's hand can be seen in its many streams and ponds and lakes and lateral water hazards. His influence has been dramatic; and because among contemporary designers his knowledge of the golf game at all ability levels is

second to none, that influence has been beneficial. The landscape makes the course; the architect makes the holes. And the player makes pars, birdies or bogeys. And if he enjoys doing it, the architect has done a good job.

India

Founded in 1829, Royal Calcutta is the oldest golf club anywhere in the world outside the United Kingdom. Indian golfers recognise it as their "Royal and Ancient" and accept is as the supreme authority on their sub-continent.

Originally there were only 30 members, all members of the British East India Company or the Army in the days before India became the jewel in Britain's imperial crown. The first course was laid out at Dum-Dum, a north-eastern suburb of Calcutta – a damp, flat area which today is the site of the city's international airport. The club moved several times, until it settled on its present land to the south of the city. The problems the course designers met, however, remained the same: the unrelieved flatness of the land, the heat, the humidity and the annual monsoon.

To grass the course the designers settled on a special type of *dhoob* grass, which is similar to Bermuda and is now almost universal in sub-tropical courses in the Far East. To relieve the flatness of the course, most of the huge tees and most of the small greens are elevated. And great use has

been made around the course of dozens of what are locally called "tanks" – water-storage ponds attached to a system of channels designed to deal with the monsoon rains.

Thousands of trees have been planted and the ponds are lotus-filled. (Sometimes they are also filled with small children, many of whom dive for balls). Indeed it is these tanks that are the main feature of the course; another is the very long teeing ground. The first hole (366 yards) is a dogleg par-4 with a large tank short of the green. The second, a par-3 of 156 yards, has a tank on the right of the fairway and another on the left of the green. The 4th (525 yards) has a channel running all the way along the side of the fairway on the right, ending in a tank behind the green. On the 7th (455 yards) this tank again comes into play: there is no way to the green for the approach shot except across about 100 yards of it. Thereafter all the holes bar one (the par-5 15th) have tanks that are either in play or threaten the misdirected shot. It is a most unusual yet most agreeable course.

In 1874 England's oldest club, Royal Blackheath, presented Royal Calcutta with a medal to be played for annually. Calcutta sent a silver cup to Scotland's Royal

---

The Royal Melbourne is a course which might have been a seaside links but with careful planting has been given the feel almost of parkland.

and Ancient in 1883, also for an annual competition. In the 1965 Indian Open at Calcutta, Major P.G. Sethi had the distinction of beating five-times British Open champion Peter Thomson. It is a club with a great tradition and one which produces excellent golfers.

Royal Melbourne

Royal Melbourne is the course that set the scene for golf in Australia. It was founded in 1891 and with due ceremony Club president J.M. Bruce drove the first ball off the first tee wearing what was to be the club uniform: a scarlet coat with gilt buttons, knicker-bockers (the forerunner of plus-twos) and a tartan tam o'shanter.

After a very few years the land which the club rented was sold for development and a new site had to be found. Happily land was made available in Melbourne's sand belt, an area of scrub, heather and sand dunes close to the sea. "Happily" because after much of the scrub had been ploughed up and the ti-trees removed, rich sand-based soil was found underneath, a perfect medium for the construction of an almost traditional golf course.

This original course was a good one, but not a perfect one. In 1926 Dr. Alister Mackenzie was called in to suggest major alterations. Former Australian Open Champion Alex Russell assisted him and the final result was two courses, the West, designed mainly by Mackenzie, and the East which was designed mainly by Russell. A composite, with holes from the two courses, was arranged for the Canada Cup (now the World Cup) in 1959 and 1972 and for the Eisenhower Trophy (the amateur world cup) in 1978.

The current championship course is 6,946 yards in length with a par of 71, and Mackenzie's work has made it a fearsome test of golf. Almost every hole is doglegged and the many fairway bunkers cry out for caution when only boldness will win the day. The greens are extremely fast – a Mackenzie trademark.

The 1st hole makes a fairly gentle introduction to the course.

There are few sights more enchanting than rich green grass in the desert. The Royal Emirates course is a favorite tournament venue now.

It is a 424-yard par-4 starting with a wide fairway and finishing with slight turn to the left. But the par-5 2nd (480 yards) is a different matter. There is a dogleg right and to reach the ideal position one had to drive over an enormous bunker. There is then another bunker on that line to the green and a big greenside bunker on the right of it. The 6th (428 yards) again has a sharp right-angled dogleg with several bunkers and a mass of heavy rough right at the angle. And so it goes on.

The fairways undulate around the many corners and the three par-3s have sloping greens and sand traps everywhere. Royal Melbourne, however, while being a severe test of talent is visually a beautiful course and for the average handicap golfer is a real pleasure to play.

Deserts

Golf has been played for many years in Africa and Arabia, and even in parts of Australasia, on many strange surfaces. On some courses there have been "browns" instead of greens – putting surfaces of which the grass-

less soil is held together less by an oil-based bonding agent. On some others the player or his caddie carries a mat with him from which to strike the ball wherever it may lie.

Perhaps the most unusual are the desert courses of the Persian Gulf, many of which are still in play. The first such course was opened 50 years ago in Bahrain. Saudi Arabia was the first of the states to conceive of a grass course. When this was opened as a 9-holer about 30 years ago, the Saudis also had eight sand courses. There were also sand courses in Bahrain, Abu Dhabi, Dubai and Quatar.

But times are changing fast. Perhaps the most striking symbol of this change has been the building of the Emirates course in Dubai. This now hosts one of the first tournaments of the European Tour, the Desert Classic. It is a really beautiful green course in a sea of sand hills. The land was donated by Sheikh Mohammed bin Rashid Al-Maktoum, the Minister of Defense. Yearly maintenance costs come to around £1 million. The course and clubhouse cost 10 million U.S. dollars to build, they say. Each day some 750,000 gallons of desalinated water are pumped up to the course along an 18-mile pipeline.

The first Karl Litten Desert Classic was played in March 1989 and

was won by England's Mark James with rounds of 68-68-72-68 and a birdie on the first extra hole of a play-off against Australian Peter O'Malley. The prize list then included players from Sweden, France, Scotland, Ireland, Argentina and Denmark. All the players were complimentary about the course, which combines difficult approach shots with subtle greens – real grass greens.

A second course is now planned nearby and there is no doubt that the greening of the desert has begun in earnest. However, membership of these new green courses is hugely expensive by European standards; so play will doubtless continue on the real sand courses of Arabia where the fairways as well as the greens consist of rolled sand-and-oil and the rough consists mostly of rocks. Golf is a test of skill and cunning, not necessarily of agriculture.

Malaysia

There is a great course in Malaysia which represents a classic case of the triumph of determination over disaster. The course was left a ruin as a result of war: it suffered seriously from Japanese occupation from 1941 through 1945. Then there's the rain. How do you keep a golf course in good condition when there are at least 100 inches

of rain every year and sometimes more than 150 inches?

But Royal Selangor proves it can be done. The course, outside Kuala Lumpur, Malaysia's capital, dates back to 1921 and the club to 1893. It was founded by two Scottish coffee planters. The club's archives record the first match: Scotland versus The Rest! The original course was in the Petaling Hills, but in 1918 this was taken over for development as the capital grew in size. A new site was found by the Selangor Department of Forestry on swampy ground a little further out and nine holes were opened in 1921 and 18 in 1931.

The first problem facing the designers was drainage, the second was deciding which type of grass to use. The English architect Harry Colt was called in for advice. Bermuda grass was used initially but later Serangon grass, the particular type used successfully at Royal Singapore, was introduced. The result was a world-class golf course now frequently used for the Malaysian Open Championship.

To help deal with the rains, the greens are crowned with steep side slopes that allow the water to run off readily; they also, of course, allow golf balls to run off, too! Since the course is flat and open, although it has plenty of attractive trees, the greens provide the main tests of skill for the straight hitters.

On the second nine, however, water also plays its part. There is a large lake on the left on the 488-yard par-5 13th tending to force the player toward the right half of the green – which, of course, is the less easy side. There are lakes too on the final three holes. On the short 17th (147 yard) one plays from between the trees out over a scenic lake; and then on the 435 yard 18th one must drive over the corner of another lake to a particular area on the dogleg right which will give one a view of the green around the encroaching trees. The green is well bunkered, and as a finishing hole in any championship this 18th would be regarded with respect by even the greatest golfers.

PLAYING TO PAR

Par is an internationally accepted standard representing the score a competent golfer would be expected to achieve on each hole and for all 18 holes of a round added together. It is assumed that two putts are taken on each green.

Par figures are determined by distance. For men any hole of 250 yards (228 meters) or less is rated par-3; from 250 to 475 yards (434m) the rating is par-4; holes longer than that are rated par-5. An exceptionally long hole may be rated par-6, but there is no standard minimum length for such a hole. Par-figure distances for ladies are less, but there are no internationally recognised standard distances for them.

Par is "what you would expect," and it has gone into the language with this meaning, as in the oft-used phrase "That's par for the course."

Professionals play to beat par, "scratch" players at least to equal it, handicap players to equal or improve on it nett of their handicaps. On each scorecard holes are numbered from 1 to 18; attached to each is a number on the *stroke index*, also from 1 to 18, showing where handicap strokes may be deducted. Thus a 10-handicap player will deduct a stroke from his gross score on holes where the index rates the holes 1 to 10 in terms of difficulty; a 2-handicapper deducts a stroke only on holes marked 1 and 2; and an 18-handicapper deducts a stroke on every hole. Those with higher handicaps will receive two strokes on the relevant holes, 36-handicappers getting two on every hole.

In strokeplay events the handicap golfer arrives at his nett score by deducting his handicap from the total number of strokes he has taken to complete a round.

For any player, therefore, "playing to par" involves more than just hitting the ball. The design and condition of the course have to be taken into account, as do each player's personal strengths and weaknesses.

Among the human factors that make golf difficult for so many people is the fact that when one is on the tee almost every hole looks longer than it is. On a par-4 hole

Above: Greg Norman at Sawgrass during the 1988 Tournament Players Championship unleashes one of his powerful drives.

Right: Payne Stewart watches his ball fly out of the sand at Oakland Hills in the 1985 US Open . . . and into the hole!

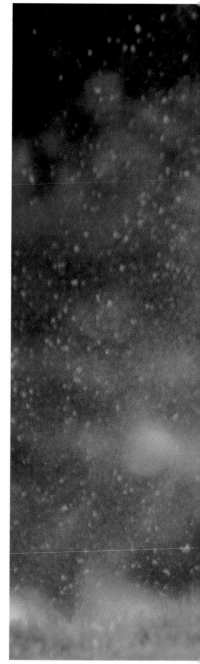

MAGIC

In his book *This Game of Golf*, Henry Cotton recorded an amazing occurrence. He was playing in the 1936 Italian Open, which he went on to win. Before the final round Joe Ezar, an American trick-shot artist as well as a tournament pro, had been astounding the crowd with an exhibition of trickery. The president of the Sestrières club said that it was strange Ezar hadn't broken the course record of 67.

"How much if I do?" said Ezar. "One thousand lira," replied the president. "How much for a 64?" asked Ezar. "Four thousand," said the president. "Okay," said Joe, "I'll do a 64." He then borrowed a cigarette pack from the president and wrote down what he would score hole-by-hole. Next day Ezar scored his 64 hole-by-hole as he had written it down on the cigarette pack, even though on the 9th he had needed to hole a 50-yard chip for his 3.

Joe Ezar came second in the tournament to Cotton. Maybe he should have borrowed the pack sooner.

MURRAY

Fifty years ago the Scottish-American teaching pro Stuart Murray, who owned a driving range and par-3 course at Natick, Mass., set down his simple formula:

Learn to swing the clubhead.

Learn to hit the ball straight.

Start with the very shortest shots.

When you can hit the ball straight for 50 yards, go on to 75. Then to 100, and so on.

Discover your five favorite clubs.

Play every course in a way that matches those clubs.

---

the green may be a quarter of a mile away but it will look even more distant. For the average golfer this should mean just two reasonable wood shots or two long-irons and an approach with a 7 or 8-iron. From the tee the chances of achieving this may look extremely remote – and what is called the "hit impulse" takes over, often with disastrous effects.

The professional can reach the green of a 500-yard hole in two shots with little difficulty. So can many amateurs, although with less precision. Those who can hit the ball 200 yards off the tee will be left with, say, two 150-yard shots, or one of 175 yards and a short approach of only 125. High

handicappers should be able to reach the green (one is talking here only in terms of distance) in three reasonable shots plus a short chip shot.

But every hole is different – even when it is the same length as another. Distance must always therefore be related to the design of the course and a player's strengths or club preferences.

The basic advice, given by teachers ever since the game began, is to play each shot so as to make the next shot as easy as possible. It is, of course, a counsel of perfection, but it should be in every player's mind all the time. The expert will be aiming for a precise spot on the fairway or the green. The high-handicapper

would be wise to aim for an *area*, the size of the area depending on his or her handicap.

It follows from this that it is vital that a player makes himself aware of his strengths and weaknesses, and of the distances he gets with an easy swing with the clubs he likes best.

Consider, for example, a downhill hole of 330 yards with a bunker on the right of the fairway at 180 to 200 yards, quite severe rough on the left and a deep ridge running across the fairway at about the same distance. The pro and the confident long-hitter will go for the green. But the medium-handicapper who tends to push or slice the ball would be sensible both to aim left and play short.

The regular hooker will aim right. The high-handicapper will probably be short anyway and would be wise to aim for an area of the fairway that will give him the widest safe approach to the green.

Then there are doglegs. The class player will use whatever club is likely to take him to or beyond the angle of the dogleg – unless that is, the situation is such that he can cut the angle off altogether. The high-handicap player will be well advised to use the two clubs that will get him to the angle and not to be greedy. Which club the class player takes and which the handicap player takes will vary from player to player depending on their personal strengths and abilities.

Nick Faldo, in winning the 1987 Open at Muirfield, did every single hole of his final round in par figures – 71. In the U.S. Open of 1932 Gene Sarazen played 28 holes, from his 45th to his final 72nd, in exactly 100 shots. Only nine of these holes were birdies. Practicing for the 1926 British Open the legendary Bobby Jones played Sunningdale Old in 66 shots. He had 13 pars, took 33 shots and 33 putts. It was called "the perfect round;" but if he had putted really well he could have scored a 60.

Course management and good putting are what bring low scores. But good course management alone can insure that a golfer will consistently "play to par."

Par-3s

At first sight the questions posed to the player on any par-3 hole are few and straightforward.

Do I go for the green or do I lay up close to it?

If I go for the green, which part of it do I go for?

If I lay up, which side do I go for?

And what club do I use?

But there are one or two other aspects which will probably need to be taken into consideration, too. For instance, where should I tee the ball?

Under the rules you may tee the ball anywhere within the boundaries set by the tee markers, even if your feet are actually outside one of the markers. And you can tee up anywhere within two club-lengths *behind* the imaginary line between the markers. Not all teeing grounds are absolutely flat, so naturally you want to find a level area to tee on. But there is more to it than that.

Which side of the teeing ground gives the better view of the area you are going to aim for? And which side best accomodates the type of shot to be played? Although geometrically there is only one straight line from the tee to the green or to the chosen landing area for the ball, visually there is often a choice. The geography of the hole, the trees, bunkers, water, can alter the geometry.

Then the top-class golfer may wish to play a fade or a draw, a decision which again will influence his choice of the best teeing area. And the high-handicap golfer may wish to take out some insurance against a slice, hook, push or pull, if one of these is his most frequent error. Here expert opinions are sometimes at odds. Many instruct the handicapper to play away from trouble, to tee up on the

Left: José-María Olazábal goes for the green at the 15th at Valderrama during the 1989 Volvo Masters. It is a shot requiring extreme precision. Even from a forward tee the average golfer would be wise to play just short of the green.

right, for example, if the trouble is on the right. But this may not be the best advice, especially if it causes a slicer to open his stance still further than usual, since an even wilder slice may result. On long par-3s, if a player is unlikely to reach the green with the tee shot, he is probably best advised to give himself plenty of room on the tee, so to speak, and to aim for the widest area that is trouble-free on the fairway and leaves him a

reasonable pitch or chip on to the green for his second shot.

Everywhere on the golf course the basic law applies: play to make the next shot easy. But, alas, there are some par-3 holes where it is extremely difficult to enforce the law. One of these for instance is the famous, or infamous, 12th at Augusta National where perhaps more hopes have sunk during a major tournament than anywhere else in the world.

Above: Tom Weiskopf in action at Augusta. On the par-3 12th during the 1980 US Masters he took a decabogey 13, ending up in Rae's Creek three times.

The 12th at Augusta is only 155 yards in total length. The green, however, is only 10 yards deep. And although it is 35 yards wide, many of those yards slope down either to the water in front of it or to one of the three bunkers. And, they say, it is haunted. (When it

Ben Crenshaw drives on the 12th at Augusta National in the 1984 US Masters. This is reckoned to be one of the world's greatest par-3 holes.

was built an ancient Red Indian burial ground was found on the site).

It is certainly haunted in the memory of some of the world's top players. Tom Weiskopf took 13 on the hole in the 1980 Masters. He put so much backspin on his tee shot that it spun back into Rae's Creek. He dropped a ball well behind the creek and repeated the shot with a wedge. He dropped again and dumped the ball in the creek. Then he

splashed down yet again. Finally he managed to stop the ball on the back of the green, and took two putts to finish the hole.

Dow Finsterwald had previously held the record with an 11. Gary Player has actually putted off the green twice in a Masters. Jack Nicklaus took a double-bogey 5 in 1981 when he lost to Tom Watson – by just two shots. Payne Stewart in the final round in 1985 put his ball into the bunker at the back of the green, then knocked it out past the hole and down into the creek. Nick Faldo found the same bunker in 1990. The ball was plugged. As he looked at the hole all he could see was water; he knew he could easily do a Payne Stewart. The ball rolled down 15

feet from the hole to the very edge of the green. He made the putt, which was just as well as his arch-rival Ray Floyd chipped in at the 12th from off the green.

Curtis Strange got a hole-in-one on the 12th in 1988. "It's the only way to defeat the hole," he remarked – and threw the ball into the creek anyway.

What makes the hole so difficult? For the pros it is first the pin placements and secondly the unpredictable wind that swirls around in the pines. This makes club selection very awkward. It also sows doubts in the minds of the players and makes it difficult for them, at the last moment, not to try to steer the ball. For members of the club playing the hole

from the front of the tee it is not so bad. They are nearer, can take less club and won't hit the ball quite so high in the air.

"This is the way to play the hole," an Augusta member once said: "Swing easy and take just too much club." Here endeth the 12th lesson.

But much the same could be said of the famous Postage Stamp hole at Scotland's Royal Troon, the 126-yard 8th. This, with the 7th at Pebble Beach, is the shortest hole in championship golf – but it wrecks a lot of cards. In 1950 the German amateur Herman Tissies entered the record books by taking 15 shots on this hole. The tee shot is downhill to a tiny green set in a sandhill with a deep

bunker in front of the green and two deep bunkers on either side. Herr Tissies contrived to visit all three.

In 1923 Gene Sarazen came to Royal Troon for the Open but, partly because of this short 8th hole, he failed to qualify. In 1973, now aged a venerable 72, he returned for a nostalgic round or two in the Open and hit a 5-iron on to the green and into the hole for an ace. Next day he bunkered his tee shot. But this time he holed out from the bunker. Well, after all, it was Sarazen who invented the sand-wedge, wasn't it?

Once again, though, if you can't hit the green at the Postage Stamp, make sure you hit beyond it: there is just one patch of safety there.

Par-4s

Par-4 holes are fairly straightforward for the professional and the scratch golfer but require very different strategies from the handicap player. The former after a reasonable drive can reach every par-4 in two shots at most so as Sir Henry Cotton once remarked: "It is the second shot that counts." These days if the wind is in the right direction many par-4s are one-shotters for the professionals. But for handicappers many par-4s are out of range even in two shots, in which case it is the drive and the third shot that matter most.

So for the average player the first question that arises is this: just where do I want to place my tee shot? And the final question is: where do I want the ball to be if I am to have a relatively easy third shot to play?

There are however some short par-4s which even the long-handicapper can reach readily in two shots and in a sense these are usually easier for him or her than for the professional. For instance when the 10th at The Belfry in the English midlands is a 275-yards par-4 – it can be shortened to become a 245-yards par-3 – the professional is nearly always tempted to go for the green in search of a birdie or even of an eagle-2. But as a par-4 it is not too difficult, provided a player can use the short irons reasonably well. The handicap golfer can even deliberately hit short from the tee leaving himself a 7 or 8-iron shot if these are favorite clubs.

At the southern headquarters of the British PGA in Surrey, at Tyrrells Wood GC – the first hole is a short, steep downhiller easily reached in one by good golfers although 50 per cent of the time they will find their ball in sand when they see it again. The entrance to the green is invisible – indeed the whole green is invisible from the tee. The handicapper usually plays down to a ridge in front of the steepest part of the slope and trundles the ball down to the green from there. On such a

hole for the average golfer a short, accurate tee shot is very much better than a long and probably uncertain one.

On a long par-4, say of 460 yards, the long-handicapper has little or no hope of reaching the green even in three shots. His aim must be to get close with the third shot and in an area from which he has a straight shot to the pin. Distance in this case is of little importance. It does not matter much whether he is left with a 30-yards shot or a 60-yards shot; it is getting to the safe area that matters.

For every golfer the game-plan matters. It matters for long-handicappers even though they rarely hit the ball exactly where they mean to or exactly as far as they mean to. We all still need a plan. The only way of ever learning to play to a plan is to start off by having one. And that is part of the fun. Every par-4 is different and presents different problems to different individuals. One plays each one's own way.

Par-5s

The trouble with the long holes in golf is that they look even longer than they are. A par-5 hole may be anything from around 480 yards to around 600 and the apparent impossibility of golf seems all too clear as one stands upon the tee. You mean to say someone can hit this small ball with this long stick to a designated spot on the turf seemingly half a mile away in two or three whacks? Yes, professionals do it in two shots most of the time these days and middle-handicap golfers often in three shots. And even beginners can – and one stresses the word *can* – get on that distant green in four shots, however improbable that may at first sight appear to be.

First one needs to hit the longest fairly accurate drive of which one is capable. Very few long-handicap golfers can use a driver or 1-wood with any degree of accuracy. It is important then to know which is one's longest accurate club at each stage of one's

golfing career. It may even be a 5-wood. If so, use it on the par-5s until after a few lessons you can move up to, say, a 3-wood. One advantage of using the shorter club is that one can also use it off the fairway and if one can hit the ball 160 yards with it then three shots will take one 480 yards. Even a long par-5 will then be within range of a mid-iron or even perhaps a short-iron.

The handicapping system in golf, although by no means perfect, means that, in effect, every long hole can be reduced in length to suit the individual's game. This may be the most often overlooked fact in golf. Beginners in most countries (except those following British rules) have 36-handicaps and therefore are allowed two extra shots per hole. On a long par-5 hole they can take six shots to get to the green and then with a single putt score a nett-par. Or five shots to get there and score a nett-birdie. Or five shots on the way and two putts and still score par. Or, for that matter, four shots to the green and three putts.

This is the forgotten factor in the game of many long-handicap golfers.

On the way the golfer has to take account, of course, of various par-5 hazards. There will be dog-legs, or trees on the fairway, or lakes or mounds or bunkers. Nobody pretends it is easy. It's not meant to be. Nobody would play the game if it was. But it is not too difficult to play to par, or nett-par, on the long holes if one uses not only one's head but also one's best capabilities. Some can hit the ball a long way, some can't. Some can hit the ball straight, some rarely do. But after quite a short time everyone realises the strengths of their present game. On the long holes of golf one has to pit one's strengths against the length of the holes. It may mean playing short here and hitting as far as one can there; keeping left at one place, right at another. Somewhere along the line one is pretty sure to be in trouble. The rule is: get out into the fairway and lose just one shot. Or get it back with a single putt.

Par-3s

Cypress Point and Pebble Beach

At both Cypress Point and neighbouring Pebble Beach on the Monterey Peninsula in California there are dramatic par-3s which test the worst as well as the best. At Cypress Point there are two running, the 15th and 16th. The 15th is only 143 yards but it is on the cliff edge, with the foaming ocean below, and requires a tee shot across a narrow inlet to a green surrounded by six wide white bunkers and a belt of Cypress trees beyond. The 16th is one of the most photographed holes in the golf world. This one is a fearsome 231 yards from the back tees, and the direct shot is across a much wider and windier inlet over the sea. The safe way is to hit the ball left to a wide fairway short of the green and hope for a chip-and-a-putt. On this hole a slice is fatal, particularly when the wind blows.

At Pebble Beach the 7th hole is but 120 yards long. There's no inlet, no chasm to cross. But it is a testing hole all the same. The green is tiny. It is ringed with

sandbunkers. It is below the tee. And it is on the cliff edge, subject to almost perpetual but ever-changing wind. There is no option here. You must go for it.

One of the many difficulties of golf, however, is that what the golfer sees with his or her eyes does not always correspond with what is written on the card. It may not look like 120 yards or 231 yards and if the wind is blowing those yardages can serve as little more than a rough guide.

These holes prove the point made by so many instructors, that it is absolutely imperative that you discover exactly how far you hit the ball, not only with each club but also in varying conditions. There is also a rider many would add to this teaching tip: find out how far you hit the ball *with an easy swing*. Not how far you can possibly hit it, but how far you hit it without pressing.

Julius Boros was once asked what he did on a drive when the wind was strongly against him. He replied: "I swing slower and more easily." Since Boros was, even in normal conditions, probably the slowest swinger among the great players of the past 60 years, his advice is worth listening to.

The handicap golfer also has to remember that the wind may exaggerate any cut spin put on the ball, so that on short holes like these it may be wisest to play not only to the left but short to the left. The second shot will also be quite short and probably no more difficult than a little chip.

Two dramatic par-3 holes, visually and psychologically. At both the 7th at Pebble Beach (*below*), only 120 yards long, and at the 16th at Cypress Point (*right*), 231 yards, you must carry those waves.

MEDINAH 17TH HOLE

This short hole – it can play up to 220 yards – has had a big influence on several championships, including two U.S. Opens, not only because of its horrendous difficulty but also because of its strategic position in the round.

The shot from the tee has to carry an arm of Lake Kadijah. When it has done that it has also to carry, or possibly avoid, a wide bunker shaped like the wings of a bird of prey. But if it has been hit only a shade too hard, the ball will

almost certainly find another sand trap at the back of the green, which is also trapped on either side. And the green has what, even to many tournament pros, are unfathomable borrows.

In the U.S. Open of 1949 Cary Middlecoff and Clayton Heafner came to the 17th tied for the lead. Just behind them was Sam Snead. Middlecoff just managed to save his par. Heafner did not; he hit wide and then bogeyed the hole. When Snead stood on the tee he was tied with Middlecoff, too. The flag was on the right of the green. Snead took a 1-iron and pushed his shot just wide of both the front bunker and the green itself. He

was in the light rough but not too far from the hole. He decided to run the ball to the hole like a long putt. The long grass slowed the ball down and it stopped eight or nine feet short. Sam failed to make the putt. All three parred the final hole, Middlecoff taking the title by one shot. And Snead never did manage to win a U.S. Open.

In the 1990 U.S. Open Ian Woosnam was challenging for the lead in both the third and the final round when he came to the 17th, which was playing to 168 yards. He took a six one day and a five the next and dropped out of contention. The trouble was, he said, that he knew what shot to play but

Hale Irwin drives while Greg Norman waits his turn at the 17th at Medinah. It was a vital hole which helped put Irwin on the road to victory in the final round of the 1990 U.S. Open.

not what club to take. He aimed to drop the ball just over the front bunker in the fringe grass one day, to let it run up to the hole. In the third round he took an 8-iron, and dumped it in the lake. Next time he took a bit more club and dropped the ball in the bunker at the back. Then, appreciating how steep the green's downslope was, he hit a gentle sand-iron but failed

OLYMPIC

(CALIFORNIA)

The 220 yard 3rd hole at Olympic Lakeside, outside San Francisco, is an unusual one for the United States. The fairway is wide open, although there are bunkers near the green both to the left and to the right. But there is no water in front of the green – indeed, no hazard at all in the direct line. You drive from an elevated tee, down the hill across a green sloping fairway to a friendly green in a charming setting. And you can, if you wish, drop the ball short of the green itself and let it run on toward the hole. It is a hole with choices.

The most famous encounter here was that between club pro Jack Fleck, the outsider, and Ben Hogan, the master, in the 1955 U.S. Open. Fleck it will be recalled, tied Hogan over the 72 holes with a total of 287. Hogan had been steadiness itself – 72, 73, 72, 70. Jack Fleck had balanced two poor round of 76 and 75 with two fine ones of 69 and 67. On the play-off the events on the 3rd gave Fleck the feeling that Dame Fortune was on his side.

What happened was this: Hogan played first and with his 2-iron struck the ball truly to the center of the green, to within four feet of the flag. Fleck then missed one of the green side bunkers by no more than six inches. His ball bounced forward and finished six or seven yards from the hole. He then sank the putt. To his own and the admiring crowd's amazement, Hogan then missed.

Fleck later said that it was on that hole that he appreciated Hogan was human after all. He went on to play another sub-70 round and to beat the master by three shots in one of the biggest upsets in Open history.

The moral of this might seem to be that he who sinks the putts wins the prizes – a moral underlined by the extraordinary career of the South African Bobby Locke, who hooked every tee and fairway shot, although not very far, but kept on scoring in the 60s when

This photograph of the 3rd hole at the Olympic Lakeside course at San Francisco tells the whole story – sloping fairway, tiny green, trees all around. In the 1955 U.S. Open it was Jack Fleck's "lucky hole."

to get out of the fringe grass. He then took three putts.

When playing this type of hole the average golfer must be sure to take enough club, even if it means going into the bunker at the back. But aim to one side of the green if you can to avoid that fate. Hit into the light rough, if you like. But then do *not* use your putter from the fringe, or even a straight-faced iron. Chip the ball into the air over the fringe and let it run to the hole. Make sure it gets to the hole, the pros say, so that if it overruns you have an uphill putt coming back. Uphill is easier than down-hill. You are less reluctant to hit the ball firmly.

his game looked worthy of only the mid-70s. But there is more to it than that.

On long par-3 holes such as this the average golfer, if he or she plays sensibly, can be pretty sure of getting onto the green in two shots and should never be tempted to go for broke, except

for fun or just as an experiment.

The 8th at Lakeside is only 135 yards at its longest and is quite different from the 3rd in many other ways, too. It is straight but heavily trapped. There is a large bunker in front of the green, two bunkers on the left, one on the right, and finally two behind the green. On such a hole you *must* go for the green.

The 15th is a rather similar hole set within an oval framework of trees, the green trapped everywhere except back left, but it is a little longer at 147 yards. Go for it: you have no option.

WENTWORTH

(ENGLAND)

The 14th hole on the famous West Course at Wentworth in Surrey, for long the home of the World Matchplay Championship, is rarely mentioned in the guides and atlases. Maybe people don't like to talk about it.

It may be this hole as much as anything else which put Jack Nick-laus off playing in this knockout tournament – he has not played competitively at Wentworth since 1971, a fact usually put down to his having objected to a referee's ruling. But Nicklaus favours downhill holes. On the courses he designs there are very few uphill holes and certainly no uphill par-3s. But the 14th at Wentworth West is uphill. Exceedingly uphill.

It is 179 yards from the back tee. You hit up to a two-level green, the levels also going uphill. There is a rough bank at the back, rough to the right, a bunker on the left of the green and trees and bushes all around.

It is very difficult even for pro-fessionals to be sure of a par at this hole and birdies are most unusual. If the flag is on the top level and the ball just fails to make that level, it will roll back and may even roll clean off the green. A shot that is straight but long will go up the bank at the back – but it may not roll down on to the green: the rough *clings*.

Those who can play a low-fly-ing, long-running shot will be able to deal with this hole as well as most professionals. Those who hit high shots with lots of back-spin, however, need to be metic-ulously accurate. For everyone the decision as to which club to take on the tee is difficult but vital. For average golfers the best advice may be to think of a num-ber – and take two clubs longer.

Below: The 222-yard par-3 8th hole, viewed from the tee, on the Dutch links at Kennemer. It is currently one of the toughest courses on the European Tour.

KENNEMER

On the European tour in 1990 the Dutch course at Kennemer was voted the toughest of the lot by many pros, and the short 8th hole the toughest of the tough.

Kennemer is a seaside links where the wind blows free. It is a place of huge sand dunes and tumbling rough, yet has a softer feel to it than the links of Scotland. The grass is greener, the fairways wider and more obvious and there are wild flowers on the swelling sandhills.

The par-3 8th hole plays to 222 yards from the back tee. It is slightly downhill but there is no fairway to speak of until the last 30 yards or so before the green. There are two bunkers on the right of the green and, as if these were not enough, there is a steep down-slope beyond them. There is a bunker on the left, too; but the chief danger there is the bumpy, treacherous rough. Drop the ball there and you feel you may never get it out.

Frequently even the pros have

to use a wood off the tee because of the wind. For them it can be a very tough shot indeed. Nor is it an easy shot from the forward tees. On most days the ideal shot will be a straight, low, wind-cheater and the average golfer is advised to have this shot in his or her bag when venturing to Holland.

The winning shot here, naturally, is the one that finds the green. But the safe shot, the sensible shot, is one that stops the ball somewhere in the flat area immediately in front of the green.

There are actually 27 holes at Kennemer and the championship course is a composite taking in the 18 most difficult ones. The 15th is only 163 yards but once again it is downhill over rolling wild sand dunes growing thick rough. To make matters worse, the flat space in front of the green is almost filled with bunkers. It demands a high ball on to the green. The 17th is rather similar but the land by the tee slopes frighteningly. However it is the 8th that most players remember. It is a great hole.

The other par-3s at Wentworth are quite different. At the 2nd (155 yards) you hit from an elevated tee to an elevated green, with a deep chasm in between. Bunkers cut into either side of the hill on which the green stands. But there is a useful bank behind the green. This is a hole where you must *not* be short. Play for the bank at the back, if you like – but never, never, never play for the front of the green – here lies trouble.

The 5th is 191 yards and fairly

flat, although the green unexpectedly falls away from you, but the 10th is quite testing. Once again you are on an elevated tee playing to an elevated green up to 186 yards away. But this time there is a copse of trees on violently sloping ground to the right and rough and a steep bank on the left. The advice is to take at least one more club than the yardage suggests. Play the 10th well and you will not be so scared when you arrive at the cruel 14th.

Vilamoura

Designed by Frank Pennink, the English architect and one-time Amateur champion who was born in the Netherlands, Vilamoura, in Portugal, is Sunningdale with much more accent on the sun. Built on the beautiful hills of the Algarve beyond the holiday beaches, the course has a distinctly English country feel about it. The holes sweep down the tree-lined fairways to the level ground in majestic succession, but of course they are not English trees: they are cork trees and umbrella pines.

The course is a long one with a par of 73, but it is the par-3 holes that are its special feature. The first that one meets is the dramatic 4th hole of a little over 160 yards. The tee shot is over a glittering lake. The overhanging trees on the right feel to be dangerously near the line of the shot and two or three lower down encroach upon the green. It is a crowned, two-level green, too, and is surrounded by bunkers.

The real danger here is of trying to "steer" your tee shot. The trees around the tee, the island in the lake, the cork trees near the green and the sand traps around it produce an almost irresistible urge to do that very thing. One has to

The 4th hole at Vilamoura is as difficult as it is scenic. The tee shot is over the lake. The green is turtle-backed and there seems to sand everywhere.

remember, to impress upon one-self, that a long or a clever shot is not required – just a nice, easy, relatively short shot with an iron. What could be simpler? The danger is in the mind not in the surroundings.

The 10th is virtually the same length but is a totally different hole. No great drama here, just a chasm in front of a shallow green and bunkers and trees right behind it. It is rather like the 2nd at Wentworth West in England, only without a forgiving bank at the back.

If you hit too short the ball will fall on stony ground and bounce away down among the flanking trees. If you hit too long and miss the bunkers the ball will run down another slope and finish among some other trees. You *must* hit the green. There is simply no alternative.

So to the 15th (168 yards), where in front of the tee is a sloping valley and in front of the green on either side are two deep bunkers. The green is wide and looks inviting, but it is very shallow and behind it once again are sand and yet another steep slope down among the tree roots. Here it is possible to play short if you wish, although the ball will almost certainly bounce left across the slope, but if you have survived the other short holes that may seem rather cowardly.

You have to be absolutely certain that you have the right club in your hand for the distance involved. Hopefully, all that practice at average distances now pays off.

Royal Melbourne

The Royal Melbourne West course presents a beautiful and savage test of golf. There are fast fairways like the links of Britain, combined with gorse, heather and the unique trees of Australia. And one of its severest tests is the 5th hole, which is also the 5th on the composite course which hosts many a championship.

The 5th hole is a hole of 176

yards. There is a valley in front of the tee and a steep bank in front of the green. There's a steep bank behind the green too. There are five bunkers half circling the green and heather and gorse and Australian rough to the side of it. The green is lightning fast.

The course had been designed originally by Dr. Alister Mackenzie and he had made this and the 7th hole especially difficult. In the late 1930s the head greenkeeper Claude Crockford made a few adjustments to slightly lessen the hole's agony.

The 5th now requires an iron shot firm enough to climb the bank, but not so firm that it goes over the back. It also demands a straight shot, for it is exceptionally difficult to get down in two from any of the five bunkers because of the speed of the green.

Ben Crenshaw won the individual prize when the World Cup was held at Royal Melbourne largely because he coped so well with this hole and the other par-3s. His putting suited the greens. Lee Trevino, on the other hand, considered them "unputta-

ble" and said he would never willingly play the course again.

Almost immediately after negotiating the treacherous 5th you are faced with the 7th, where Mackenzie originally had the green hidden at the top of a hill. The hill has been removed – at least, the top of it has. But strange slopes are still there, particularly on the green, which is protected by bunkers; and in front of the green are small bushes, heather and rough. It is a hole where even the best players take double bogeys. What chance have the rest of us? Well, actually,

just as good a chance as they have. If you can pitch and putt, you can be a match for anyone, as "Old Tom" Morris said.

On every hole, if you don't think you can reach the green, there is a relatively safe place either to one side of it or short of it. So the handicap player has to survey the scene with cool commonsense. If the shot to the green seems too long or too risky, where is the spot which will provide a safe and reasonable lie? How far away is that spot? The hole may be 150 yards away, as the

The 5th hole on the West course at the Royal Melbourne in Australia bears all the hallmarks of a design by Alister Mackenzie — sand, slopes and hollows.

7th here can be, but the safe spot may be only 100. What club and what kind of stroke will get you reasonably near that spot? That's the question.

Of course, if a straight shot of 150 yards is nothing to you, go for the green. And as you walk down to the green make sure you have your best putting stroke with you.

KILLARNEY

When one arrives in Killarney in the Republic of Ireland one's first instinct is probably to put away the golf clubs and go get some paints and canvas and brushes. The sheer loveliness of the place is inspiring. There are four beautiful lakes and two golf courses and in the background rise the Irish

mountains named Macgillicuddy's Reeks.

The two courses, Killeen and O'Mahony's Point, can be made into a composite championship course and when they are, the 18th of O'Mahony's Point becomes the splendid finishing hole. Yes, at Killarney you finish on a par-3.

The hole measures 200 yards from the back tees. The green is

perfectly visible, an inviting emerald circle half surrounded by tall pines and luxuriant bushes. The lake is on your right, almost lapping the tee. The view is stunning, the blue-green lake widening out toward the green foothills of misty-blue mountains in the distance.

Ah, but there's no fairway. The shore of the lake sweeps in on a rugged curve to take a big bite out

of the line to the green. You've got to go for it. A slice will put you in the lake, a short fade on the shore. A hook will send the ball into the thick undergrowth, or into rhododendron bushes; an over-emphatic draw – if you are lucky – will be intercepted by one of no less than four bunkers guarding the green at back left.

On the left hand side of the green, between the bunkers, the

ground forms a grassy bank, beyond which there are more bushes. The right hand side of the green is protected by pine trees and rough. But the green itself is generously proportioned and in front of it is a reasonably wide patch of flat ground.

The good golfer, and the young golfer, naturally go for the green. The handicap golfer has to remember the vital basics:

Alignment.   Club selection.

Posture.   Swing.

Correct alignment is more vital on the 18th at O'Mahony's Point than anywhere else on the course, or on most other courses for that matter. It is poor alignment that causes most slices and most slices here end up in the water.

Then we have to be sure we have not only the "right" club but a club we trust, for we are going for the flat ground in front of the green and it matters little whether we are on the near edge of it or the far edge of it so long as we are on it.

Killarney is one of those places where one comes to realise that all that practice, all that attention to the basics, was well worthwhile.

This must be one of the loveliest finishing holes in golf, the 18th at Killarney. For the handicap golfer its beauty makes up for its harshness. The fish will gobble every sliced shot.

Par-4s

St Andrews

The 17th hole at St Andrews, Scotland, "the home of golf" is one of the greatest par-4s in the world. Nobody designed it; it happened. It is 461 yards long. Good golfers have to drive (preferably with a slight fade) over a corner of a building to an area of fairway they cannot see. If they drive left not only are they quite likely to be in the rough but they have a noto-rious pot bunker right on their line to a very shallow green. If they are on the right, the correct line, they will be on a road or up against a wall if they hit a mite too hard and both are "in play." When they make the green it is long as well as shallow and has mystifying swales on it. Jack Nicklaus says he plays this hole as a par-4½. In four rounds if he makes two 4s and two 5s he is satisfied.

In the 1978 Open Champion-ship the talented Japanese golfer "Tommy" Nakajima, having hit two glorious shots to the ege of the green, putted his ball into the dreaded Road Bunker and for a long time couldn't get out of it, eventually taking a 10. (The bunker is now sometimes called "The sands of Nakajima.") In 1984, when Tom Watson was fighting it out with Seve Ballesteros on the final round, he took a 2-iron when he needed a 3-iron from a perfect position on the fairway, and his ball went through the green down the bank at the back, over the road and fetched up against the wall. In that instant, Watson's challenge was done for. And that empha-sises another aspect of the terror the hole can inspire: if you make a mess of the Road Hole in the final round of the Open, there's only one more hole – almost certainly it's too late to repair the damage.

In the 1990 Open Scott Hoch put himself out of the tournament on his second brush with the 17th. He faded his tee shot out-of-bounds, hit his second ball too far left, dropped into a fairway bunker, just got out, was short of the green in six and then three-putted. José-Maria Olazábal scored excellent pars in the first two rounds, then in his third he putted over a swale into the in-famous bunker and took three more shots to get down. Russell Weir hit his second shot on to the road – whence it bounced over the wall into the crowd! Peter Jacobsen was another who took a putter from off the green and found the "sands of Nakajima." But Robert Gamez, the brilliant rookie on the U.S. tour, playing St Andrews for the first time, got two birdies and two pars.

The man who was champion in the end, Nick Faldo, played the hole as a par-5 on the last two days and had few problems. On the third day he hit his tee shot too far left; then, to avoid the Road Bunker, he hit his second farther left, almost on to the 18th tee, and got down with a long chip and two putts. On the fourth day he hit his second (a mid-iron) short of the right side of the green and took three more to get down. It was enough: by that time he was five shots ahead of the field.

Faced with this type of hole the wise handicap golfer reminds himself of some elementary arith-metic: 150 + 150 + 150 = 450 yards. That leaves 11 yards = 1 chip + 2 putts. On the safe assumption that he receives one stroke at this hole, that's par for the course.

A panoramic view of the extraordinary 17th hole, know as the Road Hole, at St Andrews. From the tee the shot is blind, over the sheds on the right.

BACK TO AUGUSTA

Few, apart from its members and the tour players who qualify for the Masters, get the chance to play at Augusta National. But the nature of many of its holes offers the handicap golfer insights into playing strategies. "Amen Corner" at Augusta consists of the par-4 11th hole, the par-3 12th and the par-5 13th. They are all crucial holes. But in the opinion of several players, including Gary Player, the 11th is the most crucial of the three. For one thing, it comes first. Play this hole well and you could be on a run of birds. Play it poorly and you could be on the hook.

Player believes it is vital to hit your drive down the left side of the fairway so that the second shot can be hit away from the water which protects the left-hand side of the green. This is professional talk. The average member probably sees things differently.

If you are not going to get on the green in two shots (and at 450 odd yards not many handicap golfers will) the hole is a perfectly reasonable three-shotter. And, if you opt to play it that way, you will be in the best possible company. Ben Hogan, the most consummate shot-maker the game has ever known, never went for the pin on his second shot, arguing that the ball could be deflected into the water if it struck the bank in front of the green. He would put his second on the right front fringe, and make his par with a chip and putt. In your case the drive should be as central as possible, the second should be down the right side and the third should be on the green or on the

The 11th at Augusta National can be a cruel hole, as Ray Floyd experienced when he lost the 1990 Masters to Nick Faldo here. It is part of the formidable Amen Corner.

right-side approach to the green.

Do not hit the third or fourth pin-high to the right, however. Only Lary Mize can hole a chip from there and win the Masters in a play-off. The average member at Augusta will feel he has done well if he gets down in three more from there.

Writing about it is very easy, actually playing the game is more difficult. But this is definitely a case of discretion being the better part of valor for the average golfer – and for accuracy being the better part of distance. Augusta's fairways are wide. There is very little, if any, rough. The temptation therefore is to hit hard. But the rational thing to do is quite the

opposite. The high-handicapper in particular must take it easy on any hole he or she meets in their golfing life which bears any resemblance whatsoever to Augusta National.

The 17th, although only 400 yards, is another critical hole. There's no trouble on the fairway. So it is the second shot that counts for long hitters, and the third for the rest of us. Scott Hoch in the 1989 Masters dropped his first shot to par here during his final round. He went through the green and down a bank with his second shot and was at once in serious trouble. He had to pitch out of the rough on to a severe downslope. He played it superbly, the ball almost lipping the hole and stopping 3 feet past; but he missed the return putt.

Moral: It is the shot to the green that matters most to us ordinary humans, however short it is.

Par-4s of Pinehurst

Pinehurst No. 2 in North Carolina is considered by many to be Donald Ross's masterpiece. Ross came to Pinehurst in 1900 from the village of Dornoch in the Scottish Highlands, northernmost of golf's imperishable shrines. Golf has been played on the links there for well over 300 years. And the links provide a great natural golf course.

Originally Pinehurst was a links course in the heart of the countryside. Today, as its name implies it is forest course, but Ross's signature is all over it. He reckoned a golfer should be ready to play every different kind of shot, but should never have to face an un-fair hazard. The Pinehurst greens are protected as often by swales and mounds as by sand bunkers. The fairways are not difficult, but they demand precision shots if a player is to score well, whatever his or her handicap.

The 5th hole measures 438 yards. It has a longer feel about it than the card suggests. One reason is that there is a ridge 100 yards or so in front of the tee hiding the rest of the fairway and the distant green from view. On the other side of it is a gentle valley which bears left on its way to a mounded green with bunkers on each side of it. For the big hitter the way in to this green is from the right unless he can draw the ball accurately; but it is where his second shots finish that matters.

There are no dreadful hazards in the way, but the entrance to the green is narrow viewed from a distance and thus requires a second shot of great precision. But the average golfer will play the hole as a 3-shotter; and for him the entrance is fairly wide in relation to his approach shot with a short-iron. Depending on where his second finished, he may be called on for a bump-and-run to the hole or a full wedge.

The 8th from the tournament tees is a much longer hole – 468 yards – and runs downhill then uphill with a slight dogleg to the right. There is one bunker just off the fairway on the right at driving range, but otherwise there is no trouble if you keep on or near the fairway until reaching the green. Again the green is on a rise and slopes in such a way that from a distance it will hold only a really well-struck shot. From close-to it once again demands skill with the short approaches.

Ross was one of the great masters of strategic design: his courses invariably offer different ways of playing to par on each hole; the penalties they exact for poor shots are always in proportion to the degree of error, and the golfer is usually offered the chance to play himself out of his difficulties by thoughtful golf. In short, Ross's courses are rewarding rather than punishing. And for the average golfer what they reward most is some dedicated practice with the middle and short irons.

The 5th green of the No.2 Course at Pinehurst is so well guarded by sand traps that for the professionals an accurate tee shot down the right is vital.

FOURS AT HARBOR TOWN

Harbor Town Golf Links on Hilton Head Island, South Carolina, is one of the newest tournament courses in the United States. But it is home to the oldest golf club – whence the name of its premier tournament, The Heritage Classic. Harbor Town claims a direct line of succession from the South Carolina Golf Club, believed to have been founded in 1786 at Charleston (though whether its members actually played golf, and, if so, where, is unknown). The present links were designed by Peter Dye and Jack Nicklaus and were opened in 1969. It is a course of great beauty with a multitude of trees and water protecting 15 of the holes.

There are wide fairways, flat shallow bunkers and no hills. Most of the greens are unusually level. What's the problem? Much of the problem is in the mind and much of the rest of it in the shapes of the oddly bunkered greens. The trees hug the fairways and on the doglegged holes – some left, some right – copses of trees appear to narrow these wide fairways or to impede the necessary second shot. And then the bunkers, although flat, are shaped and angled in thought-provoking ways. It's a thinker's course, all right.

For the professionals the 1st and the 3rd (380 and 383 yards respectively) are these days a 3-wood and a wedge. For good amateurs they require a good drive and, say, a 5-iron. For middle-handicappers they ask for a drive and maybe a 5-wood. For high-handicappers it's probably two wood shots and a 7-iron. The fairways are wide, nearly 50 yards, and there's little trouble about, except perhaps a bunker and a pond on the left before one reaches the green. The trouble is the green is very small. On the 9th, a very short par-4 of little over 300 yards, the green is horseshoe-shaped, partly enclosing the

At this difficult, windblown 18th at Harbor Town, at least you can see the lighthouse at the end of the fairway. On the way there you must beat the tidal marsh.

bunker at the back, and guarded by another at the front. In spite of the shortness of the hole, it may make sense for the high- or medium-handicap player to lay up short of the front bunker with

his second shot, relying on a pitch and, hopefully, a single putt to secure his par.

The 18th at Harbor Town has Calibogue Sound on the left and out-of-bounds on the right. It is a hole of 458 yards from the back tees. The tee shot is over the edge of some salt marshes and these keep encroaching on the fairway the farther along it one goes. Close to the green a long sand

trap adds to the pressure put on a player by the marshes. Unless you approach the green from the right, all this is on one's line.

For the average golfer the message is: Drive to the right, then stay on the right. And unless a miracle has occurred and you have struck two excellent shots, play the third just short of the right of the green. It's a thinker's course. Think strategy.

TROUBLE AT OAKMONT

Oakmont in Pennsylvania has been the scene of more championships than any other course in North America: 13, including six U.S. Opens. It's tough. In the 1927 U.S. Open Tommy Armor was the only pro to break 300. When Hogan (then at the height of his powers) won in 1953 he finished just one-under par – and six shots ahead of anyone else! Arnold Palmer and Jack Nicklaus both had that score in 1962. But the course is playable. In 1973 Johnny Miller went round in a breathtaking 63 course record.

Why is Oakmont so difficult to score on, except during four hours of genius? Well, the greens are huge and faster than greased lightning; the fairways are often extremely narrow at critical points; and there are 190 sand bunkers. These conditions make the par-4s very difficult for professionals to birdie and equally difficult for ordinary humans to par, even using their handicap strokes.

The par-4 3rd hole has a line of bunkers called the Church Pews just off the left hand side of the fairway. Each strip of sand is separated from the next by a strip of grass. The Pews are a severe threat to those who draw or hook the ball off the tee. Those who fade the ball are little better off, for there are clusters of orthodox bunkers on the right at the same distance. Then there are more bunkers left and right on the approaches to and beside the green, and also some lone trees, fringing the fairway, which impede a long approach shot that is made from the center or left side of the fairway.

The 5th is only 379 yards from the back tee. Again there are bunker clusters to left and right of the fairway. There is also a crumpled downhill slope to the green and a ditch in front of it. There is a long semi-circular bunker around the right side and back of the green and two others on the left.

The 17th and 18th make the finish particularly testing. Both are par-4s: the first is only 322 yards and the other a long 456 yards, much of it uphill. The short 17th doglegs left. It has bunkers on the inside of the angle, and these must be carried if the second shot is not to be forced to fly over the bunkers that hem in the green. When Ben Hogan won in 1953 he made both holes look simple. On the 17th his tee shot

Arnold Palmer caught in the Church Pews bunkers at Oakmont during the 1983 U.S. Open. Palmer plays the recovery shot in his inimitable, aggressive style.

ran the gauntlet of the bunkers and rolled on to the green. On the 18th a tremendous tee shot left him a 6-iron shot; then his approach finished six feet from the flag. Result: two birdies.

But what does the ordinary mortal do? One answer is to play each hole backwards; that is, to study a distance chart of the holes and ask yourself: "Where is the best place for my ball to be for the final approach shot to the green?" To be sure of getting there, where would be the best place to hit my second (or third) from?

An English teaching pro, Reg Knight, once wrote a book titled *Learn Golf Backwards*. Not a bad idea at all.

FOURS ON THE NATIONAL

The National Golf Links on Long Island, New York, came by the name because Charles Blair Macdonald who founded it wanted the course to represent the best of British golf on American soil. He had been a student at St Andrews, the home of golf, and 30 years later after establishing a course in Chicago he became determined to provide the United States with the finest traditional course in the world outside the British Isles. He made several trips back to Britain, making notes about the best holes he encountered, and The National was the result.

The 2nd hole at this course was inspired by Royal St George's at Sandwich in Kent; the 3rd reproduces a hole from Prestwick, the original home of The Open; the 4th comes straight from North Berwick; and the 7th and 13th include elements of famous holes at St Andrews.

The 2nd for the best golfers requires a drive that carries more than 200 yards over a cavernous bunker, emulating the notorious Sahara, the old 3rd at Sandwich. This is simple enough these days, except for the average club member, who must either play from a very forward tee or else lay up short of the trap. As the hole is only 274 yards, playing short is the only sensible course.

It is thought that when he designed the 7th Macdonald had the great 17th (the Road Hole) at St Andrews in mind. There, of course, the drive is over the roof of a building (in the old days, the roof of some railway sheds) and then the second has to be either very, very accurate or blessed with good fortune. There are no railway sheds at The National: instead you are confronted by what looks like half an acre of sand and scrub. As at St Andrews, the green is protected by a pot bunker at the front left. From the tournament tees this hole is (just) a par-5 of 478 yards, but from the very forward tees it is a par-4. This again reproduces at least the spirit of St Andrews, where the 17th is regarded by most people as a par-4½.

View from the tee of the formidable 426-yard 3rd hole at The National. It is modeled along the lines of the 17th at Prestwick (sometimes called "The Alps"). The hole requires a long, accurate tee shot and then a blind approach over high dunes.

The 14th (365 yards) demands very straight shooting. The tee shot must carry a wide expanse of water. Moreover, if you hit too far left you may end up on the 12th green; too far right and you will be on a beach or a road. Over the water the fairway doglegs right before the green, the entrance to which is pinched in by bunkers at left and right. It's a very tough short par-4. But, as Blair Macdonald himself said, he always gave the handicap golfer a way out: ". . . by taking a course much as a yachtsman does against an adverse wind, by tacking."

The moral? Know your strengths – but don't try to overreach them.

FLYING AT WINGED FOOT

When you get into any bunker at Winged Foot you are in a really big bunker. Here Tom Kite manages to get out of one from a terrible lie.

Winged Foot at Mamaroneck, New York, is another one of those courses where playing to par is difficult, particularly if one is not a fine bunker player. There are two courses, the West being considered the more difficult. Both were designed by A.W. Tillinghast, whose instructions were, "Give us a man-sized course." On the West course he specified 10 par-4s of more than 400 yards, one of just under 400 and only one shorter one. They are all heavily bunkered.

Winged Foot was commissioned by the New York Athletic Club so Tillinghast made it athletic. His basic philosophy was always to make every hole require a controlled shot to a closely guarded green and for the Athletic Club he altered the formula to read "a *long* controlled shot to a closely guarded green."

This design philosophy makes any course a monster for the low-handicap amateur but an easier one for the high-handicap player. The low handicapper has to be able to hit his drives some 230 yards off most par-4 tees and after that probably take a wood for his second shot. The long-handicapper needs to hit two straightish shots of around 180 yards and then just a short iron. True, there sometimes seems to be a lot of trouble just off the tee – but a duck-hook or a super-slice will put the player in serious trouble. When trees hem in the tees they have to be ignored.

The 1st hole, 446 yards from the back tee, has a nasty sand trap on the right of the fairway at about high-handicap distance but otherwise is perfectly straightforward until you reach the environs of the green. There you can find any one of four huge bunkers. The 2nd hole is 411 yards and is very similar, except that it doglegs right instead of left. On the 4th, another dogleg left, there are traps just off the fairway at around long-driving distance; then huge bunkers either side of an extremely tricky green.

The 17th for a professional like Jack Nicklaus is "a text-book test of golf." Amateurs will understand all too well what he means. From the back it measures 444 yards. It doglegs right and at the elbow of the dogleg are four massive bunkers. Then it is all-clear until one reaches the narrow, curvaceous green with deep, deep bunkers on either side.

If he is going to prosper on a course of this type, the long-handicapper needs first to learn how to hit a straight ball most of the time. Not a long straight ball, just a straight ball. Then he or she needs to know how to get out of sand. This knowledge should include not only the usual explosion shot with a sand-wedge but the special shot used in wet or hardbase bunkers, when one hoods the face of an ordinary wedge and hits firmly down on the ball.

Armed with these two techniques and a straight ball, courses like Winged Foot can be great fun.

TURNBERRY

There is about most Scottish golf courses an atmosphere of wild abandon. It is this that has to be fought as well as the golf course. Stand on the back tee of the 9th at Turnberry and the wind may rage at you. You are standing on the edge of a gaunt granite cliff which tumbles down behind you to a rock-strewn tousled sea. There's a lighthouse on the next promontory, to the left of your line of

drive, and farther left across the sea are Ailsa Craig and the mountains of Arran.

In front of you is a narrow causeway leading up over the forward tees and then a rock-strewn hill to a narrow fairway. And narrow in Scotland means *narrow*, this fairway being in parts only 20 yards wide. On either side of it the land falls away into thick rough. From the back tee you must carry the ball more than 200 yards dead straight to be reasonably confident of reaching safety. The ball

may bounce another 50 yards; and if it does you are left with another 200 yards to a swale-back green hemmed in by rough hillocks.

From the front tees the hole is not so frightening but there's still the humpbacked fairway and the hillocks of the rough to contend with. And probably a stiff wind from the sea.

Yet there is a beauty about the course which once you have experienced it is irrestible. It was here in 1977 that Tom Watson and Jack Nicklaus had one of their

many head-to-head battles. Jack had two glorious final rounds of 65, 66. But Tom shot 65, 65 to win by that single shot on the final green.

Here too the greatest women golfers have had their own momentous tussles. In 1921 Cecil Leitch (really Cecilia) got her revenge against Joyce Wethered, who had taken the British Ladies' title from her the year before. Cecil Leitch won 12 national titles including the British, French and Canadian Opens; Joyce Wethered

became the supreme woman golfer of her time – and possibly of all time.

All this shows that for all its wildness and its sometimes scary nature, Turnberry can be tamed and its twelve par-4s – all but one of them over 400 yards from the back – can be successfully negotiated by the thoughtful golfer. The average player, however, has to overcome the constant temptation to press, to try to hit the ball too strongly. Golf is a game of opposites. We aim left to fade the

This is the 9th at Turnberry where you have to defeat the elements, particularly the north-west wind, as well as the terrain. Ray Floyd gives it a go.

ball right, aim right to draw the ball left. We hit firmly on short chips and gently on long tee shots when the sea winds blow. That tee shot on the 9th does not need strength; it calls for elegance – a smooth and graceful swing that will stand up to the vagaries of wind and weather.

ROYAL DORNOCH

Royal Dornoch is miles away from your tree-lined, well-manicured golf courses, both literally and in spirits. It is as far north as the great links go, 60 miles north of Inverness in Scotland and 600 miles from London, England. It was on common land and for many years after its opening in 1877 cattle and sheep roamed free over the course. Tom Watson calls it "a natural masterpiece."

The railway was extended north from Inverness in 1900 and soon Dornoch with its wild links became a summer retreat for ardent golfers. These included Joyce Wethered and her brother Roger, both famous golfers, who reckoned they could hone their games to perfection here.

Among the par-4s the 14th hole, 448 yards long, is considered the masterpiece. Named Foxy (all the holes at Dornoch have names) the hole runs along the shoreline and changes direction a couple of times as it runs toward and then skirts the left side of a great dune resembling a Pacific Ocean swell. Finally, as it approaches the green, the fairway moves to the right and climbs toward one of the small plateau greens that are Dornoch's signature. On this hole there are no bunkers, no water, no hazards. You just have to be able to play all the shots, that's all.

Top-class golfers on form make this an elegant two-shotter: they draw their tee shot so that it curves left, with the fairway, at about 240 yards; then, for their approach, they hit a medium- to long-iron (depending on the wind) with a controlled fade into the green. A birdie here is a very satisfying experience for even the best players.

Although the greens are not quite as hard as they used to be, this one, like most of the others, encourages the bump-and-run shots, which the handicap golfer will probably use here as his third shot. You *can* use the soft-landing pitch if you like but only if you can stop the ball dead. In the old Scots handbooks they use to illustrate several different types of bump-and-run, from the straightforward running shot to the "run-over-a-hillock." This last was done by, so to speak, hooking the ball with a straight faced club, a closed stance, an in-to-out swing and a turn of the wrists.

As well as the Wethereds the great J.H. Taylor, five times British Open winner and a great rival of Harry Vardon, used to take the train to Dornoch to improve his game. For this is the way to do it: practice all the shots, even if only at short range. Run a few. Stop a few. Hook a few. Cut a few. Have a picture in the mind of the beautiful 14th at Royal Dornoch.

This photograph shows the 11th fairway but it has been taken from the short 6th at Royal Dornoch, where what you see is what you get. This is where Donald Ross, one of the first of the great Scottish golf course architects was born. His old home course was, and is, a tough one.

St Mellion

Jack Nicklaus designed what has already become a famous course at St Mellion in Cornwall, just over the river from Devon. It was built on steeply rolling farmland and presents golfers with very different challenges from those found elsewhere in Great Britain.

The par-4 3rd hole says it all. It is not very long – 373 yards – and it is downhill; but it is wickedly difficult unless a player uses his head as well as he uses his club-head.

On the left from the tee is a steep, crumpled, rugged bank, and on the right an even more rugged chasm growing thick grass and tumbling steeply down to a path in front of thick woodland. The fairway rolls and undulates down the hill and round slightly to the right. On the right, protecting the chasm, so to speak, is a convenient bunker; convenient in the sense that a sliced tee shot that lands there at least will not tumble down toward the path or stop half way down in the clinging rough. A little farther on there is a bunker on the left, and the entrance to the green is narrowed and twisted by yet more bunkers.

Professionals have to approach this hole with great care. It is no good their blasting away off the tee. In that respect the hole favors the short hitter; but only in that respect.

You have to *think* about this hole. How likely is it that you can reach the green in two shots? If it is unlikely, what sort of shot would you prefer to play for your third? To get to that area, where should you play your tee shot? Once again, you are arriving at a game plan and your club selection by working back from green to tee. The answers to these questions will depend on the state and nature of your particular game.

Many a handicap golfer tends to slice. If you do, going for a long tee shot makes absolutely no sense at all. So the question is: with what club do I hit my straightest shots? The answer might be a 5-wood, or a 5-iron, or even a 7-wood. You should be brave enough to take the club that suits, regardless of the number on it. For this is a short downhill hole, and if your handicap allows you a stroke on it, there is no need for a long shot on any part of it.

The shot to the approaches to the green is the crucial one. The person who can pitch well will sensibly play to the center of the fairway 10 yards or so short of the greenside bunkers. The one who chips well will play to the left of the green, perhaps to the edge of the bank that runs down that side of the hole.

The first tournament played here, in 1987 – just two years after the course opened – was the Ladies' British Open. It was won by Alison Nicholas, one of the smallest and shortest hitters on the women's tour. To play this kind of course, and especially this sort of par-4, you need brain more than brawn.

Jack Nicklaus designed this hole (the 3rd) on farmland on the edge of Cornwall. It is not a long hole and it is downhill. But, as can be seen, it is a great test of golf.

Panoramic view of the greens of both the 9th and the 18th holes at The Belfry. On the right is the water which has so tested even the greatest Ryder Cup golfers.

For whom the Belfry tolls

By now the most celebrated par-4 hole in England is the 18th at The Belfry, at Sutton Coldfield in the Midlands, home of the British PGA. It is the hole that settled the Ryder Cup both in 1985 when Europe won for the first time and in 1989 when the United States and Europe tied.

The 18th at The Belfry is a very long par-4 of 474 yards: another couple of yards and it would be a par-5. From the professionals and top amateurs it requires two long shots over water, a feature unique in British golf; between the two stretches of water, the hole doglegs left. In 1985 the Scot Sam Torrance assured Europe of victory with a long and well-drawn tee shot and a mid-iron approach that enabled him to score a birdie three. In 1989, however, many of the world's best golfers came to grief here.

Paul Azinger, Payne Stewart, Mark Calcavecchia and Nick Faldo all hit into the lake in front of the tee when trying to repeat Torrance's shot of four years before. Seve Ballesteros took the safe route, left himself a long second and from a poor lie near a bunker hit his ball into the second stretch of water. For the Europeans only the Irishman Christy O'Connor, Jr and the Spaniard José-María Can-izares played the hole really well and allowed Europe to tie the match. O'Connor played the two shots of his life, a safe wood across the narrow part of the lake and a superb 2-iron to within four feet of the flag – an effort that was matched in the crucial final singles by Curtis Strange, who beat Ian Woosnam.

For self-confident long-hitters this hole is sheer temptation. The carry on the perfect line off the tee is 220 yards. This leaves one with a long-iron shot to the green over the second tongue of water. But if one takes the more direct line the carry is perhaps 240 yards and one may be left with only a 7-iron shot to the pin. If there is a match to win, who is going to play safe?

For the average golfer the distances from the forward tees are not so great; but the temptation is still there. Only in a matchplay situation should a player give in to it. In strokeplay commonsense should prevail. Take the safe route. It is often said that in match-play one should nevertheless play

HISTORY AT LYTHAM

Royal Lytham and St Annes is a links in suburbia. No sea washes the edges of the course, instead there is a railway line along one boundary and lines of substantial Victorian houses along the other. But it is a course which seems to have been made for history. Bobby Jones won the first of his three British Opens here – the only American to prevail at Lytham. Here too the South African Bobby Locke, the Australian Peter Thomson and the New Zealand left-hander Bob Charles all won. And it was at Royal Lytham in 1969 that Tony Jacklin ended the long drought of British open winners.

The 17th and 18th, two par-4s, have often proved to be the crucial ones in championships. One shot by Bobby Jones on the 17th in 1926 is commemorated by a plaque set in the ground by a fairway bunker. Jones came to the 17th level with Al Watrous. He hit the longer drive but it fell into the fairway bunker on the left, some 175 yards out on this 413-yard hole. Watrous, playing his approach first, put his ball on the green in two, leaving Jones in an apparently impossible situation. But Jones took his mashie (equivalent to a 5-iron) and, hitting the ball clean, put it to about 15 feet from the flag. Watrous three-putted and Jones went ahead.

The 18th in those days was 386 yards. For Jones, as for so many others, it was decisive. He only had to play it sensibly, which naturally he did, to make his par and win the championship.

To play the 18th sensibly today is not at all easy. The hole has been lengthened to 412 yards. At about driving distance from the tee are seven strategically placed bunkers. The most menacing one for long hitters is the one furthest along on the left. To hit right to avoid it means risking an almost impossible lie in the rough. So the safe landing area is quite small. Tony Jacklin in wining here

played the hole perfectly: his key thought was "tempo." Gary Player however nearly threw an easy victory away on this same hole in 1974. Leading by six shots when arriving on the 17th tee he hit his ball into the rough and nearly lost it. On the 18th it looked as if he might repeat the performance. His second on this occasion was far too strong; it overran the green and stopped under one of the clubhouse windows. He had to hit a kind of left-handed shot with his putter to get it back on the green and was lucky to be able to do that.

The lesson of Lytham for the average golfer is to imitate Jacklin when coming to par-4s like these and concentrate on tempo or

rhythm. The further we go on a golf course – if we are not in a golf cart – the more important does rhythm, a sustained quiet rhythm, become. One can easily lose it if tiredness takes over or if, like Gary Player, one becomes a mite careless. Some teachers say to count "One-and . . . two," the "one" starting the backswing, the "and" coming at the top and the "two" accompanying the swing through the ball. Or think of swinging in waltz time, making it a nice, slow waltz, too.

Seve Ballesteros at Royal Lytham chipping up to the 18th hole at the end of the 1988 British Open, which he won. He clearly expected to hole the shot and missed only by inches.

the course, get one's pars and let the other person press for birdies. But this is not altogether true. Most golf is played at matchplay and in every match situations will occur when one has to "go for it."

The Belfry also boasts the shortest par-4 in championship golf, the 275 yard 10th hole. Played off the front tees this is more truly a par-3. Either way it is "Temptation Corner." The green is tucked away to the right with water in front and to the left, and with trees, bushes and a steep bank to the right and behind. This hole, too, will play differently in a match to the way it plays in a strokeplay event. As the French say: "Vive la différence!"

ROYAL ANTWERP

If it is par-4s you are after, take a trip to Antwerp, the great trading port of Belgium, drive out about 12 miles to Kapellenbos and enjoy the Royal Antwerp Golf Club. It is the second oldest club in mainland Europe, founded in 1888 by British residents. (The earliest was Pau in southern France). The original design was by Willie Park, Jr and his design was revised by Tom Simpson and Philip Mackenzie Ross in 1924. The course runs through a heathland forest rather like England's Sunningdale, only it is rather flatter. To make up for the flatness of the course there are doglegged holes everywhere, turning sharply between the long avenues of pines and silver birches and challenging the golfer to great deeds, whatever his or her handicap.

Between the 6th and the 15th there are seven such holes, two bending right and five swinging to the left. Six of these holes are more than 400 yards long. For low-handicap players the secrets of success lies in good iron play; for high-handicappers it lies in good play with their fairway woods.

The 9th, 10th and 14th all turn sharply left. On each, near the elbow, there is a strategically placed bunker. "Strategically," because their placement crucially affects the tee shot the professionals and low-handicap amateurs will play. On the 9th the long hitter will try to fade the ball away from the bunker. On both the 10th and 11th he or she will try to draw it round the bend and beyond the trap. Only if they are successful will they have a reasonable chance of a par.

For the higher handicap golfer the situation is rather different. He or she will not reach the bunkers from the tee, unless on the day the tees are far forward. So they have to make sure the traps do not threaten the second shot. On each hole they should keep right, even though it may lengthen the hole for them – but not so far right that they are impeded by the trees.

On the 448-yard 9th there is a fairway bunker guarding the hole from any shot hit from either the

This aerial view of central part of the course beautifully records the very feel of Royal Antwerp in Belgium, a great golf course in a forest.

ROYAL RABAT

Royal Rabat is a course fit for a king. It had to be: it was designed by Robert Trent Jones for King Hassan II of Morocco. The Red course, the first of the three Rabat now boasts, is the most difficult – and it is very, very difficult. Apart from anything else, it's well over 7,300 yards long from the back tees. Interestingly enough, though, the high-handicap golfer on the forward tees can hope to score almost as well as the best so long as he keeps his head.

The shining green fairways swing between lines of cork oaks, and there are flowering shrubs everywhere along the way. But this is not a natural course, and the slopes on the fairways were put there for a purpose. That purpose is to collect the slightly errant shot and take it off the fairway. Then there are the Trent Jones bunkers to avoid and the Trent Jones mounded greens to master. It all looks easy, but it isn't.

The 1st hole doglegs left. It is 409 yards from the back tee and about 350 from the front; and half way to the green, on the inside of the corner, is a gigantic bunker.

There is another one on the left of the green itself, and others on the right and at the back. Even from the front tee the average golfer must play well short of the fairway bunker, where there is plenty of width. He or she can then hit the second shot over the bunker to an area short of the green and to the right. No problem there. The hole presents considerable problems, however, for those who try for the green with their second shot.

The 3rd hole has a long narrow tee between the corks. At driving distance where the hole bends right are two big bunkers and some sentinel trees. There is a big green offset to the left of the fairway, guarded by a massive bunker to the right. This is a long par-4, 454 yards from the back, and the average golfer must be sure not to put his second shot into one of the fairway bunkers. It may pay to use a short iron for the second shot and a long iron or a fairway wood for the third.

And so it goes on until, rounding the turn, one runs into water: the much photographed par-3 9th, which requires a tee shot across a lake to an island green. Then at the 11th one meets another very long par-4, (464

The 13th at Royal Rabat, which was built within a 1,000-acre forest on the fringe of a desert. Lakes now soften the landscape but even the best find it hard to beat par.

yards), with a gentle dogleg right and water most of the way along the left side of the fairway. The mere presence of the water inclines one to cleave to the right of the fairway – giving one quite the wrong line into the heavily bunkered green! The main thing, therefore, is for the average player to aim his second shot toward the center of the fairway. The 16th is the last par-4. It measures 430 yards, doglegs left, and is another of those holes with strategic bunkers at driving range which the handicap golfer must at all costs avoid. Besides fairway traps there are two others bang in front of the green.

This is not the sort of course where, on the big par-4s, one almost automatically hits a long tee shot, followed by a long iron, followed by a pitch. One must vary the order of one's shots to the design of the course. If that is done intelligently, even the high-handicapper can outwit Robert Trent Jones.

left side or the middle of the fairway; on the right, in front of the trees is another bunker to catch the approach shot that drifts too far right. There is, however, plenty of space between these bunkers, so that what is called for more than anything else is steadiness. Steadiness and good course management, which takes into account one's own personal strengths and weaknesses.

On the 416-yard 10th hole the fairway bunker is slightly farther out and on the line from the right, so that the high-handicapper's second (or third) shot should be from the left.

THE OTHER HIGHLANDS

The Royal Johannesburg, South Africa, has two courses where a golf ball flies farther than almost anywhere else on earth. The East course is considered the more difficult. It covers just about 7,500 yards: but it plays more like 6,500. The reason is that it is 6,000 feet up in the high veldt and the thin air offers less resistance to the ball. It is a splendid feeling to watch one's tee shot sail on and on and on into the far distance of this beautiful parkland course.

Any par-4 hole here of less than 400 yards is a short par-4. But, alas, the usual definitions of par itself appear to have been amended here and we have two par-4s of more than 510 yards and two of more than 485 yards! For this reason the Royal Johannesburg is a course for good drivers. Not necessarily long drivers, either. Good drivers. It is interesting to note that Bobby Locke, the first great international golfer from South Africa, was a notably short driver. It was probably for this reason that when he first went overseas he developed the controlled hook (giving extra run on the ball) that he used for ever afterwards. In South Africa his lack of distance with a straight shot did not show: his drives were plenty long enough in the thin mountain air. Moreover, the par-4s at courses like this taught him the value of accuracy.

The Locke philosophy was to draw or hook the ball to an area from which he could reach the green with his second shot, even if it was a long (and therefore also hooked) second shot. Then, if he missed the green, he would pitch and putt for his par. But if he was on the green in two he expected to birdie the hole. Gary Player also found he had to make alterations to his swing and to his game when he left South Africa. He got extra length by building up his muscles. But his basic game plan remained very similar to Locke's: accuracy then distance.

The 11th hole at Johannesburg explains much. It is a 511-yard par-4. It turns sharp right at driving distance but there isn't a single fairway bunker or other hazard to disturb the driver's concentration. The fairway is wide and wide-open. Ah, but then the trees begin to narrow the fairway as it runs toward the green – and at its narrowest a stream crosses the fairway just in front of the green. As England's Henry Cotton used to say, "It's the second shot that counts."

On the 16th the stream runs along the left side of the course, but for much of the way it is beyond a belt of trees. Here again there's not a single hazard on the way to the green. For the handicap golfer it's half way to heaven, provided he or she has concentrated first on achieving reasonable accuracy of strike. Golf is not a game of distance, in spite of what the ads say. It's a game of accuracy. Here the distance comes with the green fee and you don't need to worry about it.

Below: The 11th at the Royal Johannesburg course. Although 511-yards from the back tees it rates there as a par-4, a result of Jo'burg's altitude.

PARAPARAUMU

On the North Island of New Zealand there is a most unusual golf course – Paraparaumu Beach. It is unusual in that it is a true seaside links and its 6,495 yards are crammed into only 130 acres. There are few large bunkers but there are swales, humps and hillocks everywhere and some very tough native grass in the rough. And most of the time the heavy sea wind blows in from the west.

It is a course with a wonderful wild, open feeling to it in spite of the narrow area in which it is confined. Beyond it the majestic

mountains form a superb back-drop to the drama of the course.

The very first hole, a 419-yard par-4, sets the scene perfectly. The drive is over 100 yards of rough to a widening fairway which turns left, and slopes gently down to an apparently unencumbered green. But the entry to the green is a landscaped model of a choppy sea: it is all small humps and valleys and leads to a somewhat similar green. It is little wonder that Bob Charles, the New Zealand left-hander who holds the course record here (62), became such a splendid putter. If you can sink putts here you can sink them anywhere.

The 3rd (420 yards) is again a real links hole. Its undulations hide the bunker to the left and in front of the green and if you hit too strong an approach shot it will run away down a deep chasm into thick, grasping rough.

The 6th hole is a par-4 of only 310 yards but it is almost impossible to hit a straight drive on it: it may be straight in its flight, but on landing it is almost certain to hit a lump or a bump or a swale and be thrown off line. And this sort of thing continues until the end. The 13th hole is unlucky for some. It is a 450-yard par-4 with not a bunker in sight (or out of sight) anywhere along its whole length, although

there is a pond off the fairway to the left which conceivably might interest the high-handicap golfer. But the fairway rolls like the ocean and the green is set on a hillock with steep sides to it and rough and (at last) a bunker at the bottom of the slope behind it.

The final hole is a long 470-yard dogleg right. This does have some bunkers, two off the fairway on the right high up toward the rough and three in front of the green. But again it is the bouncing linksland fairway that needs mastering.

At Paraparaumu you truly have to take the rough with the smooth. And you need to have mastered

View from the tee of the 450-yard 13th at Paraparaumu, with its massive undulations and stunning panorama of the Tararua mountains in the background. The fairway undulations require two precisely placed shots to obtain par.

the tricky short shots – the ones with the ball below or above one's feet – if you are hoping to score to your handicap. This is not the modern hit-and-stop kind of game. it's more the old-fashioned chip-and-run, Scottish style. But you do need also to hit a relatively long ball off the tee. It is invigorating golf in an invigorating setting.

PAR-5S

FIVES AT THE HOME OF GOLF

Originally there was no such thing as a par-5 hole in golf; indeed, no such thing as par. All golf was played at matchplay. Some holes were short, some long, and how many strokes one took was of no importance so long as the total was one less than that of one's opponent. Strokeplay came in with the first Championship, the first official Open being played at Prestwick in Scotland in 1860. We do know of some remarkable "birdies" after that, even with the primitive old-fashioned equipment, like Young Tom Morris's astounding three on what was then the 578-yard first hole at Prestwick. But overall very few players of those days even parred the what we now define as par-5s.

Nowadays, with the improvement in clubs and balls, the par-5s are often the easiest holes for professionals in a scoring sense. During the 1990 Open at St Andrews the winner, Nick Faldo, birdied the par-5 5th hole in every round and parred the long 14th in every round. Payne Stewart (joint runner-up) had three birdies on the 5th and one on the 14th. Greg Norman had one birdie and three pars on the 5th and an eagle, two birdies and a par on the 14th. Norman's eagle-3 on the 14th on the second day was called "the shot of the tournament" by *The Times*. The hole is 567 yards long. Norman hit an enormous drive and, after a safe mid-iron approach shot, put his 75-yard wedge into the hole.

Now these are not easy holes. The 5th, the Hole O'Cross (out), has a line of pot bunkers, small but deep, that eat into the right and center of the fairway at or around driving distance – and the fairway has a nasty habit of throwing well-hit balls toward them. So for the top player the tee shot must be well to the left, yet not so far left that it runs into the rough. But here's the rub: the second shot has to avoid another set of

The critical 14th at St. Andrews, known locally as "Long," shares a green with the 4th hole. Overhit your approach and you may face a 50-yard putt.

bunkers on the left of the fairway near the green, and these may now be on the direct line to the pin. There is also a pot bunker there in the middle of the fairway. Then there is a hill before the green, and if the ball is not hit far enough it will roll back toward the player. If hit too far, however, it will run to the far end of a very big green.

The 14th hole is 567 yards long. There's out-of-bounds on the right, the cavernous Beardies in front and stupendous Hell bunker on the line to the green for the second (or third) shot.

What these holes require from the best golfers, besides great length off the tee, is accuracy of shot. They also need to know the course from experience and to plot their passage from tee to green very carefully, taking

account of the strength or absence of the wind. These qualities are also demanded of the average golfer. Accuracy is usually the missing factor in the game of the high-handicapper, so what is needed is a realistic appreciation of which clubs and which shots are the safest to play.

On a hole like the 5th at St Andrews we need to ask ourselves which club will take us to the left side of the fairway, short of or to the right of Hell bunker, and then which long club we can use that will land the ball short of the Beardies, but not too short.

The Beardies also come into play on the 14th. This time we probably need the longest shot we are capable of to get beyond them. Then it's three easy shots to reach the green playing to our handicap – as long as we know how to avoid Hell and, to the left and a little further on, the Grave and Ginger Beer bunkers.

These forbidding traps have destroyed the Open ambitions of many great players on the 14th, in-cluding Gene Sarazen and Bobby Locke.

Many of the current stars opt to play far to the left with their drive, finding a haven on the 5th fairway, which gives them a clean, if lengthy second shot into the green. The average player can also play the 14th that way, using three shots instead of two.

BALTUSROL

There is a championship course in the United States which they shorten for the tour professionals: Baltusrol's Lower course. This makes it more of a test. One reason is that, for members, the 1st hole is a par-5 – but only just. It is 478 yards long. Shorten it a little and it is a par-4 – but a long one. On this basis the whole course is cut down from 7,138 yards (par-72) to about 7,050 yards (par-70). If you are playing to par this makes a big difference. Later

on in the first nine the 7th is also cut down to a par-4 for the pros. The real par-5s are left for the final, the clinching two holes.

To cut a course down to size for the best players shows just how much psychology counts in golf. So does leaving the two long holes until the last. The 17th at Baltusrol is 630 yards long. Now that really *is* long!

As a par-5 the 1st is generous for the average golfer. He or she just has to remember the basic Law of Golf Arithmentic: 150 + 150 + 150 = 450. Make the common factor 160 and you are on the green. If

the 36-handicapper makes it 130 they can, after just a short pitch at the end, be on the green in four (nett two). There is an out-of-bounds on the left and some bunkers, too, but they are very unlikely to worry the handicap golfer.

For the professionals the hole is more awkward. The left-hand bunkers may indeed concern them. And the second shot has to thread its way through eye-of-the-needle bunkers by the green. Which explains why for them the hole may be a par-4.

The 6th is another par-5 for

members but a par-4 of about 470 yards for a pro tour event. The tee shot is through a narrow avenue of trees which may worry Mr Average, but otherwise there is no serious problem so long he does not slice the second or third shot into a big trap on the right at about pitching distance from the green. It is a hole for steadiness.

And so at last he, like the pros, comes face to face with distance – the 630-yard 17th and the 542-yard 18th. The 17th seems to be largely desert and the sand that crosses the fairway almost at the half way point is indeed called The Sahara.

Jack Nicklaus plays out of a greenside trap during the 1980 US Open at Baltusrol (Nicklaus won the tournament). Note how much sand he has moved.

Before one gets there the encroaching trees seem to threaten one. And at journey's end more sand and more scrub mar the approach to a green up on a hillock. Now the Basic Law of Golf Maths is suspended and the average golfer must recall the Rule of the Accurate Club, usually a midiron. This is the club that can be relied on to perform to specifica-tion and thus can be used when the prime essential is keeping out of trouble. Once beyond the Sahara, Mr Average should reckon to stop the ball about 100 yards in front of the green so that he can readily pitch over any sand that is in the way.

The 18th is at least downhill, but there is water in the way at about second-shot length for him. He should hit short of it and then, putting all anxiety aside, hit a midiron third to the heart of the final green. On the days when this shot comes off he will realise how rewarding this game can be.

THE SANDS OF SEMINOLE

Seminole, a few miles north of Palm Beach, Florida, is a winter-resort course of considerable character. It was designed by Donald Ross, architect of so many subtle courses around the United States. Here Ross brought a touch of Scotland to the tropics.

The scene is a mixture of sand and water, palm trees bending to ocean wind, sweeping green fair-ways, great white bunkers and the Atlantic out beyond the beach. It provides one truly great par-5 and three other excellent ones. This no doubt is why Ben Hogan has always had such respect for the course and used to come here in the spring to hone his game before the start of the season.

The 495-yard 15th is perhaps the best example. There are two distinctly different ways of playing it. There is a lake shaped like a boomerang between tee and green. You can safely skirt it or you can defy it twice and in doing so shorten the hole. High-handi-cappers must skirt it and play it as a straightforward righthand dogleg. The only challenge will be the palm trees and line of bunkers on the right of the elbow. It will take two straight shots to get to the right place from which to hit another two shots to the green. But the brave man's way is a different matter altogether.

The drive then is across the widest part of the lake to what is in effect an island fairway. The four sand traps and the palms are now on the player's left, while the lake bears round from his right; indeed, it bears round so far that it is in the way of the second shot, which has to be a long iron over the water, and which may have to be faded around a small copse of palms that lead up, on the right of the fairway, to a typical Ross green, heavily bunkered and equipped with subtle slopes and borrows.

The first par-5 at Seminole, the 3rd, is a 500-yard double dogleg right. There are three big bunkers on the inside of the first bend: a little further along, the fairway bends slightly again and where it bends there is another big bunker. The professional will carry this with his second shot but the average member most cer-tainly will not. The way for him is the left-hand way, keeping to the left off the tee, to the left off the fairway and then hitting a third or fourth shot directly between the huge bunkers on either hand that protect the entrance to the green.

Keeping left is a challenge in itself for most right-handed mid-handicap and high-handicap players. One reason is that in aim-ing left they will usually open their stances and fade or slice to the right even more often than usual. Thus this sort of course helps teach the average player the discipline of correct alignment.

Above: The Atlantic Ocean and Florida beaches provide a fabulous backdrop at Seminole. Ben Hogan used to come here in the off-season to prepare for the majors.

RETURN TO AUGUSTA

The 13th hole at Augusta National, named Azalea, is peculiar in several senses of that word: it's strange, and it's one-of-a-kind. For a start it is a par-5 only 465 yards long, 20 yards *shorter* than the par-4 10th! Lengthwise, it doesn't rate as a par-5 at all. But it certainly plays like a par-5.

Gary Player has taken a 7 there; "Tommy" Nakajima once took a 13. The great amateur Billy Joe Patton was leading in 1954 when he took a 7 (hardly surprising: Ben Hogan and Sam Snead were in hot pursuit). Curtis Strange was leading in the 1985 Masters when he scraped a 6 on the hole, and eventually came second to Bernhard Langer. And yet, during the Masters the hole is eagled more often than any of the others. It's a mystery.

It is a sharply doglegged hole, turning left at just about average driving distance for professionals; the fairway hereabouts is banked, like an old-fashioned speedway, and helps the well-struck ball around the corner. Rae's Creek runs along the left side of the fairway and then crosses in front of the green. The fairway slopes to the left and toward the creek once a player is round the corner. Thirty years ago some players cut the corner by hitting over the trees on the elbow of the dogleg. But this can no longer be done: the trees are too high now.

Nowadays the long driver hopes to play a controlled draw far around the corner, which gives him a straightforward second shot to the green of from 200 to 170 yards. The player who prefers a fade, like Lee Trevino, hits the right side of the fairway and then plays short of the creek. The trouble for the long-hitter is that unless he is quite lucky he is unlikely to have a straightforward shot at all. The fairway has odd slopes and undulations in the area to which he has driven and he may find himself faced with a long-iron shot off a hanging lie. The trouble for the short-hitter is that his ball may bounce on into the creek. An additional hazard is the unseen, swirling wind which often haunts the hole.

What is more, the green although nearly 40 yards long and equally wide, is usually very firm. To hold the green from a distance demands a very high shot which lands softly. Not a lot of players can play that. So what does the average club member do with a hole like this? Since he is playing in a match rather than a stroke play event he plays to par-plus-his-handicap-stroke as sensibly as he can and lets his opponent take any risk he likes. This is a clasic case of a hole where you play the course and not the man. After all, the 13th at Augusta is rated as a par-5. In a sense, the course gives the high-handicapper an extra stroke. He can afford to take three to the creek fronting the green and another three (a pitch on to the green and two putts) to make his nett-par.

This is "Azalea" the 13th hole at Augusta National. Lovely for the handicap golfer to play, it is a severe test for the pro.

GREAT FINISH AT WENTWORTH

Wentworth West in Surrey, one of England's truly great inland pine-and-heather courses, finishes in with two totally different par-5s.

On the 17th you stand high on an elevated tee and the fairway, which slopes down from left to right, disappears from view around a lefthand bend toward the invisible green 570 yards away. A thick belt of tall trees encroaches on the fairway all the way round the bend to your left. And you know that a couple of yards behind the first trees is an out-of-bounds fence. On the right of the fairway there are more trees and (on tournament days) behind them is a car park.

Many professionals coming to this hole for the first time aim to play a draw to the elbow of the dogleg, or at least to hold the ball in the middle of the fairway. That's fine if they are consistently accurate with this shot. If they are not they risk going out-of-bounds. Most pros however aim to the right of the fairway and take the lesser risk of drifting into the smaller trees there if they hit too far. This gives them a long second shot but at least the possibility, when the weather is dry, of hitting the green. But even then they, too, need to be accurate. For that green is on the left, and up just a short bank to its left is a continuation of the o-o-b; and the right is a deep depression. In the 1989 World Matchplay final, Ian Woosnam put his tee shot into the trees on the right. The ball finished on a bed of pine needles and other detritus, but he at least could get a

full swing at it. He smashed a two-iron some 250 yards, fading the ball in to the green, where it finished 20 feet from the hole – one of the shots of the year.

This is an invigorating hole for the average golfer. For it is no good him or her being heroic. A big hook is unlikely, so the out-of-bounds does not enter the picture. One goes gently along the right hand side of the fairway until the green comes into view from the hill 150 yards in front of it, then one hits the approach short and to the left of the green where, with luck, nature runs it down to the hole side.

The 18th is a different proposition. This is a shorter hole, 502 yards from the back tees, and is a dogleg right. The thing you must *not* do here is hit your drive to the right. You hit left of center and take the risk of finishing in some rough just off the fairway. But at

The 18th on the West Course at Wentworth is a great finishing hole. An eagle three may await the champion if his drive has been perfectly centered on the fairway.

least now you can see what you are doing. For the professionals what they are doing is probably hitting a long-iron to the right side of the fairway near the green to get it to run through the gap between the bunkers and roll down the slope toward the hole. For the high-handicapper the problem is rather different: it is whether he can carry the ditch that crosses the fairway some 150 yards from the green. If not, he will have to play short of it, and then use a medium or long iron for their third to get on to the green.

The lesson is: always play so as to make the next shot easy – particularly on the 18th at Wentworth's Burma Road.

A RIGHT ROYAL LINKS

Royal Birkdale on England's Lancashire coast is a most unusual links course. It has more true fairways, as the term is understood on inland courses, and far fewer little mounds and hollows and ditches than are found, say, at St Andrews. Its dunes are more like sand hills and fairways between them like valleys. There's willow scrub, gorse, and heather on the dunes and the land in general rises and falls with a rhythm all its own.

There is one par-5 on the outward nine and three coming home. At Royal Birkdale you have to conserve your strength.

Perhaps the most famous round ever played here in a championship was Arnold Palmer's 73 (one over par) on the second day of the 1961 British Open, which he was later to win. A tremendous gale struck the Lancashire coast accompanied by lashing rain. The tented village was blown flat and there were suddenly ponds on many of the fairways. Palmer used his 1-iron so often the rumor went around that he was only using one club. He conquered the wind as much by commonsense as by his awesome power.

The 6th hole is one of 490 yards which bends to the right at about half way. At this point a long, bumpy bunker almost cuts the fairway in half, leaving only a narrow channel for the long-hitter's ball to negotiate. But to play short of this trap means leaving oneself with a very long second shot – and no chance of a birdie, which is what the tournament pro is looking for on par-5s. The long-handicapper also has to take account of the bunker or risk putting his second into it.

Birkdale runs merrily along with par 3s and par 4s of high quality until one reaches the 13th. This hole is 506 yards long from the back and looks quite open. The fairway runs almost dead straight from an elevated tee to a wide green enclosed by sandhills, willow scrub and small bushy trees. There is a ditch and some bunkers on the left but not much serious trouble. One has however to hit straight shots – or be prepared to play from awkward stances in the truly frightening rough on either side of the fairway. It is a hole for not trying too hard.

The 15th is a very long hole (543 yards) whose valley between the dunes sweeps right round treacherous islands of sand. Here, whatever one's handicap, one has to hit the longest shots one can. This *is* the hole for heroics, so far as the average golfer is concerned. He will probably not get into worse trouble by hitting long than if he tried to play at half-power all the way. Somewhere along the line a good golf course demands all the shots from all golfers.

The 17th (at 525 yards) is rather different. The drive is tight to quite a narrow fairway, cramped by the huge Birkdale dunes. There are fairway bunkers left and right and more bunkers still around the green. And, as with most of the greens on links

The long 17th at Royal Birkdale. The drive is a narrow one between a plethora of scrub-filled dunes and the long, narrow green is very deceptive.

courses, if you do not reach it in regulation figures you need to have brushed up on your chipping rather than your pitching. The bump-and-run is nearly always what is wanted here. At Royal Birkdale you learn to take the rough with the smooth and to enjoy it.

MOUNTAINS OF MOURNE

The Royal County Down course in Northern Ireland is one of the most splendid scenically but one of the most baffling golfwise.

Before the turn of the century Old Tom Morris was paid £4 – ah, how time and money change – to cross the Irish Sea and tell the club committee how best to extend their rough nine holes into a good 18-hole course. Soon after 1900 Seymour Dunn and Harry Vardon both suggested some changes. Then in 1926 Henry Colt made the first true golf-course architect's modifications. But there was no way he could alter the authentic old-fashioned nature of the course.

For a start there are blind holes everywhere. This is anathema to the tour pro: you can't see where you are going. A lot of the time all you see are the Mountains of Mourne in the beautiful background. What you meet on the other side of the hill is a matter either of guesswork or gradually acquired local knowledge. Then there's gorse and long grass and hillocks and sandpits to contend with.

The course starts right off with a par-5. From the back tees it is 506 yards long and runs down a thin, constricted valley toward its dimpled green. The sands of Dundrum Bay are on your right with the Irish Sea beyond. It sets the scene for you. Then you stand upon the second tee and don't know where your ball is going: there's a hill in your light.

The next par-5 is at the 9th, by which time you are acclimatised to the blind spots over the sandhills, which is just as well. When you do get to your ball if you have hit it a reasonable distance you have a second shot over cross bunkers toward a rather small elevated green. The 12th is another 500-yarder and the 18th even longer – 545 yards.

There are 20 bunkers dotted around the 18th. Two of them could catch short hitters, whether they slice the ball or hook it. There are three in the middle of the fairway for the long hitters, and if they fade or draw the ball to miss them there is another bunker on either side of the fairway. There is sand and rough and spiky bushes on every hand.

And yet, in spite of the trials and tribulations the course submits you to, you somehow feel that this is how and where golf really ought to be played. And once

Was there ever a grander scene in golf! The Mountains of Mourne frame the 9th hole and clubhouse, where if your tee shot avoids the golden gorse the fairway seems as wide as Ireland itself.

accustomed to the course the average golfer will hugely enjoy plotting his or her way around it. You do not drive for show and putt for dough here. You play so that on each next shot you can use one of your favorite clubs. There was a pro once who, to vary things, used to drive with his wedge and hit his second with his driver. There are one or two places where this would be very sensible, you feel at Royal County Down. It is a thinking man's course, a fun course, in the most wonderful, misty, mountainous Irish scenery. And the par-5s will make you proud of yourself.

LAS BRISAS

The par-5 holes at Las Brisas (formerly Nueva Andalucia), where the valleys run down to the sea near Marbella from the Sierra Blanca mountains, are among the most entertaining in Europe.

The course is at the center of a residential and vacation complex, and when Robert Trent Jones de-

signed it he deliberately made it tough for tournaments but enjoyable, although not easy, for holidaymakers and retired folk.

The first par-5 is the 3rd hole, 503 yards from the back tee. The direct line to the green hugs the left side of the fairway. There is a line of trees down that side and out-of-bounds beyond them; and the drive must avoid a huge bunker which is directly in the

way of a straight shot. The safe way is along the wide, undulating fairway on the right. Here there is a line of bunkers filled with crushed white marble waiting for those who go too far right. When you arrive there the raised green is heavily bunkered in the Trent Jones manner and requires a high firm pitch if the ball is to halt where the player intends.

The main feature of the 530-

yard 8th hole is water, which runs all the way along the edge of the fairway and at one point divides it. If you play the hole the direct way, one outstretched arm of water protects the green from your shot, which has to be high, precise and long. If you want to play safe, you have to hit a shot across the water and around a copse of trees on to a second, shorter stretch of fairway which avoids the water. This

green, too, is mounded and not at all easy to read. Johnny Miller scored an eagle-3 on this hole during the 1973 World Cup when he set a record score of 65 for the course. (He and Jack Nicklaus won the Cup for the United States.) The hole is interesting in that what might seem the safer way for the handicap golfer is in fact the more difficult. The pitch over the water near the green

need be no big deal if you've got a stroke in hand.

The last fiver is the 12th, 520 yards from the back. For professionals and scratch golfers the second shot, the birdie shot, is one of the world's most challenging. The drive is out over water to a wide, sloping fairway with two huge bunkers on the right. On the left is the water again which keeps eating into the edges

of the fairway. To reach the green in two the player must hit a shot over the water once more and also over a large bunker fronting the green on his direct line. The handicapper's line is over the water from the tee, a second shot along the fairway with the stream to one's left, and then a pitch back over the water to the green – a line unencumbered by sand traps.

With its pine, olive, eucalyptus

Approaching the very attractive 8th at Las Brisas one either tries a long approach skirting the water or lays up short to be followed by a pitch.

and palms and its green rolling fairways, Las Brisas is a lovely holiday course, its long holes a genuine challenge for the great golfers and a delightful adventure for the modest golfers. In its way it is a classic course.

An Island in the Sun

Can you imagine what it is like to play golf on the island of Bali in the Indonesian Archipelago, 4,000 feet up in the mountains, where it is cool and the woodlands are shady and there are lakes and streams and tropical flowers? Yes, you are right. It's idyllic.

The Handara course was built, they say, with one old Russian steamroller and two thousand local volunteers. The fairways were sown by hand with grasses imported from the United States and the watering system brought in from Australia. Actually the water has to be used, diverted and channeled rather than provided because it rains in the wet months almost on schedule between lunch and tea. The greens were all built-up to drain the water off rapidly and at the same time provide a test for talented putters.

The 1st hole is a par-5 of 500 yards, over a stream to a lush green fairway seeded with a mix of Kentucky bluegrass and a local strain of Bermuda. There is a bunker on the left at around driving distance and then the fairway narrows almost to non-existence as one plays across another stream and on to another wide lush area of fairway. There is a bunker on the right of this second area of fairway near the green and two bunkers on the right side of the green which is shaped like an hour-glass. The approach must be from the left.

The 9th (527 yards) takes one back toward the clubhouse along a double dogleg left. The tee shot is over rough ground and on the right is a picturesque lake followed by a cavernous bunker and then further on an area of tropical forest. On the left at driving distance is a single tree and a long stretch of rough ground. On the direct line to the green are two more bunkers, but the fairway widens out on the right as one approaches the green.

The 15th is 540 yards long and its main feature is a wide, deep bunker, said to be modeled on the Principal's Nose at St Andrews. The fairway is then beautifully clear until there is another big bunker right on the line to the green about 60 yards out. Keep out of these two bunkers and the hole is at your command.

The 18th is a very long hole, 560 yards with a more testing tee shot, two big bunkers, some rough and some trees on the right, and as the lush fairway curves gently round to the right there are two more wide sand traps on the left.

There is not much bounce and not much roll on this type of tropical course, certainly in the two rainy seasons. The course drains superbly, but for the average person this is not a bump-and-run type of course. It is for the long high-flyer. For the average golfer it is steadiness that pays. There is less "luck of the bounce" here and more reward for straight, steady play.

The view from behind the 15th green. A round of golf on the island of Bali is the vacation dream come true. It is up in the mountains amid the forests and the flowers and the ball flies far in the cool, light air.

WAIRAKEI: PERFECTION IN PUBLIC

They claim it is the greatest public course in the southern hemisphere and they are almost certainly right. They could claim it as the best publinx in the world were it not for St Andrews and a score of other Scottish courses. But Wairakei, half way between Wellington and Auckland in New Zealand, is a gem. It is owned by New Zealand's Tourist Hotel Corporation and is near Lake Taupo (famed for its trout-fishing) and Rotorua (famed for its geysers).

The Championship layout is almost exactly 7,000 yards long. But the Regular is just under 6,000 and the Hotel Course is but 5,193. It is the average golfer's paradise It is fairly flat; there are no great hills to climb. But you have to play your best to par the course, whatever your handicap and whichever layout you choose.

The 1st hole is a par-5 of 520 yards from the back, but much less from one of the forward tees. There is a bunker right in the middle of the fairway at driving distance, whatever your handicap, and just in front of it are a couple of trees. So you keep to the right. A little farther along on the right there is another bunker and a couple more trees. The fairway now turns left and for the long hitters there is a curving greenside bunker almost bang on their line to the pin. If you fade the ball to the right of the fairway, as most average golfers can (and will) there is a perfect short-iron shot to the green. But keep it a short-iron. There are no fewer than three bunkers behind the green which collect too strong an approach.

The most challenging par-5 is the 14th, which from the back is 608 yards long. Here there are some hills. Also a forest. And what is more, a short distance away is a geyser (hot thermal spring) which puffs out sudden clouds of steam. The hole is named The Rogue.

There's rolling ground here and 10 strategically placed bunkers, a dogleg, a tree in the middle of the fairway just behind one of the bunkers, pine trees and gorse bushes. The large green is horse-shoe-shaped – and so it should be, for luck is probably what you need. There are bunkers in front

The approach to the 14th green. It is a long hole – more than 600 yards – and it is rightly named "The Rogue." The green is shaped rather like a horse-shoe.

of it and a bunker behind it and it stands (although that is the wrong word) on a hill.

A lot of people claim it is unfair. But golf is not meant to be fair. You take the rough with the smooth and play the ball as it lies. And on the way, every now and again, you show yourself that you can really play the game. This is what the par-5s are there for. They test not just the distance one can hit the ball but one's steadiness, one's shot-making skills, one's patience and one's ability to make full use of whatever talents one possesses.

GREAT PLAYERS – MEN

As Bernard Darwin, that most perceptive of golf writers, once remarked, "There is a natural law in games by which, periodically, a genius arises and sets standards of achievement perceptibly higher than before. He forces the pace; the rest have to follow as best they can."

It has happened all through history. And the result is a general raising of the level of each game and a deeper understanding of its principles. Then from this better understanding comes a wider and more active enjoyment of the game.

Here in the pages that follow are a number of golfers, women as well as men, who have personified or still personify the Darwinian principle. Each has been, or is, or will be, a leader and each has used an individual method by which to reach the top.

For golf is a game for individuals. And it is from such golfers as these that we learn how to express our own individuality on the course and how to raise the standards of our own games, thereby increasing our enjoyment of a fascinating sport.

THE TOM MORRISES

OLD TOM MORRIS

The two Tom Morrises, father and son, were both born at St Andrews, the home of golf. Totally dissimilar in their golf games and their characters, they were the first true champions in the game.

Old Tom was born in 1821 and, like so many young boys in the "auld gray toon," began playing golf at the age of six or seven. But, unlike many others, he became completely immersed in the game and soon wished to do nothing else with his life but to play the game and help others to do the same. While still a lad he apprenticed himself to Allan Robertson, the young scion of a local family which had specialised in club- and ball-making for generations. The Robertson shop overlooked the 18th green on the

Old Course and Allan Robertson himself was the acknowledged king of the game at the time.

Between them Robertson and Tom Morris made thousands of "featheries," the earliest standard golf balls, every year. This was painstaking work, the sewn leather casings having to be stuffed with fine goose feathers to make fairly hard, round balls. So they did not have much spare time for golf, except during the long northern summer evenings. However, they played as partners in some notable money matches such as the Three Links match of 1849 against the famous Dunn twins of Musselburgh. The St Andrews pair eventually won the deciding match of the three at North Berwick after being four down with eight holes to play.

In the early 1840s the "gutty" (solid gutta-percha) ball arrived and this led to a split between the two men. Robertson was by nature a traditionalist and wanted to stick to the featherie. Morris took to the gutty at once, which lasted longer and flew further. So he set up on his own and in 1851 moved to Prestwick links as keeper of the green. It was there that the very first Open Championship was held in 1860. Tom Morris came second, two shots behind Willie Park. He shot 176 over the three rounds of the then 12-hole course. The following year however he won the championship and did so again in 1862, 1864 and 1867. With that last victory he became the oldest man, at the age of 46 years and seven months, to win the championship.

By that time he had returned to St Andrews as keeper of the green of the Royal and Ancient Golf Club. And there he remained, a gentle, much-loved and much-respected man, until his retirement in 1904. He continued to play in the Open until he was 75. For him it was playing, not winning, that was the essential joy of golf. He also became perhaps the first golf course architect, having a hand in the reshaping of such famous links as Royal Dornoch and Carnoustie in Scotland, Royal County Down and Lahinch in Ireland, and Westward Ho! in England.

Old Tom was not a particularly long hitter but was a great shotmaker, his only weakness being the short putt (as it is with so many of us). When he died aged 87 his passing was universally mourned in the expanding world of golf. He loved the game and the game returned his strong affection.

OLD TOM MORRIS
b *St Andrews 1821;*
d *St Andrews 1908. British Open 1861-2, 1864, 1867.*

YOUNG TOM MORRIS

Born in St Andrews in 1851, Young Tom Morris learned his golf at Prestwick where his father had become the greenkeeper. From the start he was a star. He won his first "exhibition match" at Perth when only 13. When 16 he turned professional and beat the great Willie Park in a tournament at Car-

Old Tom Morris devoted a whole long life to golf. He played in his last British Open when 75. Here the right hand grip is intriguing.

noustie. In 1868, when 17, he won the Open. He was the youngest winner, as his father was to become the oldest.

At this distance it is difficult to rate his game, but he was clearly a tremendous hitter. In his first Open victory he had holed the then 578-yard 1st hole at Prestwick in just three shots. No doubt there was a gale of wind behind him; but it must have been against him on many of the other holes and his total of 157 was five better than Willie Park's and 13 better than his father's had scored when winning the year before.

When he won the next year, Young Tom beat Old Tom for the title. This time he did the 36 holes in 154. But there was even better

Young Tom Morris, who really changed the whole concept of the game, wears with pride the British Open Championship belt he made his own with three successive wins.

to come. In 1870 he was round in 149 and beat Bob Kirk and David Strath by 11 shots! His 149 total was not equalled, let alone beaten, for more than 30 years. It was never even approached again in a 36-hole Open.

For the Open the Earl of Eglington had presented a Championship Belt, silver buckled and made of Morocco leather. In those days anyone who won such a trophy three years running kept it. So in 1871 there was no trophy to contend for and therefore no Open Championship. St Andrews, Prestwick and the Honorable Company of Edinburgh Golfers got together and presented golf with the silver claret jug which is still contended for today. They

agreed that nobody should ever be able to take it home for good. This was reasonable as Young Tom won the Open again in 1872, his fourth Championship in a row. In 1874 he just failed to win for a fifth time.

Then in 1875 tragedy struck. After winning a foursomes match with his father against Willie and Mungo Park at North Berwick he was handed a telegram bringing news that his wife was dangerously ill. He took ship across the Firth of Forth to reach her, but before he arrived she and their newborn child were both dead. The shock wrecked him. He did win one more famous challenge match, but died on Christmas Day of that year. A memorial marks his grave in St Andrews Cathedral.

YOUNG TOM MORRIS
b *St Andrews 1851:*
d *St Andrews 1875. British Open 1868-9, 1870, 1872.* ☐

THE GREAT TRIUMVIRATE

HARRY VARDON, J. H. TAYLOR AND JAMES BRAID

The phrase was Horace Hutchinson's, a fine amateur golfer and great golf writer: "The great triumvirate" were three superb golfers, all born within a year of each other (1870-71) one in Devon, one in Jersey in the Channel Islands, and one in Scotland – who changed and widened the whole concept of the game of golf.

Harry Vardon, J. H. Taylor and James Braid dominated the game for 25 years from the early 1890s until the 1920s. Between them they won 16 British Opens. On 17 other occasions one or other of them occupied the second or third position. And they took the game half way round the world, playing exhibitions and winning matches and tournaments in Europe, the U.S.A. and Canada.

James Braid was the oldest by a few months. John Henry Taylor was the youngest, yet the first to make his mark. Harry Vardon was the greatest and by far the most influential. But in terms of results there was very little to separate them; five Opens each for Taylor and Braid, six British Opens and one U.S. Open for Vardon. (They all won at least one Open on the European continent as well). But perhaps the most significant thing of all was that each had a quite individual style and method. Every time they met on the links they showed the world that there is more than one way to play the great game successfully.

Braid, son of a ploughman in the ancient kingdom of Fife, Scotland, hit the ball with "a kind of divine fury" according to Horace Hutchinson.

Taylor, for a time boot-boy for Horace Hutchinson's father, took a firm, flat-footed, open stance and, using a compact swing, punched the ball low and straight. He conquered the wind.

Vardon, the one-time Jersey under-gardener, took the club away around his legs, then lifted it abruptly upwards. His final upright swing-plane was considered most unorthodox. But what captivated people was the beautifully casual rhythm he achieved: he was all elegance. Using lighter-weight clubs than most golfers, he demonstrated everywhere he went the value of a smooth, unvarying tempo. He made the golf swing and the golf game look delightfully easy.

His name is immortalised in the "Vardon grip." But he did not actually invent this way of gripping the club, with the little finger of the right hand overlapping the index finger of the left. It had been used ten years before him by the great amateur Johnny Laidlay. But it was Vardon's obvious dominance that made it the standard grip, as it still is today.

In Jersey he and his brother Tom lived close by a golf course at Grouville and although they were not members of the club – gardeners weren't in those days – managed to play often enough to become good at the game. Tom left for England first, becoming the pro at St Anne's in Lancashire. When young Harry was 20 Tom persuaded him to come to England, too, and take a post as assistant at Ripon in Yorkshire. From there he moved to Bury, then in 1896 became pro at Ganton. Early in the year J. H. Taylor, the reigning Open champion, came to Ganton to play a match against him and was beaten 8-and-6. Vardon's career at the top had suddenly begun. Shortly afterwards he won the Open at Muirfield, beating Taylor by four shots in a 36-hole playoff. He took the title again in 1898 and in 1899.

Forming a friendship with Taylor, he set off with him early in 1900 to tour North America. The tour was tremendously successful, Vardon's play in particular impressing every American golfer who saw it. The two competed in the U.S. Open for the first time, too. Vardon won, Taylor was second. They then returned to Britain in time for the Open at St Andrews. There the roles were

In this painting which hangs in the Royal and Ancient at St Andrews J.H. Taylor, seated left, and James Braid watch a majestic drive by their great friend and rival Harry Vardon.

reversed. Taylor took the championship and Vardon was second. James Braid was third.

After winning again in 1903, at Prestwick, Vardon fell ill and was out of the game for some years. Recovering, he won yet again in 1911, then in 1913 sailed for America to compete once more in the U.S. Open. This time he and fellow Briton Ted Ray lost to the immensely talented young amateur Francis Ouimet in a play-off. He returned again in 1920 when 50 years old and looked like winning until a sudden gale almost blew him off the course. He came second to Ray. In 1924 at Hoylake his old rival J. H. Taylor at the age of 53 nearly won the British Open for the sixth time.

He had the lowest total over the six rounds, which included the qualifying, but finished 5th in the actual championship.

James Braid, the most powerful striker of the three, had meanwhile become the first man to win five British Opens when he won at St Andrews in 1910. Vardon followed him at Sandwich in 1911 and Taylor at Hoylake in 1913. Vardon, of course, went on to win a record sixth title in 1914, at Prestwick.

Braid was also the first man to win the *News Of The World* Matchplay title and he won that championship four times in all. He served as head pro at Walton Heath, owned then by the *News Of The World,* from 1904 until his death in 1950. He became a most respected figure at the Surrey course – though for most of his time there he was not admitted to the clubhouse.

As Bernard Darwin wrote, all three players with their very different styles exemplified the very best golfing qualities – courage and chivalry, modesty and dignity. ''Their influence as human beings,'' he added, ''has been as remarkable as their achievements as golfers.''

HARRY VARDON b *Grouville, Jersey, 1870;* d *London, 1937. British Open 1896, 1898-9, 1903, 1911, 1914; U.S. Open 1900; German Open 1911.*

JOHN HENRY TAYLOR b *Northam, Devon, 1871;* d *1963. British Open 1894-5, 1900, 1909, 1913; Matchplay champion 1904-08; French Open 1908-9; German Open 1912.*

JAMES BRAID b *Earlsferry, Fife, 1870;* d *London 1950. British Open 1901, 1905, 1906, 1908, 1910; Matchplay champion 1903, 1905, 1907, 1911; French Open 1910.* □

BOBBY JONES

Bobby Jones – he hated being called that himself, much preferring plain Bob, but that is the same by which the world knew him and by which history will always know him – was the most remarkable golfer and very possibly the finest that the world has ever known.

Remarkable because he was a real amateur and, compared with all the others whom he beat in competitions, truly played very little golf. Much of the time he was studying engineering, technology, literature and law in all of which disciplines he took degrees.

The finest? In eight years he won 13 of the world's main titles, amateur and professional. In the last of those years, aged only 28, he won both U.S. and British Amateur titles and both U.S. and British Opens. Then he retired from competition. In his five Walker Cup appearances he played in 10 matches, won 9 of them and lost a foursome. Over

36 holes he beat England's formidable Cyril Tolley once by 12-and-11 and Roger Wethered (once runner-up in the British Open) by 9-and-8.

He also tamed a fiery temperament as a boy to become a quiet, modest and courteous competitor as a man and when in the end he was overwhelmed by an unrelenting muscular disease he bore this wasting illness without complaint and with true courage. He never gave up.

When Bobby started playing at the age of seven the Jones family had a cottage adjoining the East Lake course at Atlanta, Georgia. The professional was a Scot from Carnoustie, Stewart Maiden. Bobby used to follow him around sometimes and imitate his classic swing. Maiden said he taught Bobby "as little as possible." Well, Maiden was a man of few words. Once later on, when the adult Jones felt his swing was all wrong just before a tournament and consulted the pro, Maiden said, "Bring your right foot back a shade." And that was enough.

With this Maiden swing Bobby Jones won the Junior Championship at East Lake when only nine years old. When 14 he won the Georgia State Amateur; when 15 the Southern Amateur. At 17 he was runner-up in the Canadian Open and in the U.S. Amateur. Great things were expected from him immediately and there was widespread disappointment when he had "seven lean years." Between the ages of 15 and 22 he did not win any of the 10 major championships he entered and the disappointment showed just how highly he was rated even then.

What the critics didn't know was that the eight fat years, the years of wine and roses, were just about to begin. From 1923 onward he won four U.S. Opens, five U.S. Amateurs, three British Opens and the British Amateur. In 11 starts in the U.S. Open, besides winning four times, he was second four times.

In 1930 he won the Southeastern Open at Augusta by 13 shots from the runner-up, Horton Smith, one of the top profession-

Below: James Braid gets out of the heather with some vigour at Walton Heath, Surrey, where the rough can be really rough. Braid hit, they said, with a divine fury.

Bottom: Bobby Jones drives off at St. Andrews in the 1927 British Open which he went on to win. He was immensely popular with the Scottish crowds, including the children. He was later elected a Freeman of the City.

als. In the U.S. Amateur in 1928 he had won his last three 36-hole matches by 14-and-13, 13-and-12 and 10-and-9. The great amateur Francis Ouimet, the 1913 U.S. Open winner, said, "I'd be doing well. Then I'd run into Bobby and he would annihilate me!" (He won his second U.S. Amateur title in 1931 – the year after Jones had retired!)

There was simply no weakness in Jones's game, although it is true that at Royal Lytham in 1926 he took 39 putts in the final round. However, he won that Open, anyway, so he did not need to putt well. Normally, he did. But, normally, he did everything well. His swing was slow, graceful, powerful and true. His pitching was first class, although he loved to tell of his "conversation" with his youthtime hero Harry Vardon. In the qualifying rounds for the 1920 U.S. Open at Toledo he was paired with Vardon and in the second one, at the 7th hole, both were just in front of the green with their seconds. Vardon played a bump-and-run to the hole-side. Jones tried to be clever with a pitch. He thinned it and the ball ran over the green into a bunker at the back. Embarrassed he said, "Mr Vardon, did you ever see a worse shot than that?" Vardon replied "No." And this appeared to close the incident.

But the Jones swing was in many ways very like Vardon's. They both made the game look easy.

After retirement Jones wrote two syndicated newspaper columns every week for eight years. It may seem ridiculous to encapsulate his advice in a few sentences, but here are some of his most important thoughts.

- Nobody ever swung a golf club too slowly.
- Swing smoothly to swing well. Relax to swing smoothly.
- As the English champion Abe Mitchell once said, "Move freely beneath yourself."
- Make a very full turn on the backswing and slide the hips forward "along the line" at the start of the downswing.
- Feel that you freewheel through the ball. Any last minute effort to *hit* it will be fatal.
- Use a light grip.
- Shift the ball nearer the left foot to correct a slice, nearer the right foot to correct a hook. Keep it simple.
- To play a straight shot the club should travel along the line of flight.
- The real way to enjoy playing golf is to take pleasure not in the score but in the execution of the strokes.

ROBERT TYRE JONES, JNR
b *Atlanta, Georgia, 1902;*
d *Atlanta, 1971. U.S. Open 1923, 1926, 1929-30; British Open 1926-7, 1930; U.S. Amateur 1924-5, 1927-8, 1930; British Amateur 1930; Southern Amateur 1917, 1920, 1922; Walker Cup 1922, 1924, 1926, 1928, 1930.* □

WALTER HAGEN AND GENE SARAZEN

They made an unlikely but splendid duo – Walter Charles Hagen and Eugene Saraceni (Gene Sarazen) – the carefree playboy of the golfing world, yet a champion among champions, and the younger, shorter, much more volatile and much more careful son of Italian immigrants, who first became an Open champion himself at the age of 20.

They often competed against each other. They sometimes riled each other. They frequently traveled together first-class on the Atlantic liners: "I shared a liquor bill with him on one Atlantic crossing and was staggered when my half came to $300," Sarazen later wrote. But he also said "There wasn't a mean streak in the guy." Hagen was naturally delighted when he beat Sarazen by two shots to take his third British Open title at Sandwich in 1928 but subsequently did everything he possibly could to see that his young rival won at least one British title.

Sarazen, of course, did win (in 1932) and he gave a great deal of the credit to the knowledgeable old caddie "Skip" Daniels who had caddied for Hagen when he won at Sandwich ten years earlier and whom Hagen generously "willed" to him to help insure victory. By winning the U.S. Masters in 1935 Sarazen completed "the pro Grand Slam" – the U.S. and British Opens and the U.S. PGA are the other three – the first player ever to do so.

Their first major encounter was in October 1922 in a 72-hole match billed as "The World's Golf Championship." Young Sarazen was U.S. Open and PGA champion; Hagen, already twice a U.S. Open champ and a former PGA title holder, was current British Open champion. Sarazen said he was eager to get at Hagen for one very personal reason: Hagen kept calling him "kid," as though he was a young upstart. Sarazen didn't see himself as that but, simply, as "a champion." He beat Walter Hagen 3-and-2. In doing so he played the last seven holes of the match at formidable Oakmont in 26 shots.

In the spring of the following year they sailed together aboard the *Aquitania* for the British Open at Troon. Sarazen expected to win – but he did not even qualify. Hagen came second to Arthur Havers. Then in 1924 Hagen won again, this time at Hoylake; and again Sarazen was nowhere.

Hagen had an unorthodox swing. He took a wide stance, swayed on the backswing even so, and thrashed through the ball on the downswing. Off the tee he was often in the woods, but (as Ben Crenshaw said of Seve Ballesteros many years later) he was never in trouble. He always seemed to find a way to the green. And then he sank his putts. It was Hagen, indeed, who taught the great South African Bobby Locke how to putt. (They both believed they could put "true topspin" on the ball, causing it to roll truly).

Hagen was a genius at match-play, winning the U.S. PGA five times, four of them in a row. In accomplishing this feat he won 22 36-hole matches in succession against the toughest opposition. As Sarazen said, "You couldn't rattle Walter Hagen, whatever you did." In England in 1928 he lost a 72-hole match against Archie Compston by 18-and-17. He had

The stylish Walter Hagen prepares to play out of the rough during an early Britain versus America match (in 1920). Look at that expression – he is in no trouble.

nothing but praise for his opponent and for the course. Then he went on to win the British Open once again.

Hagen is remembered also for the way he raised the standing of professional golfers all over the world. When he arrived at Deal for his first British Open they would not let him in the clubhouse – no pros were allowed in the clubhouse. Hagen hired an Austro-Daimler limousine (Sarazen later claimed was a Rolls Royce), had his chauffeur park it outside the clubhouse door and arranged for his hired footman to meet him at the 18th at the end of each round. Before long the message got home.

Gene Sarazen, with his very individual punchy swing, did beat Hagen once in the final of the U.S. PGA. It was at the 38th hole in 1923 – and this time Sarazen was the one in the woods. The ball appeared to hit the roof of a cottage and fall out-of-bounds. But

Sarazen's caddie found it safely in-bounds – and with an opening to the green through the trees. He hit a long-iron shot to within three feet of the hole. Hagen, visibly shaken for once, fluffed his pitch and lost the hole and the title. Ever afterwards he suspected that someone in the cottage had thrown the ball back into bounds. But he did not let it rankle for long.

After this Sarazen ran into a bad patch. Many people put it down to his unorthodox grip. It was a very strong interlocking grip, but with his left thumb hanging in the air off the shaft. He tried several other grips, but none seemed to work. So he went back to his own. Maybe there's a lesson there.

In 1932 his long chase for the British Open's silver claret jug was at last rewarded at Prince's, Sandwich – thanks, he said, largely to old "Skip" Daniels, the caddie Hagen had willed him. Besides the usual fee, he gave Daniels his polo coat. They say the old man wore it every day, indoors or out, until his death a few months later.

Then in 1935, in the last round of the second U.S. Masters tournament at Augusta Sarazen, the eventual winner, hit what is still perhaps the most celebrated shot in the history of golf – his 4-wood second to the par-5 15th, which went straight into the hole for an albatross (or double-eagle) two, enabling him to tie with Craig Wood. That year Hagen captained the U.S. Ryder Cup team to victory for the fifth time. Sarazen was his top player.

WALTER CHARLES HAGEN
b *Rochester, NY, 1892;* d *1969. U.S. Open 1914, 1919; U.S. PGA 1921, 1924, 1925, 1926, 1927; British Open 1922, 1924, 1928-9; French Open 1920; Canadian Open 1931; Ryder Cup 1927, 1929, 1931, 1933, 1935.*

EUGENE SARAZEN b *Harrison, NY, 1902. U.S. Open 1922, 1932; British Open 1932; U.S. PGA 1922, 1923, 1933; U.S. Masters 1935. First player to do the pro Grand Slam. Ryder Cup 1927, 1929, 1931, 1933, 1935, 1937, 1939* ☐

BEN HOGAN

In a sense 1912 was the *annus mirabilis* (wonder year) of golf. It was the year three of America's greatest champions were born. One was the sweetest swinging and the longest-lasting: Sam Snead. One had the shortest yet most miraculous career: Byron Nelson. And one became by common consent the greatest: Ben Hogan.

Ben Hogan's greatness flowered late. He had begun as a caddie alongside Byron Nelson at the Glen Garden club, Fort Worth, Texas; he tied with Nelson for the caddie's championship; he started his professional career in 1931, two years before Nelson: but he did not have his first big win until 1946 – the year Nelson, the amazing shooting star, quit competitive golf for good.

Hogan won tournaments in his early years, but never big tournaments. His over-long powerhouse swing caused him to hook the ball mightily, particularly when under pressure. Besides which, he was naturally left-handed and had taken to playing golf right-handed in his youth because he couldn't get his hands on a left-handed set of clubs. Most commentators assume that this actually gave him an advantage. He could, they said, naturally control the club with the leading hand, the left. But in truth his left-handedness was probably the major factor in the late flowering of his talent. It presented him with a difficulty he had to overcome.

Ben Hogan's relentless determination, his single-mindedness, his constant search for perfection and his sheer tough courage were the characteristics that were to make him great. "The wee ice-mon" the Scots called him when he came to Carnoustie to win the British Open at his first attempt in 1953. "He was the only golfer I have played alongside who made me feel inadequate," declared the Welsh wizard Dai Rees. "He set a standard to which we all aspired, but none of us ever reached," said the great Australian player Peter Thomson.

He won his first major championship in 1946, the U.S. PGA tournament. But he did not perfect the final adjustments to his swing – the secret of which, at the end of his career, he was to sell for a small fortune to *Life* magazine – until early in 1948. That year he won the PGA once more and also the U.S. Open for the first time. But then disaster struck.

Early in 1949 he was the victim of a terrible car crash, suffering multiple injuries and coming very, very close to death. It was feared he would never walk again, let alone play golf. But Hogan determined otherwise. Hobbling badly, he captained the victorious U.S. Ryder Cup team that year at Ganton in England. In January 1950 he entered the Los Angeles Open as an experiment, to see if he could hobble round 72 holes of golf. He could: he tied for first place with Sam Snead!

But there were greater things to come. In the summer he won the U.S. Open for a second time, and he did so after a play-off with Lloyd Mangrum and George Fazio. Still walking with difficulty he nevertheless scored a 69, four shots better than Mangrum and six better than Fazio.

In 1951 he successfully defended his Open title at Oakland Hills, considered then about the toughest course in North

The young and very dapper Gene Sarazen tees off from the 1st at Hoylake during the 1924 British Open. He was not to win the title he coveted for another eight years.

The great Ben Hogan at Wentworth during the World Cup (then known as the Canada Cup) in 1956 which he and Sam Snead won for the USA, Hogan taking individual honors.

America. "I vowed I would bring this monster to its knees," he said afterwards.

But 1953 was to be his biggest year of all. He played in only six tournaments – but he won them all. He won the Masters at Augusta, the U.S. Open at Oakmont and the British Open at Carnoustie. He won the Masters by five shots, lowered the course record for 72 holes at Oakmont by 11 shots, and broke the competition record at Carnoustie with a 68 in the last round. He had reduced his score in each round – 73, 71, 70, 68 – and everyone there was convinced that if he had needed it he would have scored a 65 in that final

round. After Carnoustie, there was not enough time for him to return home to prepare for the U.S. PGA, which most people would have expected him to win, too. As it is, he remains the only player ever to have won three of the four professional majors in a single year.

By now he was rated the best shotmaker the game had ever known; and there will surely never be a better one. At the end, it was his putting that let him down. He never tried a change of grip, as old Sam Snead did so successfully. He never returned to putting left-handed, which might have saved his game. Maybe he felt he had already reached the top of golf's Everest and so had nothing to prove. He continued to play in the U.S. Open and the Masters, coming close to winning again in the Open three times;

and in the 1967 Masters, at the age of 54, he played one faultless round of 66, covering the back nine in 30 glorious shots. He was still the master shotmaker.

His book *The Modern Fundamentals of Golf*, so beautifully illustrated by Anthony Ravielli, has become a basic textbook on how to swing effectively. The fundamentals for him were, and are, the grip, the stance, the turn, the plane, the action of the right elbow and the squared and bowed-out left wrist through impact. He was the first to stress the vital value of staying on-plane, visualising the plane as an imaginary pane of glass sloping down from the shoulders to the ball. The swing must never be allowed, he said, to shatter the glass. And when parallel to the ground the club must also be parallel to the slope of the imaginary glass.

His own personal secret he never urged upon others. This, he revealed in *Life* magazine, was to open the clubface as he swung back and to cup his left wrist at the top of his swing. It cured his hook. But he knew it would never cure a slice, which is what so many amateurs are plagued with. The action that produces a firm hit with a squared clubface "along the line" through impact is the one the average golfer has to discover through trial and error for himself.

BENJAMIN WILLIAM HOGAN
b *Dublin, Texas, 1912. U.S Open 1948, 1950-51, 1953; U.S. Masters 1951, 1953; U.S. PGA 1946, 1948; British Open 1953; 63 U.S. tour victories. Ryder Cup 1941, 1947, 1951; World Cup 1956 (with Sam Snead) and individual winner with 277.* □

Byron Nelson

As with Hogan, Byron Nelson's first years on the American tour were not successful. He had married young. He wasn't making any money. And he blamed his clubs. Then his wife Louise told him, straight: "Honey, the trouble is YOU!" And he knew she was right.

He set to work studying the methods of the masters of the day, the men who were regularly raking in the shekels; and, taking what he thought was the best from each, started a five-year transformation. Things began to go right in 1937 when he won the U.S. Masters; but they didn't get truly right, in his opinion, until 1939-40. He won the U.S. Open in 1939, the U.S. PGA in 1940, the U.S. Masters again in 1942 and, after a blank period of top golf during the war, the U.S. PGA again in 1945.

That year was his miracle year. He set winning and scoring records which are very unlikely ever to be approached, never mind equalled. He had already won 13 out of the 23 tournaments he entered in 1944, but not all the other top professionals had been playing then. This was not the case in 1945. They were all back on the course: Hogan, Snead, Damaret, Revolta, McSpaden . . . the lot. Nelson won 19 of the 30 tournaments he entered, *11 of them in a row!* He was second in seven of the other tournaments. His stroke average was 68.33 strokes per round and his average margin of victory in strokeplay events was an astounding 6.3 shots.

Nelson put down his own recipe in the June issue of the American magazine *Golfing* in 1948. First, he stood closer to the ball. He said that he had soon proved to his own satisfaction that that it is "next to impossible" to stand too close to the ball. He then bent forward just enough to allow his arms to hang freely from the shoulders and clear of his body.

Next, he restricted his hip turn. And he started his backswing with a slight lateral shift of his hips. This he felt allowed him to start the clubhead straight back from the ball, improving his accuracy. Then he cut out any "rolling" of the wrists as the clubhead neared impact. Instead, he felt he kept the back of his left hand toward his objective – square to the arc – at least 30 inches before impact and the same distance afterwards. This meant, he said, that he no longer had to worry about rough. Using this wrist action he was consistently down the fairways.

There was one new element in the Nelson swing which he did not mention: he gave up hitting against a firm left side and used his knees to drag the clubhead down and through.

Although a big man, Nelson was not constitutionally strong. This, and possibly the feeling that he had nothing left to prove, made him retire early to his ranch in Texas. He did win the French Open in 1955 when on a European vacation and he also played in the British Open. But he had retired confortably on his laurels. And what laurels! Nobody is ever going to equal his record in 1945.

JOHN BYRON NELSON, JNR

b *Fort Worth, Texas, 1912. U.S. Open 1939; U.S.Masters 1937, 1942; U.S. PGA 1940, 1945; French Open 1955. Ryder Cup 1937, 1939, 1947. Eleven tournament victories in a row, 1945.* □

SAM SNEAD

Samuel Jackson Snead, "the affluent hillbilly" who really did start out as a barefoot mountain boy, had (and probably still has) the most fluent, the most graceful and the most effective swing in world golf.

Above: Sam Snead digs his way out of a sand trap at Las Vegas, Nevada, in 1969.

Below: Byron Nelson won the U.S. Open trophy in 1939. Nelson retired after his miracle year in 1945.

"Sam doesn't know a dam' thing about the golf swing," his old rival Ben Hogan once remarked. "But he does it better than anyone else."

It is said of him that he never had to learn. He saw how it was done, mainly by watching his elder brother Homer. Then he went out and did it. One of his early clubs he carved out the bough of a swamp maple. He was a natural. His great assets were fine hand-eye coordination and an extremely supple and athletic physique. At the age of 70 he could still bend down and pick the ball out of the hole without bending his knees.

He began winning tournaments almost from the moment he started on the circuit in the United States in 1933. In 1990 he was still top of the official U.S. PGA list of tournament winners with a total of 84. This figure did not include his many wins as a Senior or more than 50 victories overseas and in Canada. In 1974 he was second in the Los Angeles Open and third in the U.S. PGA. By that time he had already won the US

Seniors' title six times. He could still play as a senior or a "junior" at will.

The only blemish on this long and very successful career has been his inability to win the U.S. Open. He came very close four times and fairly close seven times, but he just couldn't make the birdies on the last couple of holes. But he won the Masters three times, the U.S. PGA three times, the British Open once, and the Canadian Open three times. Yet it is not for his victories that he will be remembered so much as for his swing. Nobody could fault it; everybody would wish to copy it. To do so you need to be lissom. If you are, Sam Snead's own recommendations include these:

● Feel oily.
● Grip lightly.
● Swing back "into the slot," the feeling being that one's hands enter the same "slot" at the top of every backswing.
● Turn, don't sway.
● Never look back.
● Play one hole at a time.
● When you practice, practice rhythm.

Finally, "Thinking instead of acting," he has always insisted, "is the No. 1 golf disease." Take it easy. Trust your swing.

In 1960 Sam Snead had a bad case of the yips on the greens. On his way back from opening a new course in Israel he stopped in Rome for an audience with Pope John. He told a member of the Pope's staff that he had brought his putter along, on the chance the Pope would bless it.

"I know, Mr Snead," said the monsignor. "My putting is hopeless, too."

"My goodness," said Sam, "if you live here and can't putt, what chance is there for me?"

SAMUEL JACKSON SNEAD

b *Hot Springs, Virginia, 27 May 1912. U.S. Masters 1949, 1952, 1954; U.S. PGA 1942, 1949, 1951; British Open 1946; Canadian Open 1938, 1940-41; U.S. Seniors" PGA 1964, 1965, 1967, 1970, 1972, 1973. Ryder Cup 1937, 1939, 1947, 1949, 1951, 1953, 1955, 1959; Vardon Trophy 1938, 1949-50. World Open 1956, 1960, 1961, 1962.* □

THREE WHO BROKE THE MOLD

HENRY COTTON

When the British Open came to Sandwich for the seventh time in 1934 no Briton had won the tournament for 11 years. Walter Hagen, Bobby Jones, Tommy Armor, Gene Sarazen and Densmore Shute had turned the title into an American monopoly, Hagen having won the two preceding Opens at Sandwich in 1922 and 1928. Then came Henry Cotton. He was to set new standards for British professional golf, not only on the course but in society as well. He finished the job that Walter Hagen had begun.

At Sandwich he opened with a 67. Then he improved that with a 65, an amazing round which gave a name to a still famous golf ball –

the Dunlop 65. After taking 72 in the third round he was still 10 shots ahead of the rest. He felt ill before the start of the final round and only just managed to break 80. It didn't matter: he won by five shots.

Three years later at Carnoustie he demolished the entire U.S. Ryder Cup team, which included Sam Snead, Gene Sarazen, Byron Nelson, Ralph Guldahl and Densmore Shute. His last-round 71, played in a howling gale and torrential rain, was reckoned to be one of the greatest golf rounds ever played there.

The six years of the Second

Cotton watches his mid-iron shot sail toward the 10th green at Sandwich during the British Open in 1938 where he had won only four years before, scoring a famous 65 in the second round.

World War put a stop to his progress (he served for a time in the RAF). But in 1948 at Muirfield he won again by five shots; his second round 66 set a new course record. He was then 41. In his 50th year he tied for sixth place, retiring thereafter to the golf course he had designed at Penina in Portugal. He was knighted on his deathbed in 1987.

Cotton believed that the basic secret of consistent golf lies in the fingers and hands. You should have the left wrist firm through impact, he said, and then hit hard with the right hand. He had pupils "sting" an old car tyre laid flat on the ground, with a club held first with the left hand only then with the right only. "But," he said, "I disguise the hit in a swing as much as possible." And, he added, "if you play golf with your hands you can play all your life."

THOMAS HENRY COTTON

b *London, 1907; d Penina, 1987. British Open 1934, 1937, 1948; British Matchplay 1932, 1940, 1946; Belgian Open 1930, 1934, 1938; Italian Open 1936; Czechoslovak Open 1937-8; German Open 1937-9; French Open 1946-7. Ryder Cup 1929, 1937, 1947. Knighted 1987.*

PETER THOMSON

In the days when there were two sizes of ball – the British 1.62in in diameter and the American 1.68in – the Australian Peter Thomson was regarded as the best small-ball player in the world, bar none.

He won the British Open on the then unwatered links five times, winning three in-a-row from 1954 to 1956. He won the New Zealand Open nine times, the Australia three times. But during this period he won only once in America (the Texas Open in 1956) and his best finish in a U.S. Open was 4th, in the Masters 5th.

It was only after he had become a Senior that Peter Thomson showed his American critics that they were wrong. The American-sized ball became standard round the world. For some three years he played fairly regularly on the U.S. Seniors circuit. In 1985 he won nine of the events.

A complex man with simple ideas about the golf swing, Peter Thomson was never just a golfer. He was also a journalist, a writer, an amateur artist and a man with a strong social conscience. When he was young, life on the American tour just did not suit him. He had more on his mind. He tried to enter Australian politics, for instance. And he chaired a foundation to help drug addicts kick the habit.

As to the golf game, it seemed fairly straightforward to him. You judge the state of the course; you plan your round; you have a definite aim on each and every shot; and you stay calm.

As to technique, you take a light, sensitive grip on the club; you take your grip first with your left hand if right-handed, and then

fairway which gave him a reasonable second shot. If that reached the green, he would expect a birdie; if not, he felt pretty sure of a par. He was generally regarded as the best tournament putter in the world – perhaps of all time. He struck his putts with a hooking action and believed that in this way he put "true topspin" on the ball. Most of his putts did seem destined to die just before the hole, yet somehow rolled gently on to fall unerringly into the center of the cup. In 1936 he was the leading amateur in the British Open. Turning professional, he won the Irish Open in 1938. Then

Left: The Australian Peter Thomson hits a drive during a US Seniors tournament.

Below: Bobby Locke, the first outstanding South African golfer, shows his oddly individual method – a big turn, a cupped left wrist yet finally a big hook.

came war and service as a bomber pilot in the Middle East. He returned a changed man. He looked much older than he was and heavier. And he had decided never to worry and never to hurry ever again. Cary Middlecoff recalled: "He never hit a foolish shot and rarely one that could be called unwise."

After winning a 16-match series against Sam Snead 12-4 in South Africa in 1946, Locke went to America and immediately won six of the 12 tournaments he entered, finishing second in two others. After winning the British Open in 1949 at Sandwich he was barred from the American tour for a time and centerd his efforts on Britain. From 1949 to 1959 he and the young Australian Peter Thomson shared eight British Opens between them.

Nobody ever swung quite like Locke and nobody ever putted quite like him. But he played his own game superbly. Shortly

bring the right hand to the shaft from behind the left; and you set up with the left shoulder up and the right shoulder down. Fixing your target in your mind you are thinking of accuracy, not distance.

Now you just draw the club back, gathering your power without any effort, and smoothly hit the ball forward to your target. It's simple.

PETER WILLIAM THOMSON
b *Melbourne, Aus., 1929. British Open 1954-6, 1958, 1965; British Matchplay 1954, 1961, 1966-7; World Cup 1954, 1959; Australian Open 1951, 1967, 1972; New Zealand Open 1950, 1951, 1953, 1955, 1959-61, 1965, 1971.*

BOBBY LOCKE

Born in South Africa of formerly Irish parents, Arthur d'Arcy Locke – known as Bobby since his childhood – was the most splendidly original golfer of his day. He learned how to swing from Bobby Jones, although it didn't look like it. And he was taught how to putt, he said, by Walter Hagen, although it didn't look like *that* either. He played the game entirely his own way.

This way was to play every tee shot with a right-to-left draw so pronounced that they called it a big hook. These drives were never very long but they always seemed to end in an area of the

The basic thought behind Arnold Palmer's swing is made evident in this great action picture – hit it hard and go for broke. Look at those forearms!

won his first Green Jacket at the Masters. He was not a man to hang about. He made the game remendously exciting. You never knew what he would do next. He quickly attracted an army of devoted fans on every course he played – Arnie's Army – who followed him at every hole. The TV cameras were always on him. The open hands of commerce called him for exhibitions, clinics, endorsements, advertising.

In 1960 he won the Masters for a second time. Then he went on to win the U.S. Open at Cherry Hills, Colorado, in the most thrilling manner. After 54 holes he was seven shots adrift of Mike Souchak. In the restaurant with some others discussing the situation he contradicted the general thesis that he was out of the hunt. "I dunno," he said, "a 65 might win." Palmer started out with six birdies in seven holes. He scored 65. He won.

Shortly after this Arnold Palmer teamed up to win the World Cup with Sam Snead at Portmarnock and then set off for St Andrews to try for the Centenary Open. He could have won it. But he tried just too hard, took three from just off the green at the 17th and another 3 from the Valley of Sin on the 18th and watched the steady Australian Kel Nagle take the title.

He was back next year at Royal Birkdale, more determined than ever. The tournament was almost decided by the first six holes of the second round when striding out into a howling gale that reduced the tented village to something resembling a bomb site, Palmer played them in three under par. Finally he won by a single shot from Dai Rees. A plaque still marks the spot from which he hit a 6-iron to the then 15th (now 16th) green from rough so tough that everyone thought he had an unplayable lie. At Troon next year, when a dry summer

before he died in 1987 he played against a Junior Champion. He lost – but he took only 27 putts.

ARTHUR D'ARCY LOCKE
b *Germiston, Transvaal, 1917.* d *1987. British Open 1949-50, 1952, 1957; South African Open 1935, 1937-40, 1946, 1950, 1951, 1955; Irish Open 1938; New Zealand Open 1938; Canadian Open 1947; French Open 1952-53; Egyptian Open 1954; Swiss Open 1954; Dunlop Masters 1954.* ☐

ARNOLD PALMER

Here is the man who set the modern game alight. His game was made for television. His looks were made for television. His personality was made for television. He "went for broke" on every shot in every game. And often enough he won.

Arnold Palmer was U.S. Amateur champion in 1954 when he decided to turn pro. He was also pretty broke. Needing money

for an engagement ring, he took a bet that he could break 72 at that beautiful, terrifying graveyard of golfing ambitions, Pine Valley, New Jersey. He was to receive $200 for every stroke below that score (nobody had broken 70 during its first 25 years). Palmer scored 68, won $800, married soon afterward and with his new wife Winnie set off on the U.S. tour in a trailer caravan.

In 1955 he won the Canadian Open. Within three years he was top of the U.S. money list and had

was making the links most unfriendly, he did the impossible again. He kept the ball in play and won with the then record score of 276.

His golf and his presence restored all the lustre to the British Open that had failed to attract many of the great American players since the war. And he was to do much the same for the World Matchplay Championship at Wentworth, which he helped start with a bang. He won the first title in 1964, beating Britain's Neil Coles in the final; then he won again in 1967, this time beating Peter Thomson.

He was to win four Masters titles at Augusta, following his first dramatic win in 1958 with equally striking victories in 1960, 1962 and 1964.

But one of the engaging things about Arnold Palmer has been his plain humanity. If you don't play safe you sometimes come unstuck. And when Palmer came unstuck, he came unstuck in spades. Besides the plaque at Birkdale there is another at the Rancho club, Los Angeles, where he hit four successive tee shots into the ocean. In the 1961 Masters, needing a par-4 at the 18th to win from Gary Player, he splashed from one greenside bunker to the other and took six. In the 1966 U.S. Open at the Olympic club, San Francisco, he led Billy Casper by seven shots with nine to play in the final round. Sparing nothing in an effort to break Ben Hogan's Open record of 276, he allowed himself to be caught by Casper – and then lost the play-off. All told Palmer won 61 tournaments on the U.S. tour and up to 1990 had won another 10 with the Seniors.

Very few players have copied Arnold Palmer's swing. You would need the Palmer attitude, not to mention his immensely strong hands and arms, to succeed with it. He has always stood farther from the ball than most players, hit through with a tremendously powerful punchy swing and finished with his arms above his head.

His advice to others is, first, to *want* to succeed. Then, having adopted an orthodox grip, to feel

that your head and your feet are the anchor points of the swing. Think of your body as a pole running down from head to feet: the clubhead revolves around the pole, like a stone in a sling. Just keeping one's eyes on the ball is no guarantee of success. One can move the head without moving the eyes (and vice versa). It's the steady head that counts in Arnold Palmer's armory. Then, he says, take the club back *smoothly*; make a big turn; start down *smoothly* with the hips; and *hit it hard*.

ARNOLD DANIEL PALMER
b *Latrobe, Penn., 1929. U.S. Amateur 1954; U.S. Open 1960; U.S. Masters 1958, 1960, 1962, 1964; British Open 1961, 1962; World Matchplay 1964, 1967. Ryder Cup 1961, 1963, 1965, 1967, 1971, 1973; World Cup 1960, 1962, 1963, 1964, 1967. 71 wins on U.S. tour, including seniors.* □

Jack Nicklaus, one of the longest hitters of his day, watches another great drive soar off into the distance. Tom Watson knows he is up against it.

JACK NICKLAUS

Jack Nicklaus has been, and remains, the complete golfer. Complete not only because of his power, his spirit, his technique and his knowledge but through his awareness of the impact of nature on a golf course, the effect on the mind and the eye of trees, shadows, water, rough, sand and slopes. The late Jack Grout, his first and only teacher, said that he studied these things from an early age even more than technique. Technique, he reckoned, comes from playing and practicing and he did both virtually every day from the age of 10 onward.

As a consequence his record of achievements is without parallel. He won two U.S. Amateur titles as a teenager, then nearly won the U.S. Open as an amateur the very first time he entered (he lost the title to Arnold Palmer by two shots at Cherry Hills, Colorado). But he did win that Open the first time he entered it as a professional at Oakmont, Pennsylvania, in 1962, when

he tied with Palmer and then won the 18-hole play-off by three shots.

He has won the U.S. Open four times (a record he shares with Willie Anderson and the only two golfers who compare with him in greatness, Bobby Jones and Ben Hogan), the PGA five times, the Masters six times. When he won the Masters in 1986 he was 46 years old. In 1990 when he had turned 50 he challenged Nick Faldo right to the end. (Jumbo Ozaki had presented him with a new state-of-the-art graphite driver which gave him back the 20 yards he had lost over the years and added, he said, an extra 20).

He has also won the British Open three times, the Australian Open six times and has been a member of six victorious U.S. World Cup partnerships. He played six times in the Ryder Cup, winning 17 out of 28 matches. Immediately he played on the U.S. Seniors' tour he showed he could be a big winner there if he so wished. If one excludes his two Amateur titles he has won 18 majors. Include them and it is 20. He has done the pro Grand Slam

twice. His record of important victories is unmatched.

The main features of the Nicklaus swing are:

- A firm wide stance
- The head cocked well to the right as the backswing starts.
- A low straight-back start.
- A late wristcock.
- An upright plane and a flying right elbow.
- The club *dragged* down by the sliding turn of the hips and legs at the start of the downswing.
- Passive hands.
- The fullest possible extension through and after the ball.

Much attention has been paid to that "flying right elbow," which traditional stylists regarded with disdain. The great Harry Vardon's elbow also "flew," although to a lesser extent. It is an inevitable result of the very upright plane Nicklaus uses. In his 40s he flattened the plane a little and so reduced the amount of "flying" his right elbow does. But all this proves is that what is important about the right elbow action is that it should come into the side approaching impact and be released as late as possible.

This release is powered by the hips and legs. They slow down when the clubhead reaches the impact area. This, says Nicklaus, produces a slinging action and the faster the hips are "whipped out of the way," the greater is the slinging action produced. And the left leg firms up at impact.

But technique doesn't win golf tournaments. Accuracy does. And accuracy is a product of control, whatever technique is used. Control is produced by the mind; by knowing where the clubhead is and how the clubface is aligned and being aware of how that alignment is related to the arc or line of the swing.

Jack Nicklaus has always maintained that the straight shot is the hardest one in golf. First, therefore, the wise golfer does not aim straight fo the pin. He aims for an "area target." Then he plays the type of shot that is most natural to them toward that area. Nicklaus likes to fade the ball, to fly it in with a slight left-to-right curve on it. If he aims 20 feet left of the pin

he can then make a 40 foot error, he reckons, and still be within 20 feet of the pin. This is rather the same philosophy as Bobby Locke's, only he hooked the ball toward the target.

Most experts would add a word of warning here so far as the average golfer is concerned. The fade can easily become a slice, which will further reduce the distance the player can hit the ball. The vital thing – as Nicklaus would agree – is to use the swing you have and use it to reach a target area every time. Course management – thinking about how to play each hole to your own best advantage – he insists is the most important forgotten factor in golf for the ordinary player.

Nicklaus is now one of the greatest of golf architects. He understands topography as well as he understands golf. On a good course, he says, the holes should "arrest and intrigue you." They should look natural. Each hole should be different. Fairways should "swing" that is, not be absolutely straight. Every hole should have rolls and breaks. So should the greens. And he never designs an all-uphill hole. If the land rises steeply he allows players to drive from an elevated tee.

Each game is a challenge, says the greatest of modern golfers. But each game must also be fun.

JACK WILLIAM NICKLAUS

b *Columbus, Ohio, 21 January 1940. U.S. Open 1962, 1967, 1972, 1980; U.S. Masters 1963, 1965, 1966, 1972, 1975, 1986; British Open 1966, 1970, 1978; U.S. PGA 1963, 1971, 1973, 1975, 1980. World Cup 1963, 1964, 1966, 1967, 1971, 1973; World Matchplay 1970. Ryder Cup 1969, 1971, 1973, 1975, 1977, 1981.* ☐

GARY PLAYER

Determined, dedicated, opinionated, powerful, a health and fitness fanatic and a positive thinker, Gary Player from Johannesburg, South Africa, has won more golf

Gary Player was often in bunkers, but never for long. He is known as one of the greatest sand shot players in the history of the game and has holed more of them than anyone else.

games internationally than anyone else in the world. Yet few people remark on the magic in his swing.

Indeed, when he came to Britain as a professional, aged 19, he was told that he was wasting his time, that his swing was nowhere near good enough for professional golf. He had at that time a very strong four-knuckle left hand grip and a pronounced tendency to hook the ball wildly. After studying some of the top British players, particularly the Welshman Dai Rees (who was his own size: 5ft 7in), Player adopted a very weak grip instead.

Now, with most golfers such a change would have taken time to effect, particularly if their games were in any case not up to professional standards. But Player won the Dunlop Masters the very next

year and with it an invitation to Augusta for the 1957 Masters.

In America he found he wasn't long enough off the tee to be sure of reaching the par-5 greens in two shots. So he began a course of serious muscle-building. Again, the effect was almost immediate. In 1958 he was second in the U.S. Open to Tommy Bolt at Southern Hills, Oklahoma. He won his first British Open in 1959 at Muirfield, his first Masters in 1961 and his first U.S. PGA title in 1962.

Meanwhile he had won the South African Open twice already and the Australian Open twice as well. Then in 1965 he won the U.S. Open. This was the only big title he was unable to win more than once. The South African he has won 13 times, the Australian seven times, the British Open three times, the Masters three times and the U.S. PGA twice. He has also won the World Matchplay title five times. Recently, he has had multiple wins in the U.S. Seniors' Open, the U.S. PGA Seniors and the British Seniors' Open.

Not a bad record, one might

think, for a man with a very suspect swing! One leading British expert said, when Player first came to England, that he "had no apparent feel for the game." But this, of course, is exactly what he *did* have.

What he also had was the conviction that because of his small size he had to HIT the ball hard. Nobody ever accused Gary Player of being a graceful swinger. And this striving for power, accompanied every now and again by a return of his old wild hook, camouflaged his innate talent for the game. He became one of the acknowledged Big Three of the 1960s and 1970s – Palmer, Nicklaus and Player.

One key to the hitter's game that he quickly discovered is *extension*. His arms are visibly extended even at the address whenever there is a long shot to hit. He extends them farther on the backswing, his right hand lengthening the left, so to speak, and his left arm bending the right arm as both approach shoulder height.

He makes a big shoulder turn, which is resisted by the right leg, so that he gets the feeling of being coiled like a powerful steel spring. In fact, muscles do not work like that; but the feeling is the same, and this feeling leads to a lateral bodily extension at the start of the downswing. The wristcock and the bent right elbow are "released" simultaneously as the hands approach the impact area and the right arm then *extends* mightily in the follow-through.

What the power hitter needs then more than anything else is confidence: confidence that the ball will go to the target area nominated in the mind; confidence that it will run or stop, depending on what action is needed. And this, for the power hitter, means constant, unremitting practice. Like Ben Hogan, his great hero, Player has never stinted himself on the practice ground. In his young days he would sometimes stay in a bunker practicing until he had holed, say, five shots even if that meant staying bunkered until the sun went down. He has the reputation now

of having been, and possibly still being, the finest bunker player of all time. When someone accused him of being lucky to hole so many bunker shots, Player replied: "Yes – and the funny thing is, the more I practice, the luckier I get."

Another feature of his swing, patently obvious in any series of action pictures, is that his head goes down and back as he hits through the ball. It has to in order to get that vital *extension*. But what stays still is the "hub" of his swing, the bottom vertebra of the upper spine at the base of the neck almost between the shoulder blades.

Not only is he a great positive thinker, but he is also extremely competitive. The most celebrated example of this was his defeat of Tony Lema in the 1965 World Matchplay Championship at Wentworth. At the first hole of the afternoon's play he went 7 down to Lema with only 17 holes to play. He fought back with relentless determination – and some truly great golf – to tie Lema at the 36th and then win the 37th. He went on to beat Peter Thomson. In 1966 at Wentworth he beat Jack Nicklaus 6-and-4. When they met in 1971 he beat him 5-and-4. In 1978 Player won his third Masters green jacket with a last round 64, gaining birdies on six of the back nine holes. Yes, he can play the game all right.

GARY JIM PLAYER

b *Johannesburg, 1 November 1935. U.S. Open 1965; U.S. PGA 1962, 1972; U.S. Masters 1961, 1974, 1978; British Open 1959, 1968, 1974; South African Open 13 times; Australian Open 7 times; World Matchplay 1965-66, 1968, 1971, 1973.* □

TONY JACKLIN

The contribution made by Tony Jacklin first to British golf and then to European golf has been quite outstanding. First he became U.S. Open champion at a time when British professionals were discounted as second-rate – and did so immediately after win-

ning the British Open. He was the first double-champion from the British Isles for almost exactly 50 years. Then a decade later, having retired from competitive golf, he returned to prove himself the most successful Ryder Cup captain ever from this side of the Atlantic.

Son of a steelworker and a dressmaker, he had to fight to make a living at the start. He did not even own a full set of clubs until he was 18. By that time he had been Lincolnshire Boys

Tony Jacklin watches anxiously as another crucial shot heads straight for the green. His winning thought was always of "tempo." By keeping his rhythm he won the 1970 US Open by seven shots.

Champion three times and Lincolnshire Open Champion once (at the age of 16). When 21 he became Assistants' Champion and Henry Cotton's "Rookie Of The Year." At 23 he tried his hand on the American tour and won the

Jacksonville Open. At 24 he won the British Open at Royal Lytham and St Anne's. At 25 he won the U.S. Open at Hazeltine, Minnesota. In that Open he led from start to finish. In the first round when Jack Nicklaus took 81, Gary Player 80 and Arnold Palmer 79 owing to the difficult conditions, Jacklin was round in 70. He finished seven shots ahead of the field, never having been seriously challenged.

In 1970 at St Andrews he played the first nine holes of that year's Open in 29 shots and seemed headed for a record score. Then a tremendous thunderstorm broke over the course. Jacklin hit his second shot at the 14th into a gorse bush just before play was suspended for the day. He finished next day with a 67, but in the final round gave way to Nicklaus and Doug Sanders. He might have won next year at Birkdale too; but the nastiest trick of all Fate reserved for Muirfield in 1972. In the final round he was up there with Jack Nicklaus and Lee Trevino and looked the likely winner. Trevino, his playing partner, after three poor shots on the 17th seemed to give up – but then wedged his fourth shot off-handedly into the hole! Jacklin, visibly shaken, chipped poorly to about 20 feet . . . then three-putted. His chance had gone. Trevino won, Nicklaus came second and Jacklin third.

He won a number of minor tournaments after that but his zest for top golf had gone. Until, that is, he was called in to skipper the European Ryder Cup team in 1983. After losing by the narrowest of margins in Florida, Jacklin's men won at the Belfry in 1985 and then at Jack Nicklaus's Muirfield Village in 1987, halving the match at the Belfry in 1989. He made an inspired and inspiring captain.

ANTHONY JACKLIN, OBE
b *Scunthorpe, 7 July 1944. British Open 1969; U.S. Open 1970; Dunlop Masters 1967, 1973; Lancôme Trophy 1970; Italian Open 1973. Ryder Cup 1967, 1969, 1971, 1973; non-playing captain 1983, 1985, 1987, 1989.* ☐

LEE TREVINO

A Mexican-American born into poverty in Dallas, the city of television riches, Lee Buck Trevino has the strangest golf swing and the merriest demeanor yet seen in tournament golf. A multiple winner of major championships, he has also defeated Fate.

After four years in the U.S. Marines he joined the staff at a local driving range and played a lot of golf on the par-3 course. He won a small bet once that he could beat one of the regulars using only a "Dr. Pepper" soft-drinks bottle. (He had been practicing with that bottle for the best part of a year.) But he also taught himself his own special golf swing with second-hand clubs, a swing that has proved one of the most effective in golf.

He stands wide open, with his shoulders aiming about 30 degrees to the left of his line-of-aim. His left wrist is cupped at the address, his right palm well behind the shaft. His hip turn is restricted. At the top of his swing his left wrist is bowed-out to an exaggerated extent. The clubface is closed. He then drags the club down and along, hitting very late against a firm left side and fades the ball left-to-right.

He says that with an orthodox swing he hooked everything and they didn't make courses wide enough for him. With his own unorthodox swing he was one of the most accurate shotmakers on the tour. He is also capable of inventing a variety of shots to deal with unexpected difficulties.

His first effort at the U.S. Open saw him finish 54th, which did little for his ego. But in 1967 his wife insisted he tried again, even pawning her valuables to pay for his entry and expenses. This time he came fifth. Next year he needed no urging and much to everyone's surprise except his own he won, breaking 70 in every round and beating Jack Nicklaus by four shots. He won again in 1971, this time beating Nicklaus in a play-off, 68 to 71. Then he flew to Britain to win the British Open for the first time. A few days later he

won the Canadian. Trevino won the British Open again in 1972, beating Nicklaus again, this time by a single shot, and Tony Jacklin by two. This was the Open when he chipped unexpectedly into the hole at the 17th when all seemed lost for him. He won other tournaments all round the world from Australia to Morocco and Hawaii to France. But one of his greatest gifts to golf has been his buoyant attitude, even when losing. Joining the Seniors in 1990 he immediately won a string of tournaments on that tour. You can't keep a good man down.

LEE BUCK TREVINO
b *Dallas, Texas, 1 December 1939. U.S. Open 1968, 1971; British Open 1971, 1972; U.S. PGA 1974, 1984; Canadian Open 1971; World Cup 1969, 1971. Ryder Cup 1969, 1971, 1973, 1975, 1981.* ☐

Above: The Mexican maestro Lee Trevino swings. Note the still head, the turning hips, the pronounced leg action and the firm hands. He stands "open" but swings "closed," yet he is extremely accurate.

TOM WATSON

Honored by the U.S. PGA as "The 1980s Player of the Decade" Tom Watson is assured of a place in history. He has won eight major titles, been awarded the Player of the Year award six times, been leading money winner on the U.S. tour five times and holder of the Vardon Trophy for the lowest scoring average three times. By the year 1990 his official earnings from tournament golf had topped $5,160,000.

He arrived on the U.S. tour in 1971 having made little impression as an amateur. They called him Huckleberry Finn because of his open, freckled face, tousled hair and generally boyish appearance. He also acquired the reputation of being a "choker": he kept nearly winning tournaments, then fading from sight.

The fact is, though, that he was learning how to win. He held a university degree in psychology, had a knowledge of mechanics and felt pretty sure that it was only a matter of time before he would be a winner. He was right. In 1975 he won the British Open at his first attempt on the long tough links at Carnoustie. In 1977 he won his first U.S. Masters and his second British Open. On the U.S. circuit he was leading money winner in 1977, 1978 and 1979. And the 1980s were still to come.

In the 1980s Watson won three more British Opens, putting himself on a par with J.H. Taylor, James Braid and Peter Thomson. He also won a second Masters, the U.S. Open, three more Player of the Year awards and 16 other tournaments on the U.S. Tour.

Below: A youthful looking Tom Watson splashing out of the sand. Not perhaps quite as splendid a bunker player as Gary Player he has been an even better pitcher.

In that first Open at Carnoustie an unexpected birdie putt gave him a tie with Australian Jack Newton after 72 holes. Then he won an exciting 18-hole play-off by just one shot. In 1977 at Turnberry he was again in a matchplay situation and again won by that single shot. This time his opponent was the great Jack Nicklaus.

In the first round they both shot 68. In the second round they both shot 70. In the third round they both shot 65. Starting out together again on the final round Jack Nicklaus went ahead. Tom Watson pulled him back with a run of three birdies. Then Nicklaus went ahead again. Watson caught up with him at the 15th. At last at the 17th Watson went ahead by a single shot for the first time. Came the 18th, a par-4. Both hit long-iron shots bang down the fairway. Watson hit his second a couple of feet from the hole. Nicklaus hit his to the fringe of the green – but then sank a monster, curling putt for a birdie. It was a brave shot indeed. But Watson, nerveless, holed his short putt for a classic victory.

In the U.S. open at Pebble Beach in 1982 he was again in a final-round struggle with Nicklaus. On the 71st hole he was just

ahead but in the long grass off the green with an awkward shot in front of him. His caddie urged him to play safe. "Heck, I'm going to hole it!" Watson replied. And he did just that, going on to win by two shots when he birdied the great 540-yard 18th by means of a 3-wood, a 7-iron, a 9-iron and one putt.

He won the British Open again that year, at Royal Troon. This time it was his steadiness that won the tournament for him, his main rivals, Nick Price and Bobby Clampett, falling away in the final round and Britain's Peter Oosterhuis with a final flourish just failing to overtake him.

At Royal Birkdale in 1983 he won by a shot from Andy Bean and Hale Irwin with rounds of 67, 68, 70, 70. Again it was steadiness that paid. He came to the 72nd hole needing a par-4 to win. He hit an excellent tee shot, followed by a superb long iron and steadily sank his second putt.

In his two Masters wins – both again at the expense of Jack Nicklaus – steadiness won the game each time. In 1977 he shot 70, 69, 70, 67 and in 1981 71, 68, 70, 71. In four Ryder Cup appearances he won 10 of his 15 matches.

In 1984 at St Andrews one bad mistake robbed him of the chance to match the immortal Harry Vardon with a sixth British Open win. He had played rounds of 71, 68 and 66 and on the 71st hole – the notorious Road Hole – he hit the perfect drive over the "sheds" along the right side of the fairway, opening up the green. He pondered which club to use for his approach, finally (and fatally) selecting a 2-iron instead of a 3 or even a 4. The ball went through the green on to the road (which is in-play on this hole) and almost up against the wall. He finished with a 73. Seve Ballesteros closed with a 69 and won, Bernhard Langer finishing with a 71 to join Tom in second place.

As has happened to many other great players, this crucial error at the culmination of a great championship seemed to deprive him permanently of his capacity for lethal finishing, for ramming those long putts into the very

center of the cup. He had won so many tournaments by a single shot, or maybe two, that when that talent waned his power to win abruptly ceased. But his record shows conclusively that over a span of nearly 15 years, he was one of the greatest post-war players.

THOMAS STURGIS WATSON
b *Kansas City, Missouri, 4 September 1949. U.S. Open 1982; U.S. Masters 1977, 1981; British Open 1975, 1977, 1980, 1982, 1983. Ryder Cup 1977, 1981, 1983, 1989.* □

TWO FROM SPAIN

SEVERIANO BALLESTEROS

Seve Ballesteros is one of the world's greatest natural golfers. Born in a farmhouse overlooking the Royal Golf Club of Pedreña, Spain, he started playing golf shots almost as soon as he could walk, first using pebbles on the nearby beach. Then when seven years old he fashioned a home-made 3-iron with a stick which he had cut to shape himself. A year later one of his three brothers, Manuel, gave him a real 3-iron and he continued learning with that. (All the Ballesteros brothers are golf professionals).

What he learned was that a golf ball will do what it is told by the clubface: that it is the moment of impact that is the moment of truth. At that moment the leading hand (left for righthanders) mirrors the set of the clubface, which is square to the target line; its sweet-spot comes solidly into the back of the ball; and it does so traveling not just at high speed but at the *correct* high speed.

In his first year as a professional his stroke average was 74.70. Four years later, in 1981, he had brought it down to 69.80. And by the end of that year he had already won two majors, the British Open at Royal Lytham and the U.S. Masters at Augusta. By 1986 his scoring average was down to

Spain's Seve Ballesteros taught himself to get out of the sand first of all with just a 3-iron. It was the only club he had. He went on to be the most successful European of the modern years.

José-María Olazábal, Seve's natural successor, pitches toward the green during the 1989 Volvo Masters at Valderrama. It is an immaculate stroke, head back, hands firm, knees flexing.

68.92 and he had won a second British Open, a second Masters, three French Opens, three Irish, one Dutch and a Spanish; also four World Matchplay Championships.

After his first British Open win they called him the "car-park champion." In the final round he had put a crucial drive among the BBC's parked cars to the right of the fairway – and then manufactured a perfect shot to the green to win the championship. And, all along, his major strength has been his ability to manufacture telling shots from awful situations. Ben Crenshaw put it succinctly: "Seve is often in the woods, but he is never in trouble."

In 1988, after an indifferent season by his standards, he won the British Open yet again, in the final round displaying the breathtaking virtuosity that has made him the most exciting player of his time. He also won the German Open, three other tournaments in Europe and one in Japan. And, from 1983 especially, he has been

a true tower of strength to the European Ryder Cup side.

During 1989 his game slipped gradually away from him. This may possibly be because, when a natural golfer's game goes wrong, he has no fixed stroke-pattern against which to judge and correct it. Ballesteros himself would argue that this is not so, that if you have built your swing by yourself you should know exactly what's wrong. Which is correct remains to be seen. So, one suspects, does more great golf from this greatest of "naturals."

SEVERIANO BALLESTEROS
b *Santander, Spain 9 April 1957.*
British Open 1979, 1984, 1988;
U.S. Masters 1980, 1983; Dutch
Open 1976, 1980, 1986; French
Open 1977, 1982, 1985, 1986;

Swiss Open 1977; Irish Open 1983, 1985, 1986; Spanish Open 1985; Scandinavian Open 1988; German Open 1988; Japanese Open 1977; Lancôme Trophy 1983; World Matchplay 1981, 1982, 1984, 1985; World Cup 1975, 1976, 1977/ Ryder Cup 1979, 1983, 1985, 1987, 1989.

JOSÉ-MARÍA OLAZÁBAL

This young man, born in the Basque country of Spain in 1966, is the one most likely to take on the mantle of Ballesteros in the years ahead. He intensely dislikes being called the second Ballesteros, however: he says he wants to be the first Olazábal. And that may very well be how he will in the end be remembered. He is with-

out a shadow of a doubt the finest young player in Europe, including the United Kingdom, today. By the end of the 1990 season he was ranked No. 3 in the world.

In 1983 he was Boys" Champion in Britain, in 1985 Youth Champion. Already Amateur champion of Spain and Italy, in 1984 he took the British Amateur title. Immediately on turning professional he won the Swiss Open and the Sanyo in Spain and finished second in the European Order of Merit. Paired with Seve Ballesteros in the 1987 Ryder Cup he helped win three matches out of four. In 1988 he won the Belgian Open and the German Masters. In 1989 he won the Dutch Open, and once again partnered Seve in the Ryder Cup, emerging as the top points scorer.

It was in 1990 that he made his mark in the United States. In the World Series at the Firestone Country Club he annihilated the cream of the American tour by the ridiculous margin of 12 shots. He was 15 shots ahead of U.S. Open champion Hale Irwin, 19 better than leading money-winner Greg Norman and 20 better than Tom Kite. "He was in another zone," said Paul Azinger (also 20 shots adrift). "He went to a different level. If the top 300 golfers in the world were here, nobody still would have been within six or seven shots of him."

"Ollie" has always hit the ball very straight. He now hits it long, too. He putts beautifully. How long before he wins his first major?

JOSÉ-MARÍA OLAZÁBAL

b *Fuenterrabia, Spain, 1966. Spanish Amateur, 1983; French Amateur 1983; British Amateur 1984; Swiss Open 1986; Belgian Open 1988; Dutch Open 1989; World Series 1990. Ryder Cup 1987, 1989.* □

TWO FROM GREAT BRITAIN

SANDY LYLE

A true Scot, but with an English home and an English accent, Sandy Lyle is another natural golfer, the very antithesis of his long-time English rival Nick Faldo. Son of a respected teaching professional in Shropshire, he had a successful amateur career, and on turning professional headed the European Order of Merit in only his second season. In 1984 he won both in Hawaii and in Japan, and in the following year topped the European money list once more after winning the British Open – the first Briton to do so since Tony Jacklin in 1969 and the first Scot since George Duncan in 1920.

This Open was played at Sandwich, a true links course on the edge of the English Channel. He started with a fine 68. Then rounds of 71 and 73 put him three behind David Graham and Bernhard Langer as the final round began. The west wind blew and his rivals began to make mistakes.

Birdies on the 14th and 15th put him in the joint lead. His rivals made more mistakes. Payne Stewart was coming up fast behind him. But he came to the 18th knowing even a bogey would win for him. He took a bogey, fluffing a simple chip from long grass to the left of the green. But he had won. Bogey or not he proved the best man on the day.

In 1986 Sandy won on the U.S. tour for the first time. In 1987 he won the prestigious Tournament Players' Championship. Then in 1988 he won the Masters at Augusta with the shot seen round the world. At the end of the second day Sandy Lyle had a two-shot lead. He just managed to hold on to it in the third round. Over the front nine in the last round he continued to look the winner, for he was two under for the half. But Amen Corner once more cast its spell. He three-putted the 11th and hit his ball into Rae's Creek on the short 12th, taking a five. Mark Calcavecchia went ahead. Sandy caught him with a birdie at the short 16th, sinking a tricky, long, side-hill putt. At the 18th he needed a par-4 to force a play-off. Using his 1-iron for safety he hit his tee shot into the left hand bunker on the fairway. Then, improbably but perfectly, he nipped the ball out with his 7-iron on to the green where it rolled back down the slope, stopping 10 feet from the pin. He sank the putt and won.

Sandy won the 1988 World Matchplay – in the semi-final blowing Seve Ballesteros away by 7-and-6 – had more wins in the United States, and looked set to conquer the world. But suddenly in 1990 his natural swing played havoc with his game. He had the same problem as Ballesteros, only more so. But he will come back.

ALEXANDER WALTER BARR LYLE

b *Shrewsbury, England 9 February 1958. British Open 1985; U.S. Masters 1988; French Open 1981; Italian Open 1984; Lancôme Trophy 1984; Scandinavian Open 1979; Spanish Open 1983; World Matchplay 1988. Ryder Cup 1979, 1981, 1983, 1985, 1987.*

NICK FALDO

They say it was watching Jack Nicklaus win the 1972 Masters on TV that persuaded Nick Faldo to take up golf. His father sent the 14-year-old to Ian Connelly, the pro at Welwyn Garden City, to learn the swing. A natural athlete and a tall young man, Nick Faldo developed such a good swing that he won five amateur events in 1975, including the English Amateur just a day or so after his 18th birthday.

Turning pro in 1976, he did well in several tournaments. In 1977 he was 8th in the European Order of Merit and won selection for the Ryder Cup. In the singles he beat Tom Watson, then at the very height of his powers. In 1978 he won the British PGA (a feat he was to repeat in 1980, 1981 and 1989). In 1983 he played on the U.S. Tour for a while without success but returned to Europe to win the French Open. He then

Sandy Lyle during the last round at the 1988 US Masters. He won, with the help of a dazzling shot out of a fairway bunker on the 72nd hole followed by a birdie putt, and was the first Briton to do so.

won four more European titles and headed the Order of Merit. In 1984, back in America, he won the Sea Pines Heritage Classic. But things began to go wrong and he decided that he would have to re-model his swing. He consulted David Leadbetter, an English professional and teacher who had settled in Orlando, Florida.

Faldo's swing had been considered the most elegant in Europe and one of the best in the world. But he felt it was too loose and certainly not secure enough to win under pressure against the best golfers in the world. Leadbetter tightened it, helping Faldo to become one of the most consistent golfers of the day. He has always been a good middle-

distance putter and on his day an unbeatable one. So long as his putting was at its best he had become very difficult to beat.

Early in 1987, with the new swing nicely broken in, he won the Spanish Open. Then came the British Open at Muirfield. Until the very end it looked to be Paul Azinger's title, but he dropped shots at the last two holes. Faldo parred every hole in the last round and won by a single shot. In 1988 he tied for the U.S. Open but lost the play-off to Curtis Strange. He was then third in the British Open and fourth in the U.S. PGA. In the following year he won the U.S. Masters, in spite of one round

Left: This picture explains much about Nick Faldo's swing. He consistently stays "on-plane." Look at the angle of his club shaft here. A clean shot through the ball looks inevitable.

Below: Greg Norman gets out of the sand during the 1989 US Masters tournament at Augusta, which Faldo won. It remains a mystery why Norman has not won more Majors.

of 77. Scott Hoch missed a 2-foot putt to win the title on the first play-off hole (the 10th), and then on the 11th Faldo played a superlative 3-iron approach shot, then sank the 25-foot birdie putt to win.

In 1990 Faldo became the first man to win two Masters titles back-to-back since Jack Nicklaus in 1966 – and the first-ever Briton to win more than one major in America. Once again he came through on the second hole of a play-off, this time against Ray Floyd. He was later within one shot of joining the play-off in the U.S. Open, which Hale Irwin won. Then in the following month he won the British Open for a second time with an imperious display of consistent golf. He finished 18 under par, a record for a major championship. His 270 was the best score St Andrews had ever seen in an Open.

No doubt about it, he was now the World's No. 1.

NICHOLAS ALEXANDER FALDO b *St Albans, Herts, England 18 July 1957. British Open 1987, 1990; U.S. Masters 1989, 1990; British Masters 1989; British PGA 1978, 1980, 1981, 1989; French Open 1983, 1988, 1989, Spanish Open 1987; Swiss Open 1983; World Matchplay 1989.* □

Two World Greats

Greg Norman

The most exciting player to come from Australia for a very long time, tall, blond, powerful and engaging Greg John Norman is the nearly man as far as major championships are concerned. He could have won – many would say he *should* have won – at least four, possibly five. But up to 1991 he had only won one.

That was the British Open at Turnberry in 1986. His second round 63 was one of the finest ever seen on the course. He defeated some appalling weather

in the third round, taking 74, but a final 69 saw him comfortably home by five shots. But it was a different story a few weeks later when the U.S. PGA was played at Inverness. It might be said that this championship was stolen from him from right under his eyes. Bob Tway hit his drive on the 72nd hole into the rough and put his second into a greenside bunker . . . then pitched out into the hole! But the plain fact is that Norman was four shots ahead with only eight holes to play. He allowed Tway in.

In 1987 he might have won the Masters. This time on the 72nd he just missed a putt of 16 feet which would have won him the tournament, went into a play-off and after playing the second play-off hole perfectly lost the tournament when Larry Mize, who had played a poor second shot, chipped into the hole from about 40 yards away in the rough.

In 1989 at Troon he should have won a second British Open but virtually gave the title to Mark Cal-cavecchia when he drove un-necessarily into a distant fairway bunker on the last hole of a 4-hole play-off. It was as if he only knows one way to play – flat out. Critics will say that toward the end of a tournament he does not distin-guish between the shots that are possibly brilliant and those that are actually necessary.

But how can you criticise the golf of someone who, in spite of not running away with all the majors, was for three whole years until the middle of 1990 top of the Sony World Rankings? He has kept on winning other tourna-ments all around the world, in Australia, the Pacific, Britain and Europe and in America. In the United States in 1989, although playing in only 17 tournaments he came fourth in the money list, winning two tournaments, com-ing second once and third once and pocketing more than $3,000,000. In 1990 he won a tre-mendous tussle with Nick Faldo to take the Australian Masters for a fourth time.

The trouble is, golf immortality depends crucially on victories in the majors.

GREG JOHN NORMAN
b *Mt Asa, Queensland, Australia, 10 February 1955. British Open 1986; Australian Open 1980, 1985, 1987; Australian Professional 1984, 1985, 1986, 1990; Canadian Open 1984; French Open 1980; Italian Open 1988; European Open 1986; World Matchplay 1980, 1983, 1986.*

CURTIS STRANGE

On the U.S. tour they used to call Curtis Strange "The Grinder." He ground out low scores relent-lessly. He didn't look as if he was enjoying it either. His expression was serious, almost grim, and he once broke the crystal of his watch when in disappointment he banged his golf bag with a 5-iron. But then he won two U.S. Opens in succession, the first man to do so since Ben Hogan in 1950-1. It changed the popular opinion of him. And it seemed to change his attitude as well.

Strange had a distinguished amateur career, winning the East-ern, South-Eastern and Western Amateur championships, but he failed to get his U.S. tour card the first time he tried for it, in 1975. He played overseas for a year, re-turned and won the vital card in 1977. For two years he ground out unsuccessful scores. Then in 1979 he won the Pensacola Open. In 1980 he earned nearly a quarter of a million dollars on the tour, in 1985 more than half a million and in 1988 more than one million.

In 1985 he really should have won the U.S. Masters. He had a four-shot lead after the front nine on the final day but hit his ball into the water in front of the greens on both the 13th and the 15th holes. It taught him a lesson: he truly is a grinder and he should have played his normal game instead of trying to increase his lead with some spectacular golf.

His first U.S. Open win in 1988 was at the expense of Britain's Nick Faldo. Faldo had played the final hole excellently and was sure of a par. Curtis Strange bun-kered his second shot. Then he very nearly holed his bunker shot and made sure of a par-4 to tie Faldo. Next day in an 18-hole play-off he was round in a steady 71 to defeat Faldo by four shots. In 1989 at Oak Hill he beat Britain's Ian Woosnam and Americans Chip Beck and Mark McCumber by one shot to take his second Open title.

In 1987 he set a course record of 62 while playing in the end-of-season Dunhill Cup at St Andrews. Admittedly the weather was gene-rous, calm, windless, serene, but anybody who can go round the Old Course in 62 shots, whatever the weather, has to be a very fine golfer indeed. He underlines the virtues of steadiness on the golf course, more perhaps than any other recent player except Nick Faldo.

CURTIS NORTHRUP STRANGE b *Norfolk, Virginia, 20 January 1955. U.S. Open 1988, 1989. Ryder Cup 1983, 1985, 1987, 1989. First to win more than $1,000,000 in a season on the U.S. Tour (1988).*

Curtis Strange, "the Grinder," sets yet another putt rolling toward the hole in the 1988 US Open, which he won after a play-off with Nick Faldo. He won the US Open again the following year.

GREAT PLAYERS — WOMEN

It is often said, and it is probably true, that the top women golfers swing better than most men. This is because they don't try to use brute force. They resist "the HIT impulse." They have to rely on the basic laws pertaining to centrifugal force.

Accuracy derives from control of the clubface, and distance primarily from clubhead speed. Control of the clubface during the moment-of-truth – the few inches "through the ball" – is what matters most for accuracy. A wide arc and an accurately timed release of the wristcock are what matter most for clubhead speed, *provided* there is a full follow-through and finish. If you look up the word "success" in the etymological dictionary you will find its root meaning is "to follow-through."

There are many, many fine women golfers today and there have been many in the past but here are some whose play has assisted in the development of the game and all of whom have seemingly quite different methods.

Joyce Wethered, perhaps the finest British woman player of all time, goes after a vital putt in her match against Glenna Collett, America's best, at Troon.

TEN OF THE BEST

JOYCE WETHERED

Joyce Wethered was the finest golfer of her day and one of the best of all time. The legendary Bobby Jones said she was the best golfer he had ever seen – man or woman. After she had played an exhibition match with Jones in 1935 on his home course, East Lake, Atlanta, his "Boswell," O.B. Keeler, wrote: "It was the greatest match I ever witnessed."

Playing level Bobby Jones won 71 to 74. Two who played with them, the inter-collegiate champion Charlie Yates and a leading woman player Dorothy Kirby, took 76 and 84 respectively. In another level match, with Horton Smith and Gene Sarazen as partners for Joyce and "Babe" Zaharias, both men scored 71, Joyce Wethered scored 78 and Zaharias 88.

She learnt the game while playing against her brother Roger, one of the finest amateurs of his day, and his golfing friends at the great links course of Royal Dornoch. She won the first English Ladies' Championship she entered in 1920 when she was barely

19. In the final she met Cecil (Cecilia) Leitch, the most renowned woman golfer of the day. Six-down with 16 to play she produced a string of 3s and won by 2-and-1. She then won every year for the next four years.

In the British Championship she lost to Leitch in 1921 but beat her 9-and-7 in 1922. Joyce won again in 1924, 1925 and 1929. In 1925 the great American Glenna Collett had entered for the championship and Joyce won 3-and-1. Glenna Collett came over again in 1929 and both reached the final at St Andrews. The American lunched 2-up after reaching the turn in 34; but Joyce Wethered launched an amazing counter attack. Out in 35 she turned 4-up, eventually winning at the 17th.

She played golf for fun after that and had an unequalled record in the Worplesdon Mixed Foursomes: she won eight times with seven different male partners.

Her secret? In a book she wrote with her brother Roger, the last amateur to play-off for the British Open title (in 1921), she stressed body-balance, a wide stance, a rhythmic flow of movement and a very full finish (produced naturally, inevitably). But the basic element in her amazing consistency was her concentration on

the 18-inch line through the ball. "For as long as possible after hitting the ball the clubhead should follow on a line in the direction of the hole," she wrote in *Golf From Two Angles,* published in 1922. "I would ask you," she added, "to look ahead in your mind at this line . . . It is a straight line starting six inches behind the ball and continuing for twelve inches beyond it . . . Concentrate on keeping the club steadfastly moving along the line." It's the very best advice from the very best.

JOYCE WETHERED (Lady Heathcoat-Amory) b *1901. English Ladies' 1920, 1921, 1922, 1923, 1924; British Ladies' 1922, 1924, 1925, 1929; Worplesdon Mixed Foursomes 1922, 1923, 1927, 1928, 1929, 1931, 1933, 1936.*

GLENNA COLLETT

Like Joyce Wethered whose rival she became, Glenna Collett (later Glenna Collett Vare) was the best woman golfer in her home country, the United States and one of the best two in her time in the world.

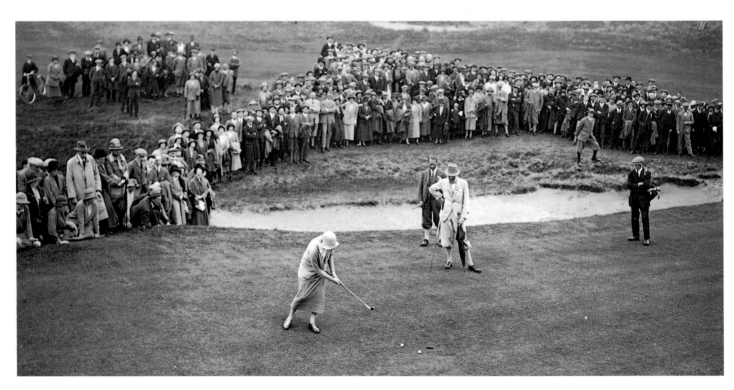

Glenna Collett (by then Mrs Vare) practicing at Sandy Lodge before a Great Britain versus USA women's match at Wentworth in 1932. Note the full swing and the perfect balance.

Like Wethered, too, her swing was based on balance, rhythm and a full turn. She had really wanted to be a baseball player when a girl but there was precious little baseball for young women and as a teenager her mother persuaded her to turn to golf. Baseball taught her the correct "hit with the hands" principle, which so many golfers, men as well as women, find so difficult to understand. Like Joyce Wethered, she hit the ball considerably farther than the other women of her day. She knew instinctively that the main factor in the long hit is clubhead speed through impact. Muscle may be useful for that little bit extra, or even for generating the highest "whirling rate," but it is not imperative.

In 1921 she, too, made the headlines by beating Britain's Cecil Leitch, who was in the United States on her way to winning the Canadian Ladies' Open and who had already won the French

Ladies' four times, the British four times and the English twice. Next year Glenna won the U.S. Women's Championship for the first time. She won the Canadian in 1923 and 1924, the then the U.S. in 1925 once again. In all she won her home championship six times.

In 1924 Glenna had been extremely unlucky in the semi-final in a way that would not happen

these days. On the first extra hole of a play-off her opponent's first putt hit her ball and bounced left into the hole. But Glenna was a graceful loser.

Joyce Wethered wrote of her, "My matches with her remain among the pleasantest of memories in championship golf. As an opponent she was unequalled in the generous-minded and sporting attitude that was natural to her ... She has taken her defeats as well as her victories with a calm philosophy that nothing can move ... If she is finding her true form then there is little hope, except by a miracle, of surviving."

In 1935 Glenna Collett played her last U.S. Women's Championship final. Her opponent was a 17-year-old Patty Berg. Glenna won 3-and-2. She retired soon afterwards, but continued to play golf to a more than adequate standard for almost the remainder of her life – until well into her 80s.

She was a great champion and the British galleries loved her as much as did her home crowd in the United States.

GLENNA COLLETT VARE
b *New Haven, Conn., USA, 1903;* d *1989. U.S. Women's Championship 1922, 1925, 1928, 1929, 1930, 1935; Canadian 1923, 1924; French 1925.*

BABE ZAHARIAS

She was nicknamed "Babe" because as a youngster she was such a great baseball player that they dubbed her the female Babe Ruth. But then she was also an all-American basketball player as well. And a sprinter, a hurdler, a long-distance runner, a high-jumper, and a javelin thrower. She was probably the greatest all-round sportswoman ever. In 1932 she won six events in the U.S. national athletic championships, and after that the low hurdles, the high-jump and the javelin at the Olympics. (The high-jump gold medal was withdrawn because she used what was then an unorthodox method).

Born Mildred Didrikson, she married a wrestler, George Zaharias, and it was he who encouraged her to concentrate on golf. Her success at the game and her very long hitting proved that it is not how much muscle you have that matters when hitting a golf ball but how efficient are the muscles that you use.

"The Babe" tees off at Wentworth during the *Daily Graphic*'s Woman's National Golf Tournament of 1951. Her power play drew the crowds and popularized the women's game.

After winning the Texas Women's. Amateur title in 1935 she was banned from amateur golf because she played other sports as a professional. But in 1943 her amateur status was restored. World War II over, she won the U.S. Women's Amateur title in 1946 and followed that with another 16 straight wins in various tournaments. In 1947 she sailed for Britain and won the British Ladies'. Then she took the U.S. Women's Open in 1948, winning again in 1950 and 1954.

That last win was only a year after an operation for cancer. The Babe didn't give up easily. She won more tournaments after that but died in 1956, a real heroine of sport. As English amateur champion Enid Wilson said, "she moved like a ballerina, as though she did not have a bone in her body." And that was how she played golf.

MILDRED ELLA DIDRIKSON ZAHARIAS b *Port Arthur, Texas, 1914; d 1956. U.S. Amateur 1946; British Amateur 1947; U.S. Open 1948, 1950, 1954.*

MICKEY WRIGHT

Mary Katherine Wright, nick-named Mickey by her father, followed Babe Zaharias at the very top of American women's golf. She was a different type of player, not an all-round athlete but a golfing prodigy. She won the U.S. Junior Girls' Championship in 1952. And she won a long-driving contest when only 15. At 17 she reached the final of the U.S. Women's Amateur, having already won a couple of tournaments; but shortly afterwards she turned professional.

In 1958 she won the first of four U.S. Women's Opens. In the next 10 years she won 70 tournaments, 44 of them in the five years 1961-4. She won the Women's PGA title four times as well as the Open, setting a record which still stands. Coming out of semi-retirement in 1979 she tied with the rising star Nancy Lopez in one tournament, but lost the play-off. In all she is credited with 82 tournament victories.

She hit the ball very long and stright, particularly with her irons, but she did not have the athletic physique of Babe Zaharias. Her game was perhaps more like that of Britain's Joyce Wethered, depending on timing, rhythm and hand action. Many regard her as the greatest woman player of all.

MARY KATHRYN WRIGHT b *San Diego, Cal., 1935. U.S. Women's Open 1958-9, 1961, 1964; Junior Girls' 1952. 82 tournament victories. Four times Ladies' PGA champion.*

KATHY WHITWORTH

In terms of tournaments won the most successful woman professional has been the Texan Kathy Whitworth. Between 1959 and 1985 she won 88 tournaments; yet, like Sam Snead among the great men players, she never managed to win her national Open.

She started golf when she was about 15. Tall and athletic, she began with her grandfather's old clubs and very soon was quite a celebrity. She won the New Mexico State amateur championship at 17 and played as a guest in several local pro tournaments. Although she said that playing at this level "frightened me out of my wits," she decided to turn pro herself and got her father and some local businessmen to sponsor her.

After the first six months she almost quit the tour. She had won nothing. She felt as if she would never again break 80. But her sponsors insisted that whatever happened she should give herself three years before making a final decision. She only needed two.

In 1962 she won two tournaments and was second in eight others. In 1963 she won eight tournaments and was second in two others. She was leading money winner in 1965, 1966, 1967, 1968, 1970, 1971, 1972 and 1973. She won the Vare Trophy (named after Glenna Collett Vare) for the lowest scoring average seven times. In 1967 she won nine times, in 1970 ten.

Suddenly in around 1979 she lost her game. The trouble, she felt sure, was mechanical and she stepped aside to find out how to put it right. By the end of 1982 she had overtaken Mickey Wright's total of 82 victories.

Her long reign at the top shows the value of knowing your own swing pattern down to the last detail so that when things go wrong you can deal with the problem. And, of course, practice until you can putt consistently well!

KATHRYNNE ANNE WHITWORTH b *Monohans, Texas, 1939. Titleholders' Championship 1965-66; Western Open 1967; LPGA 1967, 1971. Leading money winner in United States eight times; winner of Vare Trophy seven times; 88 tour wins.*

CATHERINE LACOSTE

Catherine Lacoste de Prado was a legend in her own golfing lifetime. Daughter of the famous French tennis player René Lacoste and the young lady who as Simone Thion de la Chaume had won the British Ladies' championship in 1927, she clearly started with inherent advantages.

She was Junior Champion of France in her early teens and in 1964 at the age of 19 represented France in the first Women's World Amateur Team Championship

Kathy Whitworth was the most consistent female player of all during the '60s, '70s and '80s. She was leading money winner eight times on the US Tour.

Catherine Lacoste of France was the greatest female amateur of her time and one of the finest long-iron players of all time, especially good with the 1-iron.

(The Espirito Santo Trophy). France won and young Catherine tied for individual honors with Carol Sorenson of the United States, who was British Ladies' Open champion that year. She played in every Espirito Santo match thereafter until 1970 and in 1968 won the individual title on her own.

In 1966 she won the Astor Trophy at Prince's, Sandwich, in the course of which she had a record round of 66. It is remembered as one of the greatest rounds of golf ever played on a links by a woman.

But 1967 was her great year. She not only won the French Ladies' Open but went off to the United States, against the advice of her elders, and won the U.S. Ladies' Open at her first attempt against the best professionals in America. She was the first amateur to win the title, the youngest player to win it (21), and the first non-American to win it.

In 1969 at Portrush, in Northern Ireland, where her mother had won the British Ladies' in 1927,

she too won the British. That year she also won the French and the Spanish titles and took the United States Amateur as well.

Of medium height and sturdy, Catherine Lacoste, was a hitter rather than a swinger. He long-iron play was exceptional. She was one of the few women players who regularly used a 1-iron. Her action was notable for the Hogan-like extension of her right arm in her follow-through, and her playing for her absolute determination. She played really thrilling golf and off-course was very forthright in her opinions. In her different way she was as good an amateur as Joyce Wethered – which means better than most professionals of her time.

CATHERINE LACOSTE DE PRADO b *Paris, 1945. French Ladies' Open 1967, 69, 70, 72; U.S. Women's Open 1967; U.S. Women's Amateur 1969; French Ladies' Close 1968-9; British Ladies' 1969.*

JUDY RANKIN

Although she never won the U.S. Women's Open, Judy Rankin was a leading player on the U.S. circuit in the 1970s and twice won the European Women's Open. But she has been exceptional for two other reasons: she is small – teacher Bob Toski said "She is so small, she might get lost in an unreplaced divot!" – yet she was the longest hitter pound-for-pound in American golf. And, also, she wrote a perceptive book about the special problems and needs of women golfers everywhere.

Like the great South African of an earlier era, Bobby Locke, Judy Rankin drew or hooked virtually every shot. And she drew or hooked every shot because she had what is called a very strong

The petite Judy Rankin, a leading player on the US Tour in the 1970s, proved that you did not need to be tall or muscular to hit a golf ball far and true.

grip, showing four knuckles of her left hand at the address. When he first saw this, Toski told her that if she wanted to make a living at golf she ought to change it. But she refused. The strong left hand grip, she insisted, is natural. The left hand is the leading hand for right-handers. It must not be overpowered by the right. And if the heel of the left hand leads into impact there is no need to rotate or manipulate the hands during the swing. Besides which, of course, a draw makes the ball run further on landing than either a straight shot or a fade.

Some would say that a strong grip doesn't last. But Gene Sarazen has a four-knuckle left-hand grip – and he scored a hole-in-one during the British Open when he was 70 years old! And the fact that it tends to produce a hook with most players shows that some rotation of the wrists and forearms is itself quite natural during the swing. What is necessary, whichever strength of grip is used, is that the leading wrist and hand are firm and flat or slightly bowed-out during impact particularly – *firm*.

When 14 Judy won her State amateur title. At 15 she was leading amateur in the U.S. Women's Open. After she turned pro she won at least one tournament every year except one from 1968 through 1979. In 1976 she became the first woman pro to win more than $150,000 in a single season. She also became President of the U.S. LPGA.

For women golfers, she says, the first key to good play is perfect balance. Second, most women need to sweep the ball away rather than to hit down on it. They need to turn fully and so be "behind the ball" at the top of their backswings. On the downswing the lower body *drives* and the upper half, behind the ball, follows.

Because so few courses are designed for women, Judy adds, women players need to be very much aware of when to play aggressively and when to play safely. And they should think not of hitting the ball far but hitting the ball well.

Nancy Lopez takes a full swing during the 1988 Dinah Shore tournament at Mission Hills. Lopez is another of the thoroughly modern women power players.

JUDY TORLUEMKE RANKIN
b *St. Louis, Missouri, 1945. European Open 1974, 1977; Player of The Year 1976; Leading Amateur in U.S. Women's Open, 1961; 25 tournament wins in United States.*

Nancy Lopez

With her warm, outgoing personality, a highly individual golf swing and the happy habit of winning tournaments, Nancy Lopez has drawn thousands more fans to the American women's tour.

Surprisingly, she has not yet been able to win the U.S. Women's Open. It is surprising because she is second on the women's All-Time Money List with more than $2,750,000 to her credit; because in her first full year as a pro (1978) she won nine tournaments, five in-a-row, was

Rookie of the Year, Player of the Year and won the Vare Trophy for the lowest scoring average; and because she has won the Women's PGA title three times already.

In 1985 she won five times and set a new record for a season's earnings: $420,000. She won the Vare Trophy again and finished in the top ten in 21 tournaments out of 25. In 1989 she was third in the Order of Merit, won three tournaments, and was second six times and third five times. One of her second places was in the U.S. Women's Open. By the end of the year her wins totalled 42, putting her level with Sandra Haynie and JoAnne Carner.

Nancy is perhaps the most exciting player on the women's circuit. There is in her golf a bit of Lee Trevino and a smidgen of Arnold Palmer. Rather like Trevino she bows-out her left wrist on the backswing and loops the club round to the top. Very

much like Palmer, she usually "goes for broke."

She is a very fine putter. But then, among the top tournament professionals, women or men, who isn't? Putting is half the game on average and in the professional ranks much more than half. This, says Nancy, is something the average golfer overlooks. Most golfers spend much more time practicing at the driving range or on the lesson tee than on the putting green. How many take putting lessons?

As Nancy Lopez shows, method is unimportant if you can consistently bring that clubhead through squarely along the line . . . and you can putt.

NANCY LOPEZ b *Torrance, Cal, 6 January 1957. U.S. LPGA 1978, 1985, 1989; Player of the Year 1978, 1985; Vare Trophy 1978, 1985. Tournaments won up to 1991: 42.*

Laura Davies

Sometimes called the Nancy Lopez of Great Britain, Laura Davies also started her professional career with a bang. In her rookie year she topped the European Women's Order of Merit. This was in 1985 and she was 20 years old. She was top of the tree again in 1986, won the British Ladies' Open and came 11th in the U.S. Open.

In 1987, not long after the Commissioner for the U.S. tour, John Laupheimer, had refused to allow her to play by invitation in an LPGA event on the grounds that British women had never made much impact in America, she won the U.S. Women's Open! (As British champion she could not be refused entry.)

At the end of the 72 holes at Plainview, New Jersey, there was a three-way tie between Laura,

Ayako Okamoto and JoAnne Carner. She won the 18-holes play-off quite comfortably. What amazed the other players as well as the fans was the distance she hit the ball. Her average tee shot was 255 yards against the rest of the field's 220 yards. On a par-5 hole measuring 493 yards she was the only player to reach the green in two shots. On the 18th, hitting a 5-wood for safety, she was some way ahead of the other two who were using drivers.

This long hitting would not have surprised British fans. In a long-driving contest at Stoke Poges in England in 1986 she beat the top British male amateur Peter McEvoy's best drive by 8 yards - 282 against 274.

A member of the West Byfleet club in Surrey, Laura Davies has never had a formal lesson in her life. She just enjoyed her golf, astounded the male club members with her striking, and when she decided to turn pro borrowed a thousand pounds from her mother, which she repaid in a couple of months. Tall and broad-shouldered – she is 5ft 10in in her stockinged feet – she proves that women can be hitters as well as swingers.

LAURA DAVIES b *Coventry, England, 5 October 1964. British Ladies' Open 1986; U.S. Women's Open 1987; European Ladies' Masters 1985; Italian Ladies' 1988.*

Laura Davies has been called Britain's answer to Nancy Lopez but she is a power player in her own right. A prodigious talent, she hits the ball further than most male amateurs.

AYAKO OKAMOTO

Probably the best Japanese woman golfer ever, Ayako Okamoto had already won 20 tournaments in Japan, eight of them in 1981, when she opted for the U.S. Women's Tour. In eight years over there she won 15 tournaments. Flying to Britain for the first time in 1984, she won the British Ladies' Open at Woburn Country Club by an astonishing 11 shots. She was then 34. In 1990 she flew to Europe and won the German Open. In the last round she covered the second nine in 32 shots. Her final round 67 set the pace. Cindy Rarick of the United States and Laurette Maritz of South Africa both came to the 72nd hole needing a birdie to beat her, but neither of them could manage it. In the sudden-death play-off both Rarick and Okamoto began with a birdie.

The most successful Japanese women golfer, Ayako Okamoto bases her game on the consistently straight shot. This is a fine action.

Maritz fell out. The two of them shared the next two holes but Okamoto, steadiness itself, won at the 4th.

In America in 1989 Ayako won three tournaments and was second in another two. In 1990 she won once and was runner-up twice. It is the consistent fluidity of her swing that wins for her. At 5ft 5in she is not a big hitter, but she is long enough and she hits it very straight. That's the "secret" for her.

AYAKO OKAMOTO b *Hiroshima, 1951. 40 tournament wins worldwide. British Open 1984; German Open 1990; Leading American Money Winner 1987. LPGA tour winnings to 1990: $1,739,581.*

DIFFERENT GAMES

Golf is probably unique in the great variety of different games that can be played within its general framework: strokeplay, matchplay, points-play, two-balls, three-balls, four-balls, team games, "skins games" and so on.

Stroke or Medal Play

In strokeplay, known also as medal play, the total number of strokes taken by a player is his or her competition score. The total may be taken over 18, 36, 54 or 72 holes. It is the basic game the tour professionals play, and in many countries it is the basis on which handicaps are assigned. Handicap players simply deduct their official handicaps from their total (gross) scores to determine their nett scores, thus: total 90, handicap 18, nett score 72.

The scores are recorded on an official scorecard. Totals are recorded after each nine holes and the two totals added together for the 18-hole score. Players go out in groups of two, three or four, and each player's score at each hole is marked on the card by one of his playing partners. Both the player and the scorer must sign the card at the end of the round.

Better-ball Strokeplay

In this game two players form a team and the better of the two scores on each hole is the one recorded. A similar game can be played with teams of four players. Handicap players record a nett score on each hole, depending on their exact handicaps.

On the scorecard each hole is given a handicap rating, known as the stroke index, of 1 to 18, the hole with a stroke index of 1 being the one rated most difficult. A 10-handicap player deducts one shot from his or her score on each of the holes rated 1 to 10 and counts his actual scores on the other holes.

Matchplay

This is the customary form of play in friendly matches between club members. The winner or winners are those who win the most holes outright. If one player or a partnership is four holes up with only three holes left to play, for example, the match is over. Frequently another match is then played over the remaining holes, called the "bye." Matchplay is the oldest form of golf and was regularly played at least four centuries before strokeplay was invented.

Fourball matchplay is the most common form, two players forming a partnership, with each playing his own ball. If either wins a hole outright the side wins. Handicaps are taken into account, the player with the lowest handicap giving strokes to the others where applicable.

Foursomes matchplay (called Scotch foursomes in America) has become quite a rare game. This is a two-ball contest between pairs of players in which the partners play alternate shots with the same ball. Also, each player takes the tee shot on alternate holes, irrespective of who finished the previous hole.

Greensomes has become the most popular form of this game. Here *both* partners drive off from each tee and the better drive is chosen, shots being played alternately from there. This game is sometimes called Pinehurst foursomes in the United States. In a variation of it both partners drive and play their second shots (except on par-3 holes), then select one ball and play it alternately.

Stableford

The Stableford system is very popular for competitions. Each player can acquire points on every hole, one for a nett bogey, two for a nett par, three for a nett birdie, four for a nett eagle, and so on. A score of worse than one-over par nett on any hole gets zero. The winner, naturally, is the player scoring the highest total points.

The popularity of this system derives largely from the fact that a player can have one or two really bad holes and yet still win the competition provided he or she has had several really good holes.

In a strokeplay competition where every stroke counts one, the player may play like a champion for most of the round but spoil his card with a couple of double bogeys.

The fourball better-ball format can also be used in Stableford play, the partner with the better points score on each hole counting in the total. Another variation is the aggregate version, where the points won by both partners are recorded and the team with the highest combined aggregate total wins.

Points Contest

This is a variation of the Stableford system, but in this case four points are given for a nett par. Two points are given for a nett bogey, six for a nett birdie and eight for a nett eagle. Any number of players can play this version – two, three, four or however many want to join in.

Bingle, Bangle, Bungle

This is a game with three points available on each hole. One point is won by the first player to put his or her ball on the green, one for the player with the ball nearest the hole when all balls are on the green and one for the first player to hole-out. How many strokes have been taken on the way to each point is irrelevant.

Texas Scramble

This game is played between teams of four players. All drive from each tee. The best drive is then selected and all team members play their second shots from there. The best second shot is then taken, all the team playing their thirds from that position. And so on, until the ball is holed. At the end of the round the team score is totalled up and the team handicap deducted.

Usually the rule is that each team member's drive must be used on at least four holes. This brings everybody into the game. Scrambles encourage bold shot-making and are greatly enjoyed by long-handicap players – most of whom believe they would score well if only they could drive like Jack Nicklaus.

There are two other versions of the scramble which are sometimes played. In a straight scramble all players play all the shots from the preferred positions. In a handicap scramble class A and B players play from the back tees and class C and D players from the forward tees.

Skins

Skins games, which usually involve four players, all playing against each other, are increasingly popular with TV companies and with sponsors. The basic

Above: Rodger Davis of Australia and Seve Ballesteros on the 12th at Wentworth during the 1986 World Matchplay Championship, the premier matchplay tournament.

Right: Bobby Locke drives while Britain's John Jacobs looks on, during the 1962 World Matchplay.

format is simple: if two of the players tie for best score on any hole, all the players tie. When one of the players wins a hole outright he wins a "skin"; after another tie the next hole is worth three "skins," and so on.

Straightforward skins is often played by seniors when they find themselves in a threeball, the winner of a hole getting one point and the person with the most points being declared the winner at the end of the round. Alternatively the winner of a "skin" receives a small stake from the other players, in which case there may be two winners at the 18th.

On the Perch

This is another three-ball game. The winner of any hole is declared to be on the perch. If he wins another hole before any of the others, he wins a point and stays on the perch. When one of the others wins, he is then "on the perch" and needs to win a further hole outright before any of the others does in order to win a

point. The total of points after 18 holes decides the final winner.

Low Ball and Aggregate

This is a fourball match. On each hole one point is given to the player with the lowest score and another point to the team with the lowest aggregate on the hole. If there are ties on either count, no points are awarded.

Throw-out Competition

Before play starts it is decided how many "worst holes" can be disregarded in reaching a player's final score; it might be two, three or four. At the end of the round the scores on the worst holes are subtracted, leaving the total nett score on the round.

Eclectic

In a true Eclectic competition players register their best scores on each hole throughout the season. The winner is the one with the lowest total. But a similar

system can be used in 36-hole tournaments, the lower of the two scores on each hole being used to produce an 18-hole score.

Mystery Competition

Players go out not knowing exactly what type of contest they are entering. After all scores have been posted the type of competition is disclosed.

Limited Club Competition

Eighteen-hole rounds are played with a limited number of clubs – for instance one club, or two and a putter, or three and a putter, or four. An alternative sytem is to allow extra strokes on handicaps depending on how few clubs are taken: 12 strokes for one club, 8 for two, 6 for three, 4 for four, 2 for five and only 1 for 6.

Blind Partner Event

Players go out in pairs but do not know whom their allotted partner is. This is disclosed only when

everyone is back in the clubhouse, when either the better ball or the two scores are totalled.

Bisque Par Competition

In this game players can use their full handicaps in any way they wish. They can even take more than one stroke off their score on selected holes so long as the total taken off in the end matches their handicap. The strokes taken are announced on each tee before anyone drives off.

There are many other possibilities. In some competitions players can replay a certain number of shots, in others "blind holes" are announced after the scores are in and the numbers on those holes are deducted from each player's total. Cross-country tournaments are also often organised. In a 9-hole shoot-out 10 players start out but one is eliminated on each hole either for having the highest score or for losing a chipping contest in the event of a tie for highest. At the 9th two players are left to fight it out.

HANDICAPS

Golf is a game in which the system of handicapping should allow all golfers everywhere of whatever standard to enjoy a friendly match or a competition with other players on fairly level terms. The young can play with the old, the professional with the rankest amateur, women against men, the good against the not-so-good.

Handicaps are no longer strictly tied to the concept of par, which allots a standard score for each hole on a course on basis of length alone, but on what is called the Course Rating, or Standard Scratch Score. This is based on the total length of the course adjusted for the distances from different tees, the difficulty of the course and even, on particular days, for weather conditions.

In a strokeplay event a handicap is deducted from the gross score a player has achieved over the nominated distance, usually 18 holes for amateurs but sometimes 36. For instance, a gross score of 90 over 18 holes will reduce a 20-handicap player's score to a nett 70.

For matchplay or Stableford events each hole is allotted a place from 1 to 18 on the scorecard for handicap purposes. A player with a 10-handicap will claim an extra stroke on holes marked from 1 to 10 on the card, an 18-handicapper a stroke on each hole, a 36-handicapper two strokes on each hole. In matchplay the difference between handicaps will determine the number of strokes a less-talented player receives.

In some countries the total difference is used; in other words, the 18-handicapper playing against the 10-handicapper will receive a handicap stroke from the latter on holes marked on the index from 1 to 8 inclusive. But in other countries three-quarters of the difference in handicaps is used.

A Scratch player receives no strokes. And those with a plus handicap (professionals and top-class amateurs) add the handicap plusses to their score, and in matchplay increase the number of extra shots they give to other golfers.

In the allotment and alteration of handicaps there are two basically different systems in operation around the world, the American and the British.

The American System

In the United States and those countries which follow American rules, handicaps are based on each player's current form in everyday play. In countries following the British system, handicaps are based on scores returned in official competitions.

Under the American system a player is expected to return a marked scorecard to his or her club virtually every time he or she plays 18 holes, even if only in a friendly game. For handicap purposes scores of more than two over par gross on any hole are reduced to two-over to give the handicap score. Actual handicaps are then based on the best 10 scores made over the preceding 20 rounds.

This system enables a handicap to reflect current form and means that a player has to play a little better than average to equal or improve on his or her official handicap. It has the disadvantage, though, that it cannot be monitored.

The British System

Under the British System, handicaps for men are determined by results from official competitions only, although committees are allowed to adjust handicaps at their club if the known form of any player is not reflected in his handicap – or if a player is injured or suffering any serious illness.

The Standard Scratch Score for the day is determined by officers of the club, depending on which tees are in use and, to some extent, on the weather or the condition of the course.

The major disadvantage of this system is that it takes no account of current form, or of the fact that scores in competitions rarely reflect the abilities of a player when playing in everyday matches (friendlies) with other people. And more than 90 per cent of golf is played in such matches. What is

more, some players may play in only one or two competitions each year, so that it is almost impossible to adjust their handicaps to reflect the reality of their talents. In an extreme case a senior of, say, 70 might find it takes 10 years under the British system for his handicap to be increased by one shot.

It is also possible for a younger player to have one very good day and to have his handicap reduced to beyond his actual average capabilities.

The British Women's System

The system used by British women players is more realistic. Although based mainly on competition scores, handicaps can be adjusted with reference also to "Extra Day" scores – that is, rounds played on non-competition days. For scores in these to count toward the handicap, the player signs the official Extra Day Book in the clubhouse before starting to play.

To retain or adjust a handicap, women in the long-handicap division (handicaps 10 to 36) must put in at least four cards per year. Those in the middle range (4 to 9) must enter at least six cards. Low handicappers, 0 to 3, must put in at least 10 cards.

The Australian System

Under Australian rules handicaps for men are, like those in Britain, derived from competition scores. These are related to the Course Rating which will vary according to the difficulty of a course and the weather and may be adjusted from day to day. But handicaps may be allotted either as "Australian handicaps," valid at all the clubs affiliated to the Australian Golf Union, or as "Club handicaps," valid only at a player's home golf club.

All handicaps are examined at

Nick Faldo in action on the similarly picturesque par-3 course at the Augusta National, which is played on as precursor to the main tournament – the US Masters.

the start of each year. Scores more than a year old are disregarded. And to retain his handicap a player must have at least five "live cards" on record during each 12 months.

The Callaway System

In competitions at holiday resorts or among members of golf societies where some or all players have no official handicap, the Calloway System is often usesd.

Under this system a player's handicap is determined after each round by his gross score over 18 holes minus his worst scores on certain individual holes. For example if the player scores 100 gross he can deduct the total of his three worst holes. If he has had one 9, a 7 and a 6, for example, his nett score becomes 78.

How to get a Handicap

Under the British system to get an official handicap a player must enter at least three scores, signed and attested, at a club affiliated to the national Golf Union. Such a club may be attached to a public course as well as to a private one. For the allotment of a first handicap any score of more than 2 over par is reduced to 2 over. The maximum handicap for men is 28. British women must enter at least four cards to be allotted a handicap. The maximum handicap for them is 36.

In Australia at least five cards must be entered. The maximum Australian handicap is 27, but club handicaps can go higher. In the United States men's handicaps can also reach 36.

A "Slope system" is used in America to adjust handicaps when players are at different clubs, so that handicaps derived from very difficult courses can fairly match those derived from very easy courses. The system seems likely to be introduced soon on a world-wide scale.

For complete information on the exact formulae for the allotment and adjustment of handicaps, you should get in touch with your national or regional Golf Union.

THE RULES

The basic rules of golf are simple: you play the course as you find it, the ball as it lies and the game in the true spirit of fair play. But to explain and enlarge upon these basic rules there are 34 principal regulations and more than 134 subdivisions of them, plus provisions for local rules and regulations as to the size and shape of clubs and the specifications of golf balls. The complete *Rules of Golf* are published by the Royal and Ancient Golf Club of St Andrews and the United States Golf Association.

They should be studied and understood by all golfers.

Before Playing

1. Count your clubs. You must not have more than 14 (including the putter) in your bag.

2. Do not take any artificial aid with you, such as (for instance) a distance-measuring device or a device for helping you to grip correctly or anything like that.

3. In competitions, put an identification mark on your ball, so that if it lands in the rough you can be sure it is yours. If it cannot be positively identified it will be considered "lost."

On the Tee

1. On the first tee the honor (which player tees off first) is determined by the order of the draw or starting sheet. If there isn't one, it should be determined by lot.

2. Tee off within two club-lengths behind a line between the front edges of the tee-markers.

If you tee off outside this area there is no penalty in matchplay but an opponent may require you to replay the stroke – which he probably will do if it has been a very good one. In strokeplay, however, there is a two-stroke penalty, and you must play again from the specified area.

On the Course

1. In matchplay the ball farther from the hole should be played first. In four-ball games, however, partners may play in the order they think best if one of their balls is the farthest from the green.

2. If a player plays out of turn, an opponent may require him or her to replay the shot without penalty.

3. In strokeplay the ball farthest from the hole is played first. There is no penalty for playing out of turn (unless the Committee agrees it was done by arrangement to give one player an advantage).

4. In strokeplay the player with the lowest score on the preceding hole tees off first; in matchplay it is the winner of the hole. If the hole is halved, the player who had the honor on the preceding hole tees off first. In four-ball games partners may tee-off in whichever order they prefer; in foursomes each tees-off on alternate holes.

Playing the Ball

1. Play the ball as it lies. Do not even touch it unless a Rule permits this – for instance, to identify it in the rough. In that case, tell your opponent what you intend to do – he may wish to watch you do it. But if the ball lies in a hazard – a bunker or a pond, say – you are not allowed even to identify it.

2. *Never* improve the lie of your ball, or the area of your intended swing, or your line of play, by moving or breaking anything growing (except in fairly taking your stance or actually swinging). Don't even press anything down.

3. If your clubhead hits the ball more than once, count the stroke and add one penalty stroke, making two strokes in all.

4. If you play the wrong ball by mistake: in matchplay you lose the hole, in strokeplay you incur a two-stroke penalty. These penalties do not apply however in a hazard, where you are not allowed to identify your ball. And in a four-ball game only the player playing the wrong ball is penalised – *not* his partner.

5. If your ball is moved by you, your partner or your caddie except as permitted by the rules, add

a penalty stroke and replace it. The same penalty and procedure applies if it moves after you have addressed it.

NOTES In golf the word "move" means to leave its position and come to rest in another place. You are permitted to move your ball to identify it, or if it is in someone else's line, or if you are in process of removing a movable obstruction. You have officially addressed the ball when you have taken your stance and grounded your club. For this reason, some players make sure they never ground their clubs.

6. If your ball is moved by someone else or by another ball, replace it without penalty.

Ball in Motion Deflected

1. In matchplay, if your ball is deflected or stopped by you, your partner, your caddie or your own or your partner's equipment you lose the hole. In strokeplay there is a two-stroke penalty.

2. If your ball is deflected or stopped by your opponent(s), his caddie or his bag, in matchplay you may replay the stroke without penalty. In strokeplay you play the ball as it lies, except on the putting green, where you must replay the stroke.

3. If your ball is stopped by another ball you play it as it lies. The moved ball is replaced. On the green in strokeplay, however, if your ball strikes another you incur a two-stroke penalty.

On the Putting Green

1. Do not touch the line of your putt. You are, however, allowed to brush loose impediments away and tap down a ball marker. You may also repair ball marks on your line (but *not* spike marks).

2. You may lift your ball to clean it or mark it. Replace it on the exact spot.

3. When you mark the ball, place a marker or a small coin directly *behind* it – not beside or in front of it. If the marker is on someone's line, place it one or more

putter-head's length to the side. Do not move the ball to one side and *then* put the marker behind it. Always mark the ball first.

4. Do not test the surface by scraping it or rolling a ball on it.

5. If when you are putting your ball strikes the flagstick you lose the hole in matchplay; in strokeplay it costs you two strokes.

6. If an approach shot comes to rest against the flagstick the player may move the flagstick or have it removed. If the ball now falls into the hole he or she will be deemed to have holed the approach. If it does not drop into the hole but is moved when the flagstick is taken out, it must be replaced on the edge of the hole, without penalty.

7. Always hole out in matchplay unless your opponent concedes your putt. If the putt is conceded pick your ball up immediately. In strokeplay your partners have no authority to concede a putt: you *must* hole out on every green.

Lifting and Dropping

1. A ball may be lifted and dropped under the Rules in various circumstances when not to get relief would be manifestly

Above: T-C Chen playing his infamous double-hit pitch shot at the 5th during the 1985 US Open at Oakland Hills, incurring a two shot penalty.

Right: Seve Ballesteros playing next to a water hazard. As he is not in the water he has to play the shot – and get wet.

Lost or Out of Bounds

If your ball may be lost in the rough or out of bounds you should play a *provisional* ball before going forward to look for it. If you find it in bounds, you must play it. If not, carry on with the provisional ball, taking a penalty shot. When taking a provisional, you must tell your opponent. If you don't, your provisional will automatically become the ball in play – with the penalty.

Unplayable

If you consider your ball is unplayable (anywhere else but in a water hazard), add a penalty stroke and drop either within two club-lengths, not nearer the hole, or any distance behind the spot where the ball was, keeping that spot on the line between you and the hole. If either course is impractical, replay the shot. You are the sole judge of whether or not the ball is playable.

Abnormal Ground Conditions

Casual water is any temporary accumulation of water which is visible before or *after* the player takes his or her stance. Find the nearest place which avoids the water, not nearer the hole, and drop the ball, without penalty, within one club-length of it. Similar relief is allowed if one's ball lands in ground-under-repair. G.U.R. must always be marked by the Committee.

If a hole, cast or runaway made by any burrowing animal, reptile or bird interferes with your stance or intended swing you can either play the ball as it lies or take the above relief.

If any of this happens on the putting green, place the ball on the nearest spot, not nearer the hole, which affords relief.

Finally

If any point of dispute arises which doesn't seem to be covered by the Rules settle it between you ''in accordance with equity.'' Always play golf in the true spirit of the game.

unfair; if there is an immovable obstruction in the way of your swing, for instance; if the ball is in casual water; or, under local rules, if it stops within a club's length of a staked tree. (See Rule 20).

2. When dropping stand erect, facing toward the hole; hold the ball at shoulder height and at arm's length, and drop it. If it touches you or your equipment, drop it again without penalty. If it rolls nearer the green or more than two club-lengths from where it struck the ground, it must be re-dropped. If it does so again, place it where it first touched the ground.

3. A ball must be re-dropped if it rolls into a hazard or out of a hazard or out of bounds or back where it was in the first place. A ball eligible to be dropped in a hazard must *stay* in the hazard.

Interference

A ball may be lifted at any time if it might assist another player. And you can have any ball lifted if it interferes with your play or if you think it assists another player.

Hazards

Hazards are any bunkers, lakes, streams or other water (except casual water). You either play the ball as it lies in a water hazard or under one penalty stroke you may drop it at any distance you like behind the water, keeping the point at which the ball crossed the margin of the water hazard on a line between the hole and the spot where you are dropping it.

A *lateral* water hazard is one where it is impractical, in the opinion of the authorities, for you to drop the ball behind it. In this case you can drop either within two club-lengths of where it crossed the margin or on the opposite side of the hazard but not nearer the hole. In either case you take one penalty shot.

ETIQUETTE

Golf is a game in which not only are people expected to behave in a civilised way, with thought for others, but most actually do.

Etiquette precedes the rules in the official Rules of Golf. It is the first consideration. But many newcomers to the game do not read the Rule Book and are unaware of just what they should and should not do on the course.

They may not realise that before making even a practice swing they should make sure that nobody standing near them could possibly be hit. And not only by the club, but by any pebbles or twigs or earth or anything that could be thrown up by the stroke. Nor should they play any stroke until players ahead of them are well out of range.

When anyone is about to make a stroke nobody should move or stand close to or behind them. And they certainly should not stand behind them on the line of their shot, unless asked to. (A low sun directly ahead may make it difficult for the player to see where his ball goes).

In the interests of all, players are asked always to play without delay. Don't dally over the shot. Don't stand around discussing the state of the economy or simply gossiping if the way ahead is clear. Good golfers think of the people playing behind them.

If you think you may have lost a ball on the golf course you have a maximum of five minutes in which to find it before declaring it lost. But what some newcomers to the game do not appreciate is that this does *not* mean that they may keep the players behind them waiting. If finding the ball is clearly going to take any appreciable time, you should signal those behind to play through.

When everyone has finished putting on a green, that green should be cleared without delay. Don't stand around talking. Don't mark a card there. Wait until the green is clear and you are about to move on to the next hole.

Arriving at the next tee the player who has the honor must be allowed to play first, again without delay.

The player who has the honor

Once you have reached the green, always mark the ball, as David Cooper is doing here. Also repair any pitchmarks, keeping the green in tip top condition.

is the one who has won the hole or taken the fewest number of strokes, or in a Stableford contest the one who has notched up the most points. In a fourball game either player in the partnership which has won the last hole can play first; it's up to them to decide who it will be.

On the first tee the player named first on the competition list has the honor. Otherwise the order of play should be decided by lot. You can toss a coin or ask an opponent to guess whether the number of the ball in your fist is

odd or even, or something along those lines.

Priority on the Course

Two-ball matches should have precedence over and be allowed to pass any three or four-ball match ahead of them – unless special local rules are in force that day.

Friendly matches should, in principle, give precedence to golfers playing a match in an official club competition.

If playing on your own, you have no standing and must give way to any match of any kind.

Any match playing a whole round is entitled to pass any match playing less than 18 holes.

Slow players should give way to faster ones. The rule is that if a match loses a clear hole on the players in front, it should invite the match following to pass. That is, of course, if the match following is already close behind.

Care of the Course

Before leaving a bunker, a player should always fill up and smooth over all holes and footprints he or she has made, unless there is a local rule to the contrary. If a rake is used, sand should be pushed away from the edge of the bunker last thing.

If you cut a divot on the fairway, replace it and press it down. If your ball makes a pitch-mark indentation when landing on the green, mend it. If your spikes cause damage to the green, repair it *after* everyone has putted out: remember, you must *not* repair any spike-marks that are on the line of your putt.

Don't put down your bag on the green. Don't put the flagstick back carelessly. Don't damage the hole by standing close to it. And do not lean on your putter when on the green, causing a depression.

If you take practice swings on the tee or fairway, try not to take divots. Don't damage the course. In particular, don't damage the teeing ground. Leave the course in the condition in which you would wish to find it. And with a clear conscience.

EARLY CLUBS

BRASSIE An all-purpose wood with a brass soleplate used off both the tee and the fairway. Equivalent to a modern 2-wood.

BAFFIE A lofted wood similar to a modern 5- or 7-wood.

MASHIE A hickory-shafted mid-iron which did the jobs of modern 4-, 5- and 6-irons.

MASHIE-NIBLICK A more lofted mid-iron. Equivalent to a modern 7- or 8-iron.

NIBLICK A short-range iron like today's 9-irons, often used also like a modern wedge and sand-iron.

INDEX

ACKNOWLEDGEMENTS

The Publisher would like to thank Philip Taylor and Joanna Smurthwaite for their assistance as models, to the Leatherhead Golf Centre, Surrey for supplying the equipment and to Tyrrells Wood Golf Club.

The Publisher would like to thank the following illustrators: Mark Chadwick of Allied Artists and Roger Towers of Artist Partners

PHOTOGRAPHIC ACKNOWLEDGEMENTS

The photographs reproduced on the following pages were all taken by Action-Plus Photographic and are all copyright of Octopus Publishing Group: title page, 4, 6-7, 8-9, 10-11, 12-13, 12 bottom, 14-15, 15 top, 16-17, 18-19, 22-23, 24, 25, 26 right, 26 left, 26-27, 27, 28-29, 30-31, 31, 32, 33, 34-35, 38, 39, 40, 41, 42, 43, 52, 53, 58 bottom, 59 bottom, 60 bottom, 61 bottom, 62 bottom, 63 bottom, 64, 65, 66, 68 top, 69 top, 70, 71, 72, 73, 74, 75, 78, 81, 82, 83, 84 top, 85, 86, 87, 88-89.

Acushnet 20, 21; Allsport 9, 46 left, 89 right, 159 bottom, 183, 187; Allsport/Simon Bruty 175; Allsport/

David Cannon 89 left, 103, 104 top, 109 bottom, 111, 121, 129, 166, 170, 172 left, 172 right, 173, 174 bottom, 180, 181 left, 184-5; Chrys Ayley 143; Bali Handara Country Club 154; Banff Sprigs 100-101 top; Bridgeman Art Library 158; Charles Briscoe-Knight 98-99, 108 bottom, 123; Chicot Agency 109 top; Peter Dazeley Endpapers, 6, 88, 94, 106-107 top, 108 top, 110, 115, 118, 118-19, 124, 126-127, 141, 167, 168, 169, 171, 174 top, 178, 179 bottom, 181 right; Matthew Harris 96; Hulton-Deutsch Collection 35 top, 35 bottom, 156, 157, 159 top, 160, 161, 162, 163 top, 164, 176, 177 top; Seef le Roux/SA Golf Journal 142; Hugh Owen: Memories by Owen 131; Press Association-Reuter

165 right; Tony Roberts 133; Royal Antwerp Golf Club 140; Royal Dornoch Golf Club 136; Phil Sheldon 8, 34, 69 bottom, 90-91, 92-93, 96-97, 100-101 bottom, 102, 104 bottom, 106-107 bottom, 112, 112-113, 114, 116-17, 120-121, 122-123, 124-125, 128, 130, 132, 134, 134-135, 137, 138, 139, 144-145, 146-147, 148, 149, 150, 152, 165 left, 179 top, 182-183, 186-187, 188; Singapore Island Country Club 95; Isaac Smyth 151; Sport & General 177 bottom; United States Golf Association 163 bottom; Wairakei Golf Club 155; Woodfin Camp/Marvin E Newman RWF 147.